Hoofprints
in the
Sand

Hoofprints
in the
Sand

Marc G. Mitchell, D.V.M.

This book is dedicated to:

Honey's Best. Without her, this book would not have been written. She was more than just the best horse we ever owned, she was part of an era that brought a family together in a way that none of us could have imagined. Her career lasted only ten years on the racetrack, but she gave us a lifetime of memories.

Tom and Jean Boyd, who helped my father tip over the first domino.

My parents, Harry and Elaine Mitchell...for everything. For believing in me, even when I didn't believe in myself.

My brother, Doug, who gave me the inspiration to be the best in everything that I do.

Dr. Jennifer Raaf. My wife of ten years, and best friend. She has stood by me through all my highs and lows. Without her, this book would be meaningless.

Dr. Joe Moore at the University of New Hampshire. Without his help, my life as a veterinarian may never have been possible.

This is a work of non-fiction. The events and the settings are true, however, some of the character names have been changed as deemed necessary.

TABLE OF CONTENTS

PROLOGUE

When I graduated from veterinary school in 1992, I had a plan. I was going to be an equine veterinarian. I had been groomed for the job since I was six years old. As a freshman in high school, I had already set my sights on that career choice and nobody was going to talk me out of it. My guidance counselor, Bill Tanner, certainly tried. He told me that I should consider other professions since the likelihood of a doctor coming out of Sanborn Regional High School in Kingston, New Hampshire, wasn't very good. He said I had a thousand to one chance of getting accepted. He told me that I should start looking at different choices and that there were other mountains I could climb.

It was the first time in my life that I doubted myself. I figured that he knew what kind of competition I was going to face and didn't like my chances. I started thinking that my 4.0 grade point average at a rural high school was perhaps inflated compared to those in bigger towns. My whole life up to that point, I really thought I could hang with most people intellectually.

After my conversation with Mr. Tanner, I wasn't sure anymore. For the first time, I started thinking about other careers.

My thoughts on the subject didn't last very long. I didn't care what this guy was telling me, I was going to try anyway. There wasn't another career that interested me. I had made my choice and no one was going to tell me otherwise.

He had made me so nervous about my true potential that I was concerned that I wouldn't get into college. The University of New Hampshire was the only school that we could afford to send me to and was the only school that we applied for. Most of the National Honor Society students were filling out forms like they were signing autographs. Some of my friends were applying to five or six different schools. It made me very uneasy.

When I was accepted on the early admission program at UNH, I started to wonder how much faith I could place in Mr. Tanner's advice. The first step on my quest was done.

It was a great ride over the four years at UNH. I joined a fraternity during my sophomore year, which was probably not the wisest choice for a pre-veterinary student, but it sure was fun. Even today, I wonder how I managed to keep my grades up at times. My organic chemistry final was happening at the same time as "Hell Week" (the last week of pledging where you live at the house). Somehow, I made it.

Four years later, it was time to apply to veterinary schools. At the time, New Hampshire had three contract seats with the Ohio State University. If accepted, the student would only have to pay the state tuition.

It was clearly one of my only options. The fact that it was a top five school in the country and had an outstanding equine program was a bonus.

I also applied to Tufts University. Realistically, there was no chance that we could afford it, but it was close to home, and if I didn't get into Ohio State, we might have to think about some sort of financial plan to get me there instead.

The competition for the three seats at Ohio State was tough. There were at least fifteen students from UNH vying for them. We heard from Tufts first, and don't ask me how, but I was accepted on the early admission program. It certainly wasn't my GPA that got me in. My SAT scores were good, but not crazy high. I could only assume that I nailed my interview.

Next, we heard from Ohio State. I was on the bubble. Fourth on the list. I didn't get in. The three students ahead of me were all good friends of mine, and I was happy for them, but not so much for me. My dream of climbing to the top of my mountain to become a veterinarian was in jeopardy.

We could only hope that at least one of them got into another vet school, and if they did, they would choose to go somewhere else. Although they all got accepted to other schools, they all decided to go to Ohio State. I couldn't say I blamed them. The university had a great program and the tuition through the contract was very reasonable.

Tufts became my only option. After much debate, I decided I wouldn't go. The cost of the education was ridiculous, and even if we ponied up the money, it didn't seem realistic to end up in so much debt when

I finally graduated. I would wait a year and apply for the following session at Ohio State.

Our family raced Standardbred racehorses. Since I was six years old, that was my life. It was what we did. It was in our blood. Throughout the years, we have owned or trained over two hundred horses. For a stable of three men, this is a formidable feat. During our busiest run, we were racing three and four horses a night, five nights a week.

School nights were not exempt. We would often get home at one or two in the morning from the track, and both my brother and I would have to go to school the next day. The following night, we would do it all over again. People thought our parents were insane or at best irresponsible in regard to their kids' best interest. I have news for their critics. Those were the best times of our lives.

That summer after college, summer rolled on like any other summer at the farm. In the late eighties, we were racing fewer horses than in years past, but still making the trip to the track at least two to three times a week with our stable pared down. With my brother Doug performing more music on the road in his band and as a solo artist, and with me in school full time, there was a logistical problem with racing fifteen head. With fewer horses to take care of, we found ourselves with a little more free time on our hands during the day. It suited all of us just fine.

Pool has long been a favorite hobby of mine. Whenever I could, I would shoot pool and pass the time practicing. At the end of the forty-stall barn was an old apartment. It used to be occupied by a family that stabled horses with us. When they moved out, we converted it into a recreation room with a pool table.

I had bought an old three-piece slate table for cheap money, and we had to use the tractor to hoist it into the second-story apartment. That was a disaster waiting to happen, but we managed to get it in there without killing anyone or doing any serious damage to the table.

It was late summer when the phone rang, interrupting a nice little run I had going. It was Dr. Milton Wyman, head of admissions for the veterinary school at Ohio State. I thought it was a joke.

"How would you like to become a Buckeye, Marc?" he asked me.

"If this isn't someone pulling my leg, I would love to," I replied, my voice cracking with excitement.

I was confused. How could this be? I was certain the three seats were spoken for. I thought the worst. One of them must have died. I got a sickening feeling. This wasn't the way I wanted to get in.

"We'd love to have you!" he said.

"Count me in!" I could hardly control myself. "How is that possible?" I asked.

"One of the contract seats from New York isn't being used this year, and we decided to give it to New Hampshire."

I was stunned. No way was I that lucky. I hung up the phone and announced to my brother and father that I was going to Ohio State. High fives all around. I choked on the eight ball on my next shot. My hands were shaking, my heart was pounding; there was no way I was making that shot.

I found out later that luck had nothing to do with it. My advisor during my senior year was Dr. Joe Moore. He was the head of pathology and had taken me under his wing. For my first two years, I didn't have an advisor, and he called me into his office one day to question my course schedule. I had been forging the signature of the advisor that I was appointed for over six semesters and thought he had caught me. I felt I was justified in my "illegal" actions, but was supremely worried when I walked into his office.

The guy who was my appointed advisor was an avian vet and wanted me to take all these silly classes that steered me toward avian medicine. There was absolutely no way I was going in that direction. When Dr. Moore asked me why Dr. Bird was making me take my current curriculum, I came clean. He wasn't upset so much with my forgery scheme; he just wanted me to be most prepared for the future. He set me straight from that point on.

Although Dr. Moore was too modest to tell me himself, I heard through one of my other professors that he had pulled some strings and requested that the seat be reallocated for New Hampshire students. It was an unprecedented move. I still don't know why he went out of his way for me, but if it weren't for him, it is quite possible that I would never have become a veterinarian.

I have made it a point to thank him whenever I can. When I do, he always responds in the same way. He says that it wasn't him that got me there, it was me. I still beg to differ. And I still owe him a debt of gratitude.

After graduating from vet school, I started on my quest to become an equine practitioner. There were quite a few horsemen that knew me and were waiting for me to get my license. I had clients and work, but not enough to make a living. I was forced to take on a small animal job to supplement my income until my horse business picked up. If you would have told me that I would be practicing small animal medicine while I was in vet school, I would have laughed in your face. It was far from what I had envisioned.

For ten years, I traveled the countryside treating horses. Many of my farm calls were excerpts right out of one of James Herriot's books. The grind of the winter, the risk of injury, as well as too many non-paying racehorse clients started to make me reconsider my future ambulatory work.

Walking away from my life's dream to practice equine medicine was not easy. It just so happened to coincide with our family's decision to stop racing. My world as I knew it was forever changed. In 2001, we were no longer racing horses, and I wasn't an equine vet anymore. That's when I realized that the only thing that truly defines a person is who they are, not what they do.

I started my own small animal practice in New Hampshire in 1997 and started climbing another mountain. Recently, when examining a golden retriever for a mother and her ten-year-old daughter, the young girl asked me a question that I have been asked hundreds of times.

"What made you become a vet?" she asked.

I had answered it over and over again with the same old knee-jerk response that most people wanted to hear and for the most part was true. I told her that it was because I loved animals and enjoyed the science of medicine. It seemed a perfect fit. Although there is a lot of truth to that response, there is so much more to what made me who I am and why I chose veterinary medicine.

It would be impossible to explain all of it in a simple conversation. The evolution of a boy into a man who also happens to become a vet is complex. This book is intended to show all the young aspiring veterinarians and anyone else who wonders why it is that some people choose a certain path. Throughout my childhood and young adult life, the farm and the horses that lived there taught me who I am and how to act. This is the story of why I became a vet.

HONEY'S BEST

Honey's Best cruises to victory at Scarboro Downs with Doug Mitchell in the sulky.

The sun shone brightly but gave little warmth as we unloaded the horses from the trailer. So many long nights waiting for this. So many jog miles, training trips, bandaging legs. So many preliminary races during the season to lead to this.

It was the Super Bowl of the three-year-old stakes program in the state of Maine. It may not sound like much to an outsider, but those on the inside know the weight of the stakes finals. Only eight horses are ultimately eligible from a field of as many as three hundred when the season starts. Perhaps only a quarter of those young horses even make it to the races. The ones that do make it have to earn their way to the finals by amassing enough points over the season to qualify for the event. They have to be talented enough to win, and lucky enough to stay healthy over the four-month circuit to even have a chance to qualify.

Honey's Best qualified. She did it by winning all eleven races she entered out of the twelve slated in the program. The one she missed was skipped by design since the track was in the most northern part of Maine and required an eight-hour trailer ride. Although we were of modest income to say the least, we all thought it was best to sacrifice the purse for the greater good.

Back in the early eighties, the purses averaged $4,000 to $5,000 in these races, and the winner got half that. For our family, that was a lot of money in those days. Even today, it would still be worth the trip, especially since she was the heavy favorite, and barring some unforeseen bit of bad luck, we would certainly have won that one as well.

But Honey's Best was not just one of our horses, she was one of us. And I don't mean that in the sense of her being like a person and having feelings like us, or any of that sentimental nonsense. We had foaled her on the farm and had raised her since day one. She was part of our lives like no other horse you can buy at a sale or claim in a race. She was part of a team. Our team.

The eight-hour ride to Presque Isle was not to be taken lightly. They say that during a trailer ride, a horse is basically walking the whole time in terms of energy. They need to stabilize themselves constantly as the trailer moves during transit, and without the benefit of seeing their surroundings, they are forced to compensate for balance at a higher level than if they could focus on a horizon.

After much discussion, we all felt that the stress of the ride (a total of sixteen hours in a trailer) was probably not worth it. She was far too valuable and had done too much for us to put her through it. She had earned a week off. It was the least we could do after she had already won nine in a row.

Honey's Best. The name came with power. She was a feared competitor and an unbeatable rival to most of the trainers and owners in the state. Over her last nineteen stakes races, which included her two-year-old season in which she was crowned the champion by winning the finals, she had won nineteen races in a row. A stunning feat.

Even when you are the best, it isn't always easy to win them all. She held both records for two and three-year-old fillies in the state with the fastest race time in the history of the program for both years. She was also the highest stakes money earner in history. She loomed fearlessly over her rivals.

Today she was looking for her twelfth win in a row, a clean sweep of the stakes, a perfect season, which had never been accomplished, and her share of the

$16,000 purse. As easy as it seemed from the outside, we all felt the pressure. It was palpable.

The first thing you noticed when you walked into the stable area at Lewiston Raceway (long since shut down) was the overwhelming smell of horse urine wafting from the cement floor. Most barn areas are dirt, but for some reason, Lewiston's was concrete. At the end of a night, your back ached and your nose burned from the ammonia.

In the winter, ice would form on the floor near the doorways. All the horses wore metal shoes, and that combination was sometimes a horror show coming off of the track, as the track surface was elevated about eight feet above the barn floor level. It was quite a slope from the backstretch to the barn. We never had any horses go down, but you can only imagine how many bruised or broken toes were the result of a misstep from one of these thousand-pound animals. Every once in awhile, you could hear the familiar scream of a man getting his foot squashed in the doorway, followed by a string of expletives that almost invariably ended with "...you son of a whore!" or some variation of that. It was quite laughable...when it wasn't your foot.

At the center of the long paddock was a large garage door entrance. In each direction to the left and right were long aisles that had stalls on either side facing each other. The paddock could hold about a hundred and forty head (seventy on each side). Another garage door was directly across from the entrance, where the horses had access to the backstretch. The doors were always open during racing. Always. Even if it was twenty below outside, they were open. The cement floor acted like a refrigerator in the winter. It was brutal some nights.

Just inside the entrance on the right was the concession stand. That's where you got your programs and coffee, and if you had to, something to eat. Most times, I just got a bag of pretzels or a hotdog. But there were times that, when hungry enough, I went for the burger. This was no ordinary burger. This was the Lewiston Raceway special. It was the greasiest hamburger you could find. No joke. They served it on a napkin, and before you even got it, you needed another one since the first one was already saturated with lard. It literally dripped off of the burger. I have no idea where they came from, but they were perhaps the closest thing to eating a heart attack on the planet. But, man, were they good. After soaking them with a half-pound of ketchup and ringing the fat out, it was the best-tasting burger I have ever had to this day. They have probably shortened my life by ten years, but I think it was worth it.

As we walked into the paddock, Honey drew the stares of her adversaries and I could feel the eyes upon us. I sensed that some had hoped we wouldn't make the trip today, as they were all buzzing when we didn't make the trek up to Presque Isle. Sorry. We were here. And we were here to win.

The admiration for Honey was not nearly as strong as the jealousy people felt. Up until this point in our career, we didn't get much respect from the locals. We were New Hampshire natives, and Mainers didn't give much thought to those outside the circle. Honey's Best put us on the map. We had arrived.

Owners and trainers started using Doug to drive their horses once they saw how good he was. It wasn't that he had gotten any better, but Honey had opened up some eyes as to his ability. He wasn't driving a Ford

Escort in the Porsche Invitational anymore. He finally had some stock to showcase his talent, and people were noticing. They say good drivers make good horses. It's more likely that good horses make good drivers. Things had changed. People still looked at us like outsiders, but we were respected outsiders.

Honey never boasted. She didn't prance and show off like some of the stallions and adolescent colts. She displayed her beauty without a sound. She glided down the aisle with the grace of a champion. She took her spot in her pre-assigned stall for the ninth race, six-hole. She seemed to have no concern with her poor post position. She knew what she had to do.

The harness slipped over her back easily, as it had all summer. Deep breath. Doug and I were quiet. The gravity of the race was hitting both of us. He slung the race number six over her flank and we both looked at each other in disgust. We didn't need to say a thing. The biggest race of our lives, and she drew the six-hole. Typical. Never had the number six looked so ugly.

Honey looked so much better in red. That was the one-hole. What we wouldn't give to have the rail today. Slam dunk. But the six-hole was a completely different beast altogether. She would have to overcome the outside post by either pressing early or coming from behind and pressing late. Little did we know at the time she would need to do both.

As we fastened the number on and finished our silent stare of disdain, Honey was seemingly unaffected by our displeasure and sighed as though bored. She had been here before. The six-hole was nothing new. She had won from every post position they threw at her. It didn't matter. She was, after all, "The Beast."

That was the nickname she had earned over the last six months as she dominated her peers. It fit her. She was exactly that on the track. A beast.

I tightened the girth around her belly. Circling to the front, I started up with the bridle.

If there was one thing that was annoying about Honey, it was her antics with her head. She loved having the front of her face rubbed. It was her thing. Anytime you would come close to her, she would throw her head at you in an upward fashion and ask for attention. And the more you patted her forehead (and she liked it as rough as possible), the more she would start throwing her head at you for more. At times she could throw you clear across the shed-row. Cute. I guess. It was annoying for sure. In fact, it became quite obnoxious.

As I went up over her ears with the bridle, she gave me a warm-up shove as if to say, "If you're going to put that thing on, you had better make it worth my while."

I whispered back to her, "Not now, Honey, we have to go out onto the track," as I continued to apply the straps around her ears.

Wrong answer. In her best attempt to imitate a rhinoceros, she threw me back about three feet, nearly into the sulky of another horse passing by the stall.

I thought to myself, "Thanks, Honey, this is just another reason they don't like us; we don't know how to handle our horses."

I looked back at her, half amused, half agitated, and saw a white trail of debris in her nostrils. She coughed. Mucus flew from her mouth. My mind shut everything off except her. I now understood the meaning behind tunnel vision. It was surreal. This wasn't happening. I felt myself getting cold. Doug felt it too. She was sick. It was worse than we had thought.

A few days ago, she had coughed a few times at home but it had hardly seemed an issue. People cough all the time; no one calls the doctor right away. It will pass, we had thought.

It didn't. I grabbed a towel and wiped her muzzle, and she gently nudged back at me. I wanted to make sure that nobody saw the discharge coming from her nose. I didn't want anyone else to see that she was sick. Someone could report it and maybe even have her scratched because of it. Looking back, I think I just wanted it to go away. Once wiped clean, she didn't look sick, and I didn't want the reminder of what we were up against.

Before we left the barn that day, we all knew she had some sort of upper respiratory infection, and although we had initiated treatment with antibiotics, it wasn't responding very quickly. We actually discussed scratching her from the race. That discussion was fairly short-lived. Doug was emphatic. She was racing. Thank God he was pragmatic and didn't let any idealistic thinking get in the way.

Weren't we being hypocritical? We had certainly talked a good game when we protected her from the long trailer ride to Presque Isle. And now she's sick, we're going to race her anyway? The thought of the hypocrisy crossed my mind and for a moment I wondered what this all meant in the philosophical sense of who we were as humans and all that horseshit.

My father became the collective conscience. "Let's take her temp. If she's got a fever, she'll make the decision for us."

Two minutes. Felt like an hour. Normal. We loaded her up.

That's right, guys, don't get me involved. I'll probably start talking about the greater good and look like a complete idiot by the time I finally agree with you anyway. I mean, seriously, she was racing. There really was no need for discussion, was there? Not really.

My mother, Elaine (we call her St. Elaine for her often annoying habit of doing what's right and always playing by the rules), at some point in her infinite pursuit to play the role of making sure everyone is doing what was correct and just, questioned whether Honey would be okay if we in fact raced her. Although she would often complain that she was always outnumbered three to one during arguments between us, I was quite sure this was one of those times that she was throwing out the St. Elaine Card, knowing full well that it would be trumped by the Ace of Testosterone. Who was she kidding? She wanted her to race as badly as we did. Maybe more.

When we got to the track and looked at the program, I was curious to see what the morning line (odds) would be on Honey. We rarely, if ever, bet on her. Call it superstitious, but we didn't like to concern ourselves with the gambling part of the game with her. Sure, we bet on other horses in our stable, but Honey was different. There was enough stress of racing her week after week than to worry about picking horses for a trifecta and perfecta and all that nonsense.

Today's line on Honey was one I had never seen on a horse in all the years of racing. Instead of having numbers like 5:1 or 8:5, there was a single word where the numbers should have been. Barred. At first we didn't know what to think of it. It seemed that she was such a prohibitive favorite that the track felt too much money would be wagered on her, and her alone, that they would end up losing money. She was barred from wagering.

To the bettors, she in fact wasn't in the race. If she won, it didn't matter to the bettor. The horse that finished second would be declared the pari-mutuel winner, but the actual winner of the race won the purse. Every once in a while you will see this when there is a three- or four-horse field and they bar show wagering. I have even seen a horse at one of the fairs barred from wagering because of a clerical error on the program and the bettors were not seeing the right information about the horse.

Now they had barred Honey for being too good. Talk about a jinx. What next? Were they going to stick pins in a little Honey's Best voodoo doll?

We all knew that she in fact wasn't that much better than the rest of them. Yes, she had won all her races, but some of them were a struggle. She had come from eighth place at the three-quarter pole and swept the field around the last turn and just got up at the wire just three weeks ago. This wasn't a cinch. We knew that. She wasn't a machine, she was flesh and bone. Anything could happen.

Post time was only ten minutes away. My father and mother had gone up to the grandstand to watch the race with the family. My aunts, uncles, friends... it was a circus. It seemed like my whole lineage was there. My parents needed to be there to entertain and obviously take their guests into the winner's circle when Honey won. You would have thought it was the Kentucky Derby, without the big hats and mint juleps. Come to think of it, there wasn't a huge crowd of people, and there certainly wasn't anybody singing a song about the state of Maine before the race. Actually, it was nothing like the Kentucky Derby, but to us, you couldn't tell otherwise.

That left just Doug and me in the paddock. The pressure was mounting. We were now in silent mode. There was really nothing else to say at this point. The pre-race strategy had already been gone over ad-nauseam in the truck and in the paddock by the three of us (Doug, my father Harry, and I).

Giving your driver too much to think about can be devastating. You never want to over think a race. Almost always, things arise in a mile that you can't foresee, and any pre-race judgment would be deemed useless if not distracting. Best to advise and put faith in the driver you chose. Sort of like what a caddy will do for his golfer in a pre-shot routine. He won't tell his man how to hit the ball, just give him factors like wind speed, green slope, distance, and the like. It's up to the professional to digest all that information in his head and have it manifest itself through his hands.

Five minutes before post now. We were fortunate enough to have a driver that was not only smart, but race savvy. He was able to make adjustments on the fly that most take too long to do. If Honey were to lose, it likely wouldn't be from driver error. Even if it was, we were all comfortable that when the error was made, it was made with the best intentions and probably seemed to be the right choice at the time.

The paddock judge called us out to the track. The butterflies in the stomach were real. I couldn't believe how nervous we both were. It was insane. We made our way down the urine-stained cement and headed toward the door to the track. I checked her up (term used to attach the bridle to the harness to keep the horse's head from dropping to the ground, rendering driving impossible) and led her outside. Still no words exchanged. Finally, I broke the silence. "Good luck."

I had never checked up one of Doug's horses and not said those words. I stopped short of perhaps jinxing him, as I sometimes kidded with him by saying, "See you in the winner's circle."

Doug quietly quipped back, "Thanks, we'll need it."

He didn't say, "I'll need it." We were all on that track when Honey raced. This was a team like no other I have ever been a part of. We won and lost together. Today was no exception. In fact, it was the pinnacle of what we had put together as a family. This was why we raced. This was why we put the hours in. Dozens of foals that we raised and raced were never even close to what Honey's Best had accomplished. For some reason, we were blessed with this animal. It was overwhelming.

She disappeared around the tote board on the other side of the track, as the paddock was located on the backstretch. I didn't make eye contact with anyone. I just stared down at the ground, listening to the announcer over the loudspeaker. I caught bits and pieces of his pre-race line-up through the cold breeze from across the infield. As the wind shifted and blew toward us, I could hear him almost as if I were in the stands.

"These are the three-year-old Maine Stakes pacing fillies, traveling a distance of one mile for a purse of $16,587."

I heard the number, had seen it on the program, and the idea of how this would help us with so many things that we didn't have, including money for college, was numbing. I couldn't think about having it. We needed to race first. Couldn't get ahead of myself.

The announcer went on..."Number one is Flicka Swift, a winner of over $3,000 this year..."

"She's not much," I thought. "Shame to waste the one-hole on her. If only we had drawn the rail." Forget about that now. She didn't.

"Number two is Race Me Tonight..."

Another one that Honey should crush.

"Number five is Brittany Three, she is owned..."

The announcer's voice broke off through the cold breeze. Brittany Three. We had discussed her in the paddock. She was a reasonable threat. She was peaking late and had just won last week in the other division handily. Honey was still better, but this filly was coming into her own, and we all thought she was at least a threat.

"Number six is Honey's Best!" The announcer's voice would have come through a hurricane.

I looked up and opened my eyes and saw her across the track. I was awestruck at her gracefulness. I envisioned her crossing the wire so many times before. They say that a champion racehorse knows where the wire is and will not stop driving until he or she gets there. If that's the case, The Beast was a champion. Years later, when we watched her race as an adult, she would win literally by whiskers in some unbelievable finishes. She got up at the wire. She was amazing.

The announcer came back to my ears, "She's owned by Harry Mitchell and driven by Doug Mitchell. This year she has turned into a pacing machine. With eleven wins in a row, undefeated in the series, she has summed over $18,000 this year and is titled Maine's richest filly in history."

I smiled nervously. It really was incredible. But all that didn't matter right here, right now. Anything could happen. She was not invincible. But she was. I was torn between reality and fantasy. I was making her something she wasn't. There were world-class horses at the Meadowlands that would destroy her on the track. But they weren't here. This was our time.

The starter called the field to the gate. "This is going to happen," I thought. "Win. Lose. It's going to happen." I watched her pass by me as the car picked up speed. Doug gave me a nod that said a thousand things.

Thirty seconds seemed a lifetime, and the horses were off and the race had begun. Historically speaking, the higher the purse, the crazier the drivers become in trying to win. It seems that their aggression is magnified in these big races. Horses on the program that never show early speed are suddenly leaving the gate like the race ends at the quarter pole. It seemed like all eight horses were gunning for the front.

Honey was not just exceptionally fast, she was exceptionally fast off the gate, and often times was able to race wire to wire. Not today. Even with her brilliant gate speed, Doug hard pressed her from the start and was only able to settle fourth.

"How fast are they going?" I thought.

For Honey to have to settle meant they were flying. The first quarter was torrid. Flicka Swift got to the front. Certainly she wouldn't carry us home. Heading to the half, the other drivers in the race all realized this as well, and started pulling their horses to the outside to go get her when she faded.

That forced Doug to pull Honey out at the half. He had to. If he stayed any longer, he would have been swallowed up by outside flow, and as we always talked about, a race is a race, and the immortal Honey's Best would have lost.

She was first over on the outside, cutting the air on her own. She was gliding up to be the third now, second on the backside, and closing in on the leader. They took dead aim toward me and I could see her strides were shorter than normal. She was struggling. Something was wrong. This was out of character.

I had seen her too many times not to know when she was in trouble. The lead horse was hanging tough, tougher than she should be.

"Flicka Swift should be dead," I thought. "These fractions are ridiculous."

Doug feathered her with the whip and got no response. As they rushed directly in front of me, I could see the white mucus coming from her nose.

"Oh God, she can't breathe."

My heart sank. I felt her anguish. The three-quarters rifled off a quick, quick race time. She had been pressed early, used at the half, and she still had one more turn to go.

"Hang on, girl."

I looked down at the still ground at my feet, the grass dying from the oncoming winter air, unknowing of its fragile fate. I looked up, seeing our great filly being torn apart. She was trying so hard, but her lungs weren't getting enough oxygen. The field rounded the final turn, she had lost some ground there, but the front-running horse was fading and now Honey started closing in on her again. I could see Doug rocking the bike and asking her for just a bit more.

It wasn't there. Still, her desire to win drove her down the lane as she relentlessly closed in on the leader. Brittany Three, who was following her cover, was tipping three wide and taking aim at her.

"Come on, Beast, bring 'em home," I implored her quietly.

I knew she could see the wire now and was locked in. She was driving on with nothing left.

There are times, albeit infrequently, when I will ask for help from above. This was one of them.

"God, just get her there. Please. Help her."

I knew how selfish my request was. We were the ones that had decided to race her when she was sick, not Him. He had already blessed us with this magnificent animal, and now I wanted more. I didn't care. I just wanted someone to stop her pain. I asked again.

"Please, God. Carry her home."

I knew I was just kidding myself. It was a futile prayer. I whispered to her under my breath.

"You're on your own girl."

She only had a sixteenth of a mile to go to close the books on a legendary two years. With each whistle of my brother's whip, I felt her frustration as she reached for more and found nothing. Her heart pushed her forward as she finally caught the lead horse on the rail that she had been chasing down for a half mile and got a nose in front.

Honey was unaware of the three wide horse that was looming from behind, that had been drafting her cover since the quarter pole. It was Brittany Three, and she was closing in on her blind side with every step, breathing freely and effortlessly as they approached the wire. A hundred feet. Fifty feet.

With one last heroic effort from her tired legs, Honey drove on home, but was caught by the outside horse. She had been beaten. The machine had been shut down. It was over.

After snapping out of a fugue state, Doug and Honey were the last to get back to the paddock area. I unchecked her and immediately loosened her girth to allow her to breathe without the constriction of the harness. The harnesses in those days had just switched to the elastic girth that expanded during inhalation somewhat for the animal's benefit, but I still felt it hindered the expansion of the chest.

Most horses will come off the track and show obvious signs of physical exertion. The most recognizable to the lay person is sweating and increased breathing. Trainers will often boast when an exciting prospect is preparing for the races that after a particular vigorous training trip, the horse wasn't even blowing. This, of course, is in reference to his breathing. The horse is an animal that only breathes through the nose, so it is easy to see how hard they are breathing after exertion. The less a horse is "blowing" after a mile, the better shape he is in.

An old-timer in our barn would often come off of our track behind the barn, with a wet cigar hanging from his mouth, and proclaim how well his horse went. He would hold his hands close to his body to mimic holding the reins tight the whole mile to prevent the horse from going faster than he actually wanted to go and say, "I was just like this," (holding his hands to his chest), "and just look at him!" he would exclaim. "He wouldn't even blow out a match!"

Honey could have put out a bonfire. I had never seen her so distressed after a mile. She was leg weary and the mucus was now yellow and streaming from both nostrils. As we made our way down the cement to the inner sanctums of the barn area, Doug clamored out one single word just audible enough for me to hear, and only me. There was only one word that could describe everything that had occurred over the last two minutes and three seconds. It is a word that we use only when the emotion of the situation is so combustible and visceral that other profanity is just not enough. "F—k."

My thoughts exactly. And the conversation was over. He said it softly enough that Honey couldn't hear him. I'm sure she wouldn't have understood it, but I'm also sure that he didn't want her to think he was addressing her. He was addressing all that wasn't her.

That was the only word uttered over the next hour. There was nothing else to say. No excuses, no words of comfort, no pep talks to make it better. Nothing would have helped anyway. And no real good words how to describe what I felt.

Surprisingly, I wasn't angry. There was an overwhelming sense of emptiness. Not depression. Just an empty feeling. I felt like someone had reached into my soul and taken away the part that made me want to do anything. Numbness. The world was quiet around me, despite everything that was happening. There was one emotion that kept hitting me like a hammer. Empathy. For Honey. The thought of losing this race was always in the forefront of my mind.

After racing for as many years as we had, if there was one thing I knew for sure, it was that there was never a sure thing. It was killing me that the adage was true. Whenever I thought of losing, I would always think about how upset I would be for me and my family. Never once did I think about Honey. Now, that was all I could think of.

At the risk of upsetting a lot of horse people, I will make the statement that horses are not that intelligent, but there are a few things that they do understand. They know pain. They know displeasure. They know hunger. They know how to care for their young... And they know how to win.

All horses have the blueprint to want to be at the front of the pack. In the wild, it is almost always the strongest and fastest stallion leading the way. It's not that the others want to follow; it's that they are incapable of leading. They either lack the speed or the heart to do it. Honey's Best knew how to win. And she knew when she lost. Knowing that she was sick and that we allowed her to lose gave me a feeling of betrayal that I never knew I could have for an animal. There was no way to apologize to her. No way to make it up to her. She lost and she knew it. It couldn't be undone.

It was a moment that, as I moved forward to becoming a veterinarian, helped me to become the voice of the animals and to be their ambassador when no one else would speak up for them. I finally understood the meaning of being compassionate for animals and where to begin. First, listen to them. They are talking to us. Second, hear them, and act on what they are saying.

Honey's Best took the rest of that year off to recover physically, and for us to recover emotionally. She went on to be one of the most feared and respected pacing mares in New England over the next eight years. A year later, after a brilliant four-year-old campaign, she suffered another huge loss in the New England Sulky Championships when a vindictive driver took her out of the race by driving recklessly with a horse that had no shot at winning. It was a crushing blow, but nothing close to what we had experienced a year earlier. We were hardened.

As a five-year-old, she came down with a puzzling muscle disorder that sidelined her for nearly twelve months. As a six-, seven-, and eight-year-old, she became one of the elite pacing mares, racing in the Fillies and Mares Open condition every week. At times, when there weren't enough good mares to compete with her, we were forced to race her with the boys (something that few fillies can handle, just ask the Kentucky Derby owners who have seen only one filly win it in over a hundred years). Even against the boys, she was formidable, winning many of her starts in the higher class.

In 1990, at the age of eight, when most horses are on the "back nine" of their career, she set her lifetime mark (fastest win time in her life) at a little fair track called Rochester Fair. It was a chilly night in September when she overcame a rough trip and faced all colts and geldings to stop the teletimer in a time that has stood for almost twenty years. It was nothing short of magical. No filly or mare before her, or after her, has eclipsed her time.

Over her career, she amassed fifty-five lifetime
wins and $250,000 in earnings, and all of those wins
were facing stiff competition. To put it in perspective, a win to a horse in its career is like a homerun
for a baseball player in a season. This was all done
without the use of growth hormones. Her career
ended in 1993 when she had an injury that prevented her from ever racing again. She was retired
on the farm and had a foal three years later. That
colt, although promising enough, showed crazy gate
speed, but never managed to even come close to
having his mom's prowess or heart.

In 2006, the old mare was becoming more and
more arthritic with each passing year as many ag-
ing horses do. None of us could bear to see her go
through another tough New England winter as her
conditioned worsened. We all reluctantly agreed that
it was time to put her down.

On a cloudy day in late November, a soft rain was
coming down over the farm. When the barn was quiet
and only the four of us were around, we took our last
walk with Honey. We all wept together as we walked
with her one final time. The injection was given and
her beautiful dark bay body slowly collapsed to the
ground, along with all of our dreams. It was almost
unbearable.

My mother spoke softly to her through her tears.
"Oh, Honey. We love you."

Although Honey had retired over twelve years
previously, her presence on the farm was a wonderful
reminder of what we once had. When she was finally
gone, there was an eerie quietness that underscored
the end of an era.

She was buried in the same soil that she arrived on. As a veterinarian, it was the hardest euthanasia I have ever performed, or ever will.

She taught every one of us many invaluable lessons throughout her career and even posthumously. She taught us how to win with class...and she taught us how to lose. She taught us passion, empathy, strength, and, most importantly, to never give up. On that cold afternoon in October at Lewiston Raceway, she kept driving on even though she was exhausted and sick and had nothing left. She kept trying, pressing, and never gave up. She lost, but she went down swinging.

She was inspirational to me in becoming a veterinarian as she was a part of my life when I was making the transition from boy to man. She also gave us the financial means for me to even consider going on to a higher education. Without her, I am not sure it would have been possible. She brought unity and teamwork to an already close family.

When we talk about being home, there is a greater meaning to the word than just being at your house. Home is a state of mind, a peacefulness and serenity that comes with being in a place that feels right. Home is where you can rest easy, love freely, and enjoy life for its purity. Honey carried Doug home safely to fifty-four wins and me once. But more importantly, she carried all of us home. There was no way of knowing how profound her impact would be on us while she was racing because we were in the moment. Looking back, it is indescribable what she did for us emotionally, not to mention financially. She gave us more than one animal, or perhaps any person, could give.

If there was a way to thank her for all of this, I would. Maybe one day I will get the chance. If there is such a thing as a heaven and Honey's Best is there, I know one thing is certain. She's racing...and most likely winning.

"Hey, Beast, good luck. I'll see you in the winner's circle."

Honey's Best sweeps the field in the stretch with my brother Doug guiding her home on the far outside.

HARDWOOD BRET

Hardwood Bret was a nice horse. He was small and sleek, with a kind way about him, and on the racetrack he was all business. As far as geldings go, he was good to work with. He didn't mind noises and other horses in the shed-row. He had no stall vices like weaving or kicking or, even worse, cribbing. Cribbing has to be one of the most annoying habits a horse can have. Don't ask me how they figured out how to do it, but any horseman that hears that sound will tell you it is almost as irritating as your alarm clock in the morning. But at least you can shut your alarm clock off. A "cribber" will make that noise ALL DAY LONG.

What a cribbing horse does, when bored, is hook its front incisors on the stall door or feed bucket or the wall (anything he can, even after you have exhausted the means of blocking the objects he first started using), and then actually inhale air, making a large hiccupping type of noise. This, for a horse that breathes solely through its nostrils, is quite a remarkable task. But somehow a few select antagonistic animals have learned how to do what God himself decided they shouldn't.

Scientists have figured out that the act of cribbing apparently releases endorphins that make the horse feel good, so once a horse gets hooked on cribbing, you have issues. He's a cribbing junkie and will be for life. And God forbid if his neighbor sees him doing it, because these so-called stupid animals will learn from each other. Before you know it, you have a whole stable full of gasping, tooth hooking crack-horses that will ultimately drive you insane. It is best to isolate that animal to a back stall and hope he is the only one to ever do it, and then sell him.

Hardwood Bret was not a "cribber."

For the reader who is familiar with horse racing, either Standardbred or Thoroughbred, specifically those races known as claiming races, you can skip these next few paragraphs and get into the story. For all others, the following primer on claiming races will be helpful in fully jumping into my shoes and head as I recount the story of a claimer named Hardwood Bret.

Races, for the most part, are put together by a race secretary (an official) at a racetrack. The race secretary attempts to match up horses of a similar caliber. Theoretically he or she wants a race to finish with every horse noses apart at the wire. He or she may write a race condition that says..."this race is for horses that have not won more than two races this year." The trainer or owner then enters his or her horse in that race if it fits that condition.

Other conditions may be, "mares that have never won a race," or "geldings and stallions that have won over $5,000 this year," or "mares that have not won $2,000 this year." The race secretary looks over all the horses on the track and then tries to write a race condition that will provide enough horses to fill a race. Let's say you had a cheap horse that won a lot of his races early in the season. He would soon fit a condition that reads "winners over $3,000 this year," but he would get blown away by other superior horses that fit the condition. In order to make any more money that year, you may be forced to place your horse in a claiming race where he can be competitive. If you really didn't want to lose your animal, you could continue to race in the condition ranks, but he likely wouldn't make any money the rest of the year.

The claiming race is quite different. The trainer or owner comes to a decision as to what he believes the horse is worth: $2,000, $6,000, $10,000, and so on. The race secretary looks over the available horses and says, "Okay, I have enough $3,000 horses on the track to fill a race," so he puts out a race condition for horses to be claimed for $3,000 (rule of thumb: race horses are worth approximately what they earned in the previous year).

In a claiming race, the trainer or owner is saying to the public, you can buy (claim) this horse for the claiming price; however, you cannot have him until after he races this race. He is yours after the race, but the purse winnings are mine.

In this situation the trainer knows that his horse is racing against other horses that are of the same approximate value. The trainer also buys into the human frailty that exists in believing what you have is worth more than it is. Say there is a race for $3,000 claimers. Some trainers will put a horse in there that is really only worth $2,000 because they believe their horse is better than he really is. That horse is beatable. On the other hand, if someone puts a $5,000 horse in this race the horse may beat yours, but you or someone else will likely claim him for $3,000 (not a good business judgment).

In essence, the race is built to have similar caliber horses racing one another. It makes the trainer or owner, in essence, his own race secretary, making his own decision as to who his horse will race against. Now you have a rough idea how claiming races work.

The night we claimed Hardwood Bret, we had no idea what we were in for. We had been clocking him for several weeks and knew he was worthy of a claim, but waited patiently for them to drop him down to where he was more appealing to us. The night they put him in for $2,500, we knew he would soon be home at the farm. He was in to go at Scarboro Downs in Maine, and we were racing anyway, so we shipped up the two horses we had in our four-horse gooseneck trailer and made the all familiar trek to Scarboro.

The trip took us an hour and a half each way, and we made the journey at least four times a week. I swear I recognized the same woodchucks along the side of the road that grazed on the highway grass. The trip was long and boring, and on the nights we did poorly, getting home took forever. Some nights it was so bad, that we didn't even stop at Lisa's Pizza for a late night snack. Not stopping didn't make the trip any quicker. As a matter of fact, the hunger made it worse, but getting home was the priority. On those nights, we didn't want to spend another minute in Maine.

Hardwood Bret finished second that night and probably should have won, but Bret's driver was a human anchor and cost him the race. The fact that the driver was not very talented was one of the main reasons we wanted to claim him, figuring that my brother Doug could improve him by a fairly large margin. I showed up with my wash bucket, lead shank, and cooler (blanket). These were my three staples for a claim. We had claimed so many horses that summer, I felt like the grim reaper walking into the paddock.

Anyone who had a horse in a claiming race that night knew I was there to pick someone up...the bucket, the lead shank, and the cooler. It was my signature. Some people might have felt uncomfortable doing what I did, taking a horse away from someone else. And part of me did. I never liked when it happened to us, but that was the business.

But part of me loved it. It was quite a power trip for a four-foot-nine-inch junior in high school. I was ready for battle. Instead of a gun and a helmet, I had my bucket, shank, and cooler. As far as I was concerned, as soon as we gave the money to the office and signed the paperwork, that horse was mine, and I was staking claim to him.

Since Hardwood Bret finished second, he had to go to the "spit box" for a urine test. Years ago, saliva was taken for chemical/drug testing until better testing techniques were applied and urine was later obtained (the kidneys are quite the efficient detoxifier and most drugs exit via the bladder) instead of "spit." The whole idea of him going to the "spit box" only made the divorce a little messier; since his previous owners didn't own him anymore, I was responsible for washing him, yet they were responsible for bringing him to the test stall. Very awkward indeed.

After Hardwood Bret did his business, he was officially handed over to me, albeit reluctantly. Along with the horse, a list of the equipment that the horse races with is given to the new owner. This is done so that the new trainer isn't in the dark as to how the animal is rigged for the next race. This is standard operating procedure at all race tracks. The equipment card is provided by the track. This is available for the safety of the next driver.

Standardbred pacers wear hopples (pronounced hobbles, believe it or not) to keep their legs in stride. Each horse wears its own size hopple (please, in your head, do not pronounce it as it reads....it really is "hobble") varying from the little horse at fifty inches to the monster stride of sixty-two inches. This measurement is extremely important. Without the proper size, the horse will unquestionably not stay "on stride" or, as they say in the horse racing business, "make a break." When a horse makes a break, he is forced to lose ground and steer clear of the field until he once again regains stride. In most instances, it doesn't matter if you eventually get your horse back on stride, since you have lost enough ground in recovering that the race is for the most part over.

As far as Hardwood Bret was concerned, I didn't trust these guys. They just had that feel of being rats. I had paid close attention to what he was wearing on the track, so I didn't even need the equipment card. The only thing I needed now was his hopple size. Due to the importance of this measurement, there is a specific tool designed for this purpose. Conveniently enough, it's called a hopple measure. This contraption has a circular disc at each end to attach each end of the hopple. A shaft in the middle is made up of two sliding metal bars that extend until the hopple is taut. When the hopple is extended completely, the length of stride can be seen by reading the number on the shaft.

It's a two-man job. One of those men was always me when I picked up a claim. I trusted no one. I wasn't going to fall for the "make it look like we're pulling real tight to give an accurate measure when the hopple is actually loose" trick. Please. Don't embarrass yourself. Not only is it difficult to pull off, I invented the technique, so don't bother.

If you were really sneaky, you could change the hopple size on the track on the way back to the paddock before anyone saw you. Only a handful of grooms were actually capable of pulling this one off, as it was done on the fly while running next to the horse. Difficult, yes, but not impossible. This little gem was saved for only the worst of enemies and a good way to get your thumbs broken if you got caught.

Hardwood Bret measured in at fifty-four inches. He was not big by any stretch of the hopple. But he had heart. And that's something that can't be measured.

In the final moments of the exchange is where the unwritten rule of gamesmanship comes into play. If the horse is dangerous in any way, this is the time you usually will come out and warn the new owners. I would never allow a horse to go to another stable with the potential of injuring someone without them knowing about it. It just doesn't make any sense not to. It was, and still is, a gentleman's code of ethics to protect your fellow horseman. You might not like the person that claimed your horse, and you certainly hope they will fail miserably with them, but you never want anyone to get hurt or even killed.

In that moment, I asked if there was anything about Bret that I should know about. The previous owner handed me the horse and walked away. He was obviously pissed off. Hey, pal, don't put him in a claimer if you don't want him to get claimed. Don't hate the player, hate the game.

We had two other horses racing that night. One was a little stud called Economy Class (we called him Echo) and the other was C.C. Beauty. Both were decent racehorses, but neither had won that night. As Echo was a stud, we loaded him first onto the four-horse trailer up front on the driver's side and left an empty stall next to him. Although he was mild-mannered as far as stallions went, it wasn't prudent to sidle a mare right up next to him, eye to eye, in the close quarters of a trailer. You were inviting trouble. You would likely have issues at some point in the trip involving some sort of sexual harassment (verbal and physical). We put C.C. in the right hind stall and then proceeded to put in Bret next to her.

Earlier, while washing him off just outside the spit box, I had noticed a small half-dollar-sized scab over his right hip. I didn't think much of it. Lots of horses have little dings here or there. They're tough. This looked to be a couple months old, so it likely was fairly significant at the time. Maybe he went down in a race and I wasn't aware of it, but I had been clocking him for weeks, and I never saw an incident. It really didn't matter, it was fairly inconsequential. Or so I thought.

Thinking back on how we traveled in those days, I have to wonder how we ever survived. The gooseneck trailer that we used had a tack room in the front, and where the front of the trailer projected forward was a storage area above the bed of the pickup truck body. In that area, we had placed a mattress, some fairly clean horse blankets, and a smattering of pillows that always had the pervasive smell of mildew. For most horse people, this area was strictly used for its purpose...a storage area for tack. For us, it was like a sleeper car in a passenger train.

When we first started out with the four-horse trailer, we had an old short-bed 350 Chevy pickup truck that at best sat three people in the front. Most times when we raced, there were four or five of us making the journey. We really had no choice. If we wanted to get to the track, we needed to pile in, and the tack room was the only reasonable option. Later on, when Honey's Best started to make us a profit, we bought a dually pickup that could easily accommodate six people, but we were so accustomed to riding in the trailer that we continued to do so.

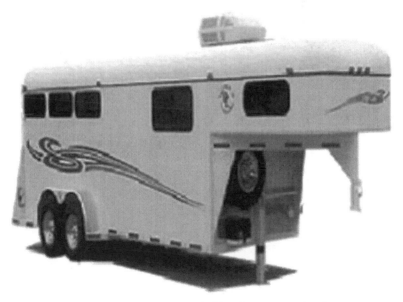

A classic goose-neck trailer much like the one we had.

You have to remember, this was a time when the helmet was still foreign to most parents with children that rode bicycles. Today kids wear helmets to roller blade. We had bought an old eight-track player and installed it into the front dash of the tack room and ran speakers to the front corners. There was a shelf above the stereo for drinks (the prototype for the cup holders of today). It was like a little fort back there.

When it was too hot, or the horses would relieve themselves, there was a crank-out window directly in the front that gave a wonderful breeze, especially at sixty miles an hour. There were some summer nights that were so hot that even the window wasn't enough to make it comfortable, unless of course you were the lucky one that got to sleep directly in line with the breeze. Those that were relegated to the alleys on the side were pretty much screwed. If you were lucky enough to get the middle spot, you were hunkered down, and there was no way anyone was getting your spot...not that night anyway.

While we were awake, we would lie face down, all facing the window to watch the road. It was way too boring to sit back along the side walls and face each other doing nothing. We figured if there was ever an accident, the middle guy would likely get thrown out like a torpedo through the little window, stripping him of his limbs on the way out. This was really the only drawback to the center spot. We also assumed that if we saw an accident coming, we were spry enough to somehow change positions and brace ourselves. Right. Clearly a thought process from an adolescent mind that had no idea what mortality really was.

We didn't talk about it much, but I know we all thought about it from time to time. Crashing, that is. We did have one stipulation for safety. When we slept, and that was almost always on the way home, we would turn around and have our legs facing forward instead. I guess we figured if we crashed while we were sleeping, at least our legs would take the first hit. Perfect. Instead of being dead, we'd be paralyzed. Well, at least the two guys on the side would be; the center guy would have been launched onto Route 95 and undoubtedly would have been spared becoming paralyzed, being dead and all. But he would have been bathed by a cool breeze getting there. Fortunately for us, we never got into an accident. If we had, you likely wouldn't be reading this.

That night, we all loaded ourselves into the trailer and started our way out of Scarboro Downs. It was a beautiful summer night in Maine. It was cool and the mosquitoes were quieter than usual with the lower temperatures. The running joke was that the mosquito was the state bird of Maine. Most nights as we left the track, we spent the first ten minutes killing the majority of them in the trailer before settling in for the trip home. There wasn't much in the way of swatting that night. We turned the FM radio on to WBLM 102.9 (the Blimp) and Cindi Lauper was singing "Time after Time."

That's when it started. The horses were acting up. This wasn't uncommon at all. Some nights, a horse would steadily talk all the way home, or kick at the tailgate every so often to let us know it didn't like traveling in the trailer anymore than we did.

This was different. It started with the normal sounds of kicking but soon escalated into a full-on thrashing. My brother yelled at them to stop it, which oddly enough, worked in many instances. This time his yells were ineffective. The trailer was rocking fairly violently at that point and we figured our father could feel the waves that were reverberating back to the pickup.

Not yet. He drove on. There were no cell phones back then. We couldn't call to the cab and tell them there was a crisis. We tried yelling through the window, but sound doesn't carry well at all through a sixty mile- an-hour headwind.

There was a little connecting doorway, a half door that you could duck through to get to the horse area. As you walked through it, you were directly at the horse's head and there was only a three-foot space to stand in. Quarters were tight. Doug and I had both jumped down in a bit of a panic to see what was happening. The noise of hooves against wood and metal and cries from one of the horses was sickening.

Something was dreadfully wrong. Scooting through the door, we saw that Economy Class was anxious and dancing around in place but not harmed. The problem was in the way back area.

The lights in the horses' stalls were ten-watt mounted bulbs covered by hard white plastic. They gave very little help when it came to vision. Their intended purpose was to keep the horses from being in complete darkness for the trip rather than give people light to see anything of importance. Headlights from traffic behind us shed enough light into the trailer for us to see what the problem was. Bret was down. He had fallen onto his right side and, by doing so, had pushed down the middle partition between himself and C.C. Beauty. She was pinned up against the right side of the trailer as Bret thrashed on his side with his hooves clamoring against the left side of the trailer. His eyes were wide, nostrils flaring, and he was petrified.

Most people are familiar with the term fight or flight, but not many have really experienced the phenomenon in person. Bret was in full-out flight mode, with absolutely no where to go. There is no reasoning with an animal in times like this. If you intervene, you likely, if not certainly, will get hurt. By this time, Doug had made his way back to C.C.'s head and was trying to release her from her stall and move her forward to be next to the stallion Echo. We knew this could be a concern—putting a mare next to a stud in such close quarters—but there really was no choice. We had to move her to keep her from getting injured.

By this time, my father had felt the tremors and had begun pulling over on the side of the highway. When he finally got the rig stopped, we had C.C. next to Echo, but Bret was still thrashing badly and on his side. He had snapped his halter off when he broke the middle partition on the trailer.

With traffic racing by us without concern and just a few feet away, we dropped the tailgate of the trailer and pulled Bret out onto the breakdown lane. We strapped an old race halter on him to control him as he clambered to his feet. The cool air of the night was gone. It felt like it was a hundred degrees out. We were all sweating profusely, but none worse than Bret. He was in a full lather and the sweat was dripping off of him. And then came the blood.

Through the flashes of oncoming headlights as we spun him in circles to control him in his frenzy, desperately trying to keep him from blindly spinning into oncoming cars, we could see that his right flank had been completely stripped of skin. It was a horrifying sight.

At that instant I knew what that scab on his side was that I had seen outside the spit box. This wasn't the first time this had happened. He had done exactly this for his previous owners, and they knew it would happen again given the right circumstances. I felt the anger start to come up through my neck with the pulsing of my already increased heart rate. How could they let this happen? These people were the lowest form of humanity I could think of. To allow an innocent animal to almost destroy himself out of spite for another person was about as low as I could imagine someone going. They knew this would happen. I gave them an opportunity to tell me if he had any issues, and they purposefully didn't tell me. Both Bret and I were now in shock. I was having trouble controlling my temper as expletives erupted from my mouth. I needed to pull it together and help extinguish the crisis at hand.

Adding to our problems, Echo was starting to get fresh with C.C. right next to him. He was whinnying and carrying on to the point where we were getting concerned that round two of what we had just seen was about to happen. My father went into the tack room and grabbed some Vick's VapoRub and applied it to Echo's nostrils. The smell of the Vick's is so strong that it masks the pheromones that mares give off that attract stallions. This is Horse Husbandry 101. We always kept this on hand just in case of this very situation. It worked.

The two horses up front settled down and we turned our attention to the very tired Hardwood Bret. He was exhausted and shivering from sweating so much and losing what was not a life threatening amount of blood but enough to make the State Police think someone got murdered on the highway when they saw it in the morning.

The wound on his side was a glistening red in the night air. It was easily bigger than the diameter of a large pizza and had the strange look of one, but one that you had stripped all the cheese off of. I was still angry. I hadn't told anyone yet in the mayhem what I had deduced from what I saw earlier in the evening.

We had no idea how we were going to get him home. What was going to prevent him from doing the same thing again if we reloaded him? Other thoughts started to flood my mind. Was he going to survive? If he did survive, how could we race him if he couldn't be shipped? How had anyone ever shipped this horse? Clearly he hadn't lived at the racetrack his whole life and never been moved. We started thinking things through, and thought that likely he either couldn't be shipped on the left side of the trailer or he couldn't be shipped next to another horse. There had to be some sort of key to unlock this horse's shipping phobia.

We decided to eliminate both concerns. Bret did not want anything to do with getting back on the thing that just caused him so much pain and distress, but we couldn't just let him stand there on the side of the highway. Sooner or later he would likely get spooked from the cars and probably get hit in the process. Watching a horse get hit by a car is something you don't want to see. Trust me. It's perhaps one of the saddest things you can witness.

We placed a blindfold over his head to calm his nerves and slowly inched him back in, this time on the right side. We slid the broken partition all the way to the left and chained it to the wall. Closing the tailgate, we pulled the blindfold off and talked to him gently, assuring him that he wouldn't go through the same pain he had just suffered. His breathing had finally slowed and the blanket we put on him had stopped his shivering. He was back, but now he had a look of uneasiness that, if you know the equine, can only be equated with pain. As the endorphins from the panic attack faded, the pain from his injury was becoming apparent. In our rudimentary first aid kit, which included some bandages, black tape, and some Phenylbutazone (strong horse aspirin), we gave Bret a double dose of pain meds to get him home.

My father pulled the truck away slowly as a test to see if he would start the same behavior that got us there. No sounds came from the back of the trailer. As we picked up speed, we could here him scramble a bit, gain his balance, and then settle down. He, too, was testing the waters. The open stall had calmed his mind as we made the rest of the trip home uneventfully.

Back at the farm, we were all concerned what we would see when we finally were able to look at his wounds. Perhaps in the heat of the moment our eyes had made it seem worse than it was. It hadn't. Although not life threatening, the extent of the injury was sickening. The blanket had acted as somewhat of a cauterizing agent as it had become adhered to the open tissue. Blood had soaked through the cotton, completely outlining the extent of the wound, and we had to peel the blanket from his raw flesh.

Living on a horse farm, you see things most people wouldn't imagine could happen. Horses getting hooked on old fence wire and sawing through tendons, eyelids getting caught on old rusty nails and ripping off, a newly acquired horse dying from having so many worms that they caused an intestinal impaction after de-worming; but none of us were prepared for this. Mostly because it had been avoidable. Most accidents happen because they are just that, accidents. This wasn't. It was driven by malevolence.

The previous owners knew that Bret had a problem shipping next to another horse and were likely hoping this very scenario would unfold. Most of the flesh on the upper right part of his flank was gone. He had abrasions on the right side of his face, and his legs had multiple lacerations from his scrambling up against the side wall.

The only saving grace was that we knew time would heal his wounds. There was really nothing to suture back together since the wound was a degloving one (complete stripping off of the skin layers). There was too large a distance to close the skin back together surgically. It would have to heal by what I now know is called "third intention." Wounds will heal if you just allow time to contract the skin together to a point where a scar will form at the center. This size of an injury would take months.

We hosed him down to clean the dirt and debris from the bottom of the trailer as well as the cotton fibers that were stuck to it. No doubt he would just lie down and contaminate it more each night, but we cleaned him up anyway. A river of water, dirt, and blood ran down the shed-row. We gave him a shot of penicillin, another shot of pain medication, this time Banamine (a more potent pain killer for soft tissue), and put him up for the night.

In the morning, the vet came out to assess him and confirmed what we already knew. We would have to let nature do her thing. If there's one thing I've learned over the years about horses it's that they have an amazing tolerance for pain and an even more amazing ability to heal soft tissue wounds. Their ability to create what horsemen call "proud flesh" or what veterinarians refer to as granulation tissue is second to none that I know in the animal kingdom. This tissue is like a skin imposter. In just a few days, a bumpy red fleshy tissue starts to grow from the exposed subcutaneous tissue.

This is very unique to the equine. As it grows in, it completely covers the wound and anchors itself to the skin edges. From here, it starts to contract like a muscle, pulling the opposing skin edges together. It does so in a symmetrical fashion from the center of the wound. It is quite fascinating. As it does this, it sets up a barrier to prevent bacteria from entering the body. The one faux pas to the whole process is that as the wound contracts inwardly, the granulation tissue gets thicker and thicker in the center and starts to mound up, much like if you tried to push two cement blocks together on a sandy beach. You could do it, but as you got them closer and closer together, the sand would build up between them. The only way to ever get those cement blocks to meet cleanly would be to remove some sand, push some more, remove more sand, until you finally got them touching.

This is where the term "proud flesh" got its name. As the skin pulls together and the granulation tissue rises, there is no way the wound will ever close. Nature doesn't really care. As long as the horse can function and the body has sealed off the outside contaminants, the animal will survive and do just fine. But in the human world, cosmetics come into play. It is fairly unacceptable to almost everyone to have a horse parading around in public with a mound of flesh the size of a soccer ball on his hip.

One would think that the skin might eventually grow over the wound, but as nature would have it, it is impossible for skin to grow uphill. It can only grow horizontally. If nothing is done, the flesh will remain there forever. Hence the very fitting name of "proud flesh." At this point, the extra tissue needs to be removed, thereby allowing yet more contraction to take place to a point where there is a new, second mound of "proud flesh" and so on until the wound is almost completely contracted to form a small scar. This requires surgery.

The really cool thing about granulation tissue is that it has absolutely no nerve endings. The surgery can be done with no sedation and nothing more than a straight razor blade. It has to be done by a very steady hand because if you cut into the real flesh underneath and you haven't sedated the animal, you are likely to get yourself in trouble. Especially if the wound is on the back legs or, worse, underneath the horse. The blade is placed almost horizontal to the skin and slicing motions are gently made to remove the tissue. It peels much like the skin of a potato that has been parboiled. But these wounds bleed. And let me tell you, they bleed badly.

Granulation tissue, for as few nerve endings as it has, makes up for it in blood vessels. If you've never seen "proud flesh" removed, you have never witness bleeding like this. With a wound of this size, you would think you were ex-sanguinating (bleeding out) the animal. But as a wise veterinarian once told us in vet school...all bleeding stops. Hopefully before the animal dies, of course, but the bleeding will stop.

When you make the first cut through, there is pale pink sheet of tissue underneath that gets exposed, and it is smooth and clean. For a brief moment, there isn't any blood, just a nice clean bed of flesh, and it would appear the surgery will go nicely without much bloodshed. In less than four seconds, however, the sliced capillaries release their fury. It covers the surgical field so quickly that you can't really tell where to cut next. Gauze momentarily helps as you dab it over the area. It clears your path for a brief instant so you can find your new margins, but then the flood gates open again in an instant. It really is a marvel to watch.

Over the next four weeks, this procedure was done six times to Bret's hip area. During his recovery, we didn't race him. We were able to keep him fit on the farm with jog miles and training trips, but he was on the shelf as far as racing went. After five weeks, the wound had finally scarred over to a point that we felt was reasonable for public viewing. It was now the size of a coffee lid. We were finally going to get a chance to race him.

We made sure we only entered three horses that night. We knew we would have to ship him alone. We placed him up two classes, to $3,500 claimers. This was quite a jump. It may not seem like much to the layperson, but to the horse, it was a pretty big deal. It would be the equivalent of going from "single-A" baseball, to "triple-A" baseball.

He drew an inside post for his first start with us. He had that going for him anyway, but he hadn't raced for over a month, so his conditioning would likely leave him "short" as we referred to horses that were not quite race ready. Still, we had to race him, and after all we had been through, we didn't want the old owners to claim him back for the same money we took him for. That would have been a complete disaster for us emotionally. Not to mention we had already spent hundreds on vet bills and he hadn't even picked up a purse check yet. No, he wasn't getting claimed back that night.

He indeed was short that night. He raced hard and got a decent trip and finished third. A moral victory for sure. He stepped up two classes after a month layoff and still raced well. We knew we had a nice racehorse.

Over the next few weeks, we continued to race him in $3,500 claimers at first and he moved all the way up to $5,000. He went on to get two wins and a second. No doubt the old owners, who were laughing when he was absent for so long, were now muttering to themselves.

The following week, I was met by his old owners after the race. They had claimed him back...for $5,000. I was in disbelief. They claimed him back for double what they sold him for. It didn't make sense. We could only deduce that he was a horse they could cheat with. That is to say, they could hold him back for a few weeks, and then when his odds were good, bet him heavy and win through the windows.

Harness racing has long been scarred by people who do this on a regular basis. It's what has made the horse racing industry's integrity be questioned. It happened more than I naively believed it did. This may be hard for some in the racing business to believe, but our stable never "stiffed" a horse. Every time our horses set foot on the track, they were out to win. That isn't to say they were pushed to the point of exhaustion for the sake of a purse check, because there were times that winning was impossible. In those instances, Doug wouldn't press a horse unnecessarily for the sake of finishing fourth instead of fifth. The point is we never intentionally lost a race in order to make a horse's odds better for the next week for wagering purposes. It wasn't the way we worked.

It became apparent that Hardwood Bret was a horse they were cheating with. His driver probably wasn't that bad after all; he just made himself look bad to ensure he lost when he wanted him to. It was no wonder he was able to race in $5,000 claimers because that's where he really belonged. And now he belonged to the same people that almost destroyed him.

When I handed him over to the groom picking him up, I found myself frozen for words. I desperately wanted tell them how much I hated them for what happened to Bret that fateful night on the Maine Turnpike. I said nothing. I couldn't. I didn't want them to know what we went through. It would be like they won again, knowing that their little plan to have him fall down in our trailer that night had worked. I was frustrated for myself and saddened for Bret. It was a long, empty ride home.

The summer drove on. Honey's Best kept winning. She was on a roll. Seven in a row now and counting. Wednesday nights were the Maine State Sire Stake nights for three-year-old fillies, and that's when Honey raced.

We had another little gelding we had bought a few months back called E.T. Vic, no doubt named after the movie character but in no way looked like him. As a matter of fact, to the contrary, this horse had one of the stouter necks of any of our stock. Kind of ironic he was named after an extraterrestrial with an extraordinarily long neck. And no, one of his hooves didn't light up.

The only thing this horse had in common with the movie character was that he had a hard time getting home. He finished second eleven times that summer with one win and four thirds. It didn't matter what class we put him in, he couldn't seem to get a win. I think the win he did get was because the front horse made a break at the wire, disqualifying him, giving E.T. the default trip to the winner's circle. He had tried his best for that bridesmaid's role yet again, but he finally got to the altar. I'm sure he wasn't happy.

To make matters worse, he seemed to get called to the spit box every week. You would think after testing him the sixth or seventh time, someone would give us a break and overlook us. Every winner gets tested and then one random horse. Random. Please. Lightning is random. This was just plain harassment.

At Scarboro, or as we affectionately called it, Scabby Row, horses that were called to the test stall were announced directly after the results were official. Most of the time, it was just after the race had finished. In some instances, when there were inquiries or delays, the announcement would come as long as five minutes after the race. An official from the paddock judge's office would also come by with a little clip with a race number on it and snap it onto the horse's halter if he was called in. If the horse wasn't there, the official would clip it to the crossties that held the horse in his stall.

After E.T. finished second…again, I listened for
his name over the intercom system, assuming he
would get called…again. It was becoming a bit of a
joke really, but I wasn't laughing. No announcement.
As a matter of fact, I didn't even hear the race winner get called. It didn't matter; E.T. finally didn't get
the random draw. Hallelujah. I was in a bit of a hurry
since Honey was in the race after the next and that
was the real reason we were there. Sorry, E.T., but
you're second billing, my friend. We have a racehorse
that actually wins in the seventh going for eight in a
row.

I stripped him down in less than two minutes. I
was the fastest groom in Maine, hands down. While
other grooms were still taking off their horses' bri-
dles, I was already walking E.T. to the wash stall. I
brought him back and threw a cooler on him, gave
him a nice long drink of water, and hooked him to
the crossties. No tag was hanging that would have indicated he needed to be tested.

Honey went on to destroy the field, setting a stakes
record for the fastest mile ever by a three-year-old filly. It was a great night. This is why we raced. You can't
buy that feeling with any amount of money. I was
pumped. We all were. Eight in a row. Unbelievable.
Three more and then the finals. It was surreal.

I unharnessed Honey slowly. There was no hurry.
She had to go to the spit box anyway, and Honey typi-
cally didn't urinate for at least twenty minutes after
the race. Including her two-year-old campaign and
this one, she had fifteen wins in a row. I think I had
a pretty good grasp of her urinating habits by then. I
knew I might as well just take my time.

There were some nights she just plain refused to go. Talk about a buzz kill. You win a big race and instead of celebrating with everyone, you're stuck in a stall full of straw listening to a guy whistle to persuade a horse to urinate that just isn't going to cooperate.

Hours went by some nights. It was awful. If any horse hadn't urinated by a certain time after the races were over, the officials would reluctantly draw blood instead. Blood is okay for detecting drugs, but urine is a much more reliable source, so they liked to wait until the last possible minute before resorting to a blood draw...especially for out-of-towners like ourselves that were obviously cheating. How else would small timers like us have such a good horse?

That night, as if she knew I was sick of her little antics, she went almost immediately. Comically enough, the guy in the urine stall knew her as well as I did and was sauntering about, getting ready for a good long night of whistling when she stretched to go. He started fumbling for the lid of the urine jar and was scrambling to get the thing under her before she voided completely. She was almost finished as he secured the cup under a withering stream as the last bit of urine came out of her. We both looked at each other with a sigh of relief. That could have been a nightmare. Pardon the pun.

And just like that, we were out of there. Doug grabbed E.T. and let me have the glory of walking the new record holder for the state of Maine out of the paddock. A good night indeed. You wish you could bottle these nights up forever. They didn't come around but once every lifetime or so. For us, it probably never would again. We loaded them up and off we went to Lisa's Pizza for a celebratory slice. It never tasted so good.

We had the night off on Thursday, and we had three horses in to go on Friday. When we got to the paddock, they were paging Harry Mitchell to the paddock office. Perhaps something to do with next week's draw. The race secretary often needed to use one of our horses in a race that wasn't filling. We would let him use a horse one week and maybe bury us in a class too high, so that he'd likely pay us back with fitting another horse in a cheaper class the following week. In any business, one hand washes the other. It didn't always work out, but it was best to stay on his good side. It was nice to have an ally somewhere. As it was, we didn't have many fans. We were from New Hampshire. They really didn't like the non-Mainers much.

It wasn't the race secretary on the paddock phone. It was the presiding judge. My father was receiving a $200 fine and a ten-day suspension from racing for failure to report to the spit box. He came out of the paddock judge's office and started explaining what went down.

"They're saying that we didn't bring E.T. Vic to the spit box the other night," he said.

"Of course I didn't. He wasn't called...or tagged, for that matter," I replied.

"Did you listen for the announcement?" he asked.

No, I was in the cafeteria playing checkers with the short-order cook, I thought to myself. "Yes, and they never called him in," I said, instead of what I was thinking.

"Apparently he got called in on a special and we left without having him tested," he went on to explain.

This was clearly bullshit. And in this case, horse-shit. But there was no debate. No jury. No hearing. They said they called him to the spit box and that was that. When I asked why he wasn't tagged, they said it wasn't necessary to tag the horse, and that they only did it to help expedite the process. Ten-day suspension. No appeal. It was what it was. I knew that it was too good a night to be true.

Amazing. It was as if Karma had to even things out. We were having one of those nights that make you alive with a passion that words can't express. And now, the frustration of this shocking news was overwhelming. I felt an inner rage starting to crest. This anger thing was becoming a theme and I didn't like it. We were on an emotional rollercoaster and it was wearing me out.

A good friend, Leah Boyd, who happens to be the daughter of Tom and Jean Boyd (owners of Honey's Best's mother) wrote a song about an old boyfriend of hers. "*You taught me life on your rollercoaster. Can't see the highs 'til you reach the lows. Dangerous curves and few happy endings. You taught me life.*" How fitting, I thought. From the mind of the girl whose family had allowed us to feel the elation from the other night came words that were an exact description of what was happening at that very moment.

I tried real hard to think about the positives of what we had just forty-eight hours ago. A sudden feeling of calmness came over me. Those bastards couldn't take that away. Moments later, the negativity slowly crept back in. The rollercoaster was coming to a stop and the ride was over. The feeling of euphoria from the other night when we were on top of the world was losing out to the current wave of darkness that was rolling over me.

They scratched all of our horses that night.

"Isn't this fun?" I thought.

This would never happen to one of these locals. They would get a slap on the wrist or more likely someone would have told them that they needed to go to the spit box. Or how about announcing it again? Maybe your microphone wasn't on, you moron. One announcement and that's it? Are you kidding me? The bagger at the grocery store gets called more than once for a spill on aisle eight. You're telling me that you made a single announcement and that was it, for something we can get a ten-day suspension for and cripple us for two weeks? This was a joke. But it was happening and there was nothing we could do. We drove all the way back to New Hampshire with three horses that never raced that night.

Spirit Special was one of those horses that wasn't allowed to race. He was entered in the first race and had drawn the rail. He happened to be in one of those races that the race secretary had owed to us. He would have "jogged", a term used to describe how easily the horse would have won. Since he was with a cheap field, he wouldn't really have had to race at top speed to win...he could "jog."

It was a widely used term. So widely used that there were variations of the term. One of them was probably my least favorite that some of the old-timers used. They would say the horse "jiggy jogged." "Dud" Nason was one of those old-timers who had, for the most part, one horse for the period of time that we knew him (about fifteen years). Marylyn's Pluff. I'm not sure how "Dud" got that nickname, but his real name was Alvin. You would have thought that over the years someone would have asked him where that nickname came from. No one ever did.

"Dud" would often wax poetic after many years following Marylyn Pluff's retirement. He would go on and on about how she won this race and that race. According to "Dud," she jiggy jogged to more victories than perhaps any horse in harness racing history.

I looked it up one day on the Internet years later. She won five lifetime starts. The way he went on and on about her, I thought she set some sort of record for lifetime wins. Five. Wow. Honey did that last month. Even if I had known this while "Dud" was alive, I wouldn't have had the heart to tell him that his mare wasn't really all that much. He believed it, and that was all that mattered. To him, she was his Honey's Best. I wouldn't have wanted to take that away from him.

Spirit Special would have jogged. Not sure he would have jiggy jogged, but the frustration of the whole Maine scene just kept mounting. These guys really seemed to have it out for us. The worst part of it was that it was my fault. If I had heard the announcement or just asked the paddock judge on the way out, we never would have been in this mess. I pictured myself leaving the paddock with E.T.

"Just take a right and go to the spit box," I thought. "Don't leave. Just take a right."

I kept walking right out the gate. The guard didn't say anything. The P.A. system was quiet. I imagined them announcing his name again for us to report to the test stall as we loaded them into the trailer. The timing had to be perfect.

I tormented myself all the way home. Perhaps being the fastest groom wasn't such a good thing. Had I not heard them call for him in my haste? No, they hadn't called him in. I always paid attention. I'd been in the spit box over fifty times that summer and never missed one call. Something had to be amiss.

It didn't matter. It was over. I used the dim dome light in the tack room of the trailer to study the program for the other two horses that didn't race. They both had good shots to win as well. The first race was probably going off right then as I agonized over the course of events over the last forty-eight hours.

"Spirit should be in the winner's circle right about now," I thought. I was beside myself.

It was what I thought was the longest ride home of my life. It turned out to be the second longest.

It took some finagling, but we were able to move all of the horses in our stable over to Doug Mitchell's name from Harry Mitchell. It cost twenty bucks a horse to make the change and we had about twelve horses actively racing. Two hundred and forty bucks. It just kept getting better. They allowed us to race the horses we had in to go on Saturday. How big of them. The way things were going, I was assuming they would have scratched them as well. They didn't.

We had a mediocre weekend with what we had going. The only win we had that week was Honey's. But that was a good one. We had to try to get back into a positive mind set. She was in to go at Skowhegan, and as luck would have it, she drew the eight-hole.

If you say eight-hole quickly, it isn't surprising that it sounds like an expletive. It's the kiss of death for a harness horse on a half-mile track. You start on the extreme outside of the field and you either have to use a tremendous amount of energy early in the race to get position or settle last and try to circle the whole field. Either way, it was a daunting task. The statistics for winning out of the eight-hole is about five percent. The winning percentage from the one-hole is about twenty-one percent. Racing on the outside of the horse on the rail over the course of a mile requires the outside horse to travel about a hundred feet longer than the inside horse, or the equivalent of about twelve horse lengths. In order to win, you had to have a good strategy, some good fortune, and a really good horse.

It was the first time Honey had drawn the eight-hole all year. She was due. It was her ninth start; it had to happen sooner or later. The trip to Skowhegan took a strong three and a half hours. As my brother would say, "It's up there."

We brought another horse with us to make the trip more interesting. To be honest, I can't remember who it was. It was all about Honey. The other horse was an afterthought. Making her task more difficult was that she had drawn the tougher of the two divisions. They weren't supposed to seed the fields, as it was supposed to be done randomly, but they weren't fooling anyone. Sneezes are random. This was a conspiracy.

One of the tougher fillies in the race was called Stephanie Direct, and there was also a blossoming Brittany Three. Stephanie Direct was notorious for her huge move going to the three-quarter pole, opening up a big lead, and then collapsing in the stretch. As a two-year-old, she would be out in front by twenty lengths at the top of the stretch and then literally almost stop. She stopped so badly one night that the horse behind her coming down the stretch almost ran over her driver. He realized what was happening almost too late and barely steered around an accident. She stole a few races this way, but almost always she got caught. Honey had nailed her at the wire many a time in her two-year-old campaign.

This year, however, Stephanie Direct was maturing. She wasn't "crawling" home anymore. She was getting stronger and lasting longer. Instead of slowing down at the head of the stretch, she was making it farther and farther down the track before tiring. Looking at the program, it was like a graph. She was definitely improving. I honestly didn't think we could win from the eight-hole.

We were all nervous, but in a strange way. These were unchartered waters for us. We never had a horse come even close to nine wins in a row. It appeared the streak was going to end. When they left the gate, the typical gate speed of the stakes program madness showed itself. Three or four horses went vying for early command. Doug settled Honey back to last. She was the prohibitive favorite and those that had backed her with their money were certainly not happy at the quarter pole. She usually had the lead or was close to it early in the race.

At the half, she was still eighth, as the horses were two by two going into the third turn. Doug had nowhere to go. It was as if they were blocking him. If he was going to have any shot at this one, he would have to go three wide up the backside and try to make a giant move. That's when Stephanie Direct started to make her patented move heading to three-quarters.

She went from fourth to the lead in just a few seconds. Honey was still eighth. The horse in front of Honey was tipping three wide, blocking Doug's three-wide move. This was crazy. I was already consoling myself about how you can't win them all and that this day had to come.

Stephanie Direct was opening up a five-length lead on the field when Doug swung Honey four deep on the backside. She was about two tractor trailer lengths away from the leader when they finally cleared the three-wide horse. That's when Honey shifted into a gear that I'd never seen her hit. She was flat-out flying. She had rested the whole mile and finally was looking at daylight instead of horseflesh.

It was at that moment that I started thinking there was an outside chance she could catch the horse out front. She circled the field four wide on the last turn and was clear of them all, except the leader, when they straightened out for home. I couldn't help myself. I yelled out to her, knowing she couldn't hear me,

"Come on, Beast, go catch that piece of crap!" I guess I figured if I degraded the lead horse, I could give her some sort of psychological fodder to let her think she was better than her. And she *was* better. She just had way too much ground to make up.

She reached the top of the stretch still seven or eight lengths off the lead. It looked like she wasn't even touching the ground. I know she could see the horse in front of her and she was taking dead aim. But Stephanie Direct wasn't stopping.

"Come on, Beast, come on, Beast," I kept saying out loud.

Stephanie Direct kept driving on, but not at the breakneck speed Honey had built up after being reined in for three-quarters of a mile. Two hundred feet to go and she had four lengths to make up. The gap was closing fast. This was going to happen. I could see she was going to get up.

She cruised past the leader fifty feet before the wire and won by three open lengths.

This was some special filly. She had refused to let us down yet again. It was one of the most amazing races I had ever seen in my life...and my horse just did it. Nine in a row.

"Hey, Maine, you might be able scratch Spirit Special, but you can't defeat the spirit of Honey's Best... and you can shove it up your..." I was as high on the rollercoaster as I had ever been, and it felt good. It had washed away all the darkness that was surrounding us. I felt like I could have run through a wall. It was the singular best feeling I had ever felt in my life to that point.

I did not forget to go to the spit box.

In order to get horses to urinate in the test stall, it requires someone to whistle to the horse. This may sound strange, but it has been the way it has been done for decades. I'm not sure how this all started or what the scientific explanation is for this, but I'll be damned if it doesn't work. I often wondered whether horses urinated because of the whistling or we whistled to the horse when they urinated and taught them like Pavlov's dog.

As yearlings on farms, when a young colt or filly is seen urinating, you can almost be certain there's a trainer nearby whistling. As a veterinarian, I always wanted to try whistling to some Morgans or Arabs on a farm call to see if they would respond, but at the risk of looking like a complete moron, I never did.

The urine collector has to be able to do two things: collect urine and whistle. Not just any whistling, mind you, it was a specific technique and sound that was universal. You don't just walk into the urine stall and start whistling, um, Dixie. No no. You start by creating the same noise as if mimicking a bomb dropping and repeat that over and over again. Different pitches and cadences are used and the timing of the repetition is modified as you go. When the horse starts to urinate, the whistler almost always starts to crescendo and pick up the pace.

If your mind was in the gutter, you might think that the horse and the collector had a thing going. At times, it was somewhat awkward...the horse grunting as it stretched to pee, and the whistling growing stronger during the act, until the climax was reached and we had our sample. Okay, maybe I'm the only one that thinks that, but until you've been there, don't judge.

At Scarboro, Stan was the master. He could whistle a show tune. I wonder how his resume for the job might have read. "Previous experience: Performed opening song for the *Andy Griffith Show* and enjoy whistling while I work." He was good. The best, in fact. If he couldn't get a horse to go, it wasn't going to happen.

Stan didn't work at Skowhegan, but the guy we hooked that night was worthy of being his understudy. Honey took about twenty minutes this time.

"Not bad, but not great, Honey," I told her as we walked back to the paddock area. "We'll have to work on that. I suspect we will be doing this a lot more in the future."

Doug had been looking at the overnight sheets that showed who was racing at Skowhegan on Tuesday of the next week. My father was hiding up in the grandstand, as he was still banished from the paddock for another three days. He was allowed in the grandstand as a patron, but sadly, he couldn't go into the winner's circle.

Doug handed me the overnight sheet and pointed to the ninth race. It was a race for $3,000 claimers. I glanced at it briefly, and it took me a moment before I saw it. Hardwood Bret. My heart sank. Those bastards were trying to steal a mile up here in God's country knowing no one would come up here and claim him. I had news for those guys; I'd be here next Tuesday, and I'd have a bucket, a lead shank, and a cooler.

It was a bittersweet moment. I was just feeling the elation of a lifetime when, moments later, I got pulled back into the negativity of these soulless lowlife degenerates. I didn't care if Tuesday was a school night, or that the trip was over seven hours in total. We were getting that horse back. If not for us…for him.

As it worked out, Doug was singing that night as he had a dual career. He was both a harness driver and a polished performing artist. He played guitar and sang. It was early in his career as a musician, so the number of gigs he did each week was minimal compared to today. He was running a Hoot Night at Ye Olde Swiss House in our hometown. Every Tuesday night, he would host an open-mic night type of format. Local musicians could come in and do four or five songs and showcase their talent—or lack thereof in certain cases. Nights when there weren't many performers, he would fill in the gaps. He brought in quite a crowd, and Tuesdays at the Swiss House in Kingston, N.H., was the place to be. It was no Studio 54, but for a small town like Kingston with just over five thousand residents, it was hopping. He really couldn't give up the gig. Besides, my father and I were more than capable of claiming a horse without our driver being there. We would make the trip ourselves, all seven hours, and bring Bret back home.

The timing worked out just perfectly as my father's suspension was ending on Sunday, and he was getting his license back. You didn't have to reapply or any-thing, you were automatically reinstated when the ten days was up. Otherwise we either wouldn't have been able to claim him or Doug would have had to give up his gig and go up there himself to make the claim. He was the only other licensed owner in our family.

When you make a claim, the track only accepts money orders or cash. We went to the bank and took out $3,100. The extra hundred was for handling fees and paperwork. I was anxious and ready to get him back. I just wanted to have him in the trailer and be on our way home. A flat tire, engine trouble, or traffic issues on our way there could throw a snafu in every-thing. We were cutting it tight for time, so I knew we needed to have a clean trip to get up there, put the claim in, and get the job done.

We took the two-horse trailer that night, since Bret would be the only one coming back with us, and the middle partition had the capability of swinging to the side, so we were fine. It would save on gas, and we could travel a little bit faster without the extra weight.

I held the cash in my hand. This was a lot of money, and it seemed like a lot more holding it. I wondered if it was really worth it. It was late in the season, and there weren't a lot of starts left before winter set in.

Although tracks raced right through the winter, we usually shut it down in December and started back up in the early spring to give our stable a rest—for both the horses and the people. The decision had already been made. We really had reached the point of no return.

It probably wasn't the soundest business decision, but this was more than just business. This was personal. As much as we wanted Bret back, we just as much didn't want them to have him. I felt like we were on a rescue mission more than a claim.

We made it to the track with only about twenty minutes to spare.

"Too close," I thought to myself.

We had to scramble around. My father had to go to the race secretary's office first and get a claim form. The racing secretary is a much more important position than the name implies. His or her job is very complex, and a thorough knowledge of the game is required to do it properly. A more appropriate name for the position might be racing director. The secretary in the title makes it sound like he or she just answers phones and takes messages, but it was much more than that.

To make it even more confusing, the race secretary had a secretary. The one at Skowhegan almost resembled a human being. She was built exactly like a pear. She weighed at least three hundred pounds and was the quintessential curmudgeon. In all the years I had known her, she had never smiled. Not once. She was about five feet two inches and had these little horn-rimmed glasses that just hung around her neck.

Her face was wrinkled like a woman in her seventies that had spent her life in the cornfields. She was probably in her fifties.

"With any kind of bad luck," I thought, "this world has to endure her for other thirty or forty years."

Without any small talk or even so much as a "How are you guys doing today" she had my father sign the forms and hand him the claim slip. She glared at us as we left.

"Listen, lady, I don't like you either so quit eyeballing me," I said under my breath.

I swear she heard me because the glare got even meaner. God had made one serious blunder when he made her. I hoped to never have to deal with her again. Ever.

My father then had to go all the way up to what they call the crow's nest at the top of the grandstand and hand the presiding judge the claim slip. Three thousand in cash for a slip of paper. As I waited outside the paddock for him to make the transaction, I wasn't sure he was going to make it. It was a long walk from the paddock to the grandstand, and then he still had to go up to the roof. My father was not one to run. I watched him walking, and not too swiftly I might add, all the way around the outside of the track to the grandstand. Would it kill him to jog? How about just a brisk walk? My God, man, move a little bit. We drove four hours up here, and now you want to cut it close?

He made it. With less than ten minutes to spare, he made it. The only way I knew that he had was that they announced that there was claim in on the race in the paddock. It was customary to let everyone in the race know that somebody had bought one of the race participants. They didn't announce the actual horse being claimed, just that there was in fact a claim in. This way no one would just leave with their horse quickly, without first finding out if they had been taken.

Hardwood Bret had the three-hole that night and was going off at 2:1. "He really should win this for fun," I thought.

I hoped he wouldn't since that would only mean the old owners would have made more money with him, and I was in a spiteful mood. The schmoo-looking excuse for a human in the paddock office had sucked the life force out of me and replaced it with a charge of negativity.

The driver on Bret sent him to the lead early but never made the top. He got parked (on the outside) the whole mile. He was gutting out a tremendous effort. On the last turn, when most horses would have packed it in, he kept coming. The driver was whipping him all the way down the lane. Most professional drivers use the whip softly on a horse's hide to get its attention and don't slash away to accomplish the goal. The majority of the hits that a driver delivers are to the shaft of the sulky, which makes a popping noise meant to stimulate the horse. The sound of the whip and the cracking are both motivators.

Their driver was clearly hitting Bret instead of the shaft.

"Leopards don't change their spots, he's still a lowlife," I muttered. I just wanted the race to be over and take him away from all this. "Hang in there, Bret, you're coming home."

He drove hard all the way down the stretch and, in a monstrous effort, won the race. Part of me felt good. He deserved it. I just couldn't stand that he did it for *them*. It didn't really matter. It was over. I just had to go get him.

I waited for the announcement. Nothing. I wasn't nervous. It had to have gone through. Maybe the same guy that announced E.T. Vic to the spit box was announcing the claim. Four minutes went by and still nothing. Now I was nervous. Something was wrong. The groom had all but stripped Bret of his harness. They were taking him to the bathing area. Hold on, boys, that's my job. You can take him to the spit box, but the new owners get to wash him. But there was no announcement yet. And no cell phones to call my father to find out what the hell was going on.

I ran back into the paddock office, all the while looking over my shoulder to see what was happening with the horse. I knew they couldn't leave right away; he still had to produce urine. I had time. Dear God, I have to face your mistake again. There she was, no smile, sitting down in her chair peering over her glasses that she now had on her ugly little wrinkled face.

"My father put in a claim for Hardwood Bret and there's been no announcement," I said in a half-panicked voice.

"I know," she said back without any emotion, "but there's a problem."

"A problem!? I'll tell you what the problem is. You're using up good oxygen! That's the problem!" I was screaming in my mind. She then explained to me that they couldn't find the money.

"Jesus Christ," I thought, "how do you lose three friggin' thousand dollars? And in a matter of ten minutes?"

It really was a conspiracy, and I finally met the leader of it. Five more minutes went by, and the troll in the office found the money. It was like a bad rendition of *It's a Wonderful Life* when Uncle Billy mistakenly hands the money over to Mr. Potter. The phone rang and the judge in the crow's nest told her that they had located the money. There was still no announcement.

"Okay, they found the money, why haven't they made the announcement?" I asked impatiently.

The wrinkled face of pure evil looked back up at me and told me that there was another problem. First the money, now what?

"In order for anyone that is not a Maine resident to claim a horse at this meet, you have to have raced a horse here, and you guys have not raced a horse here this week."

I was having a mental meltdown. Typical Maine rules. If you're not a resident of the state, you can't claim unless you've raced a horse here. The Skowhegan Fair only raced horses for one week out of the year. It wasn't like you had a huge opportunity to race here and then be able to claim. Besides, that meant no one outside the state could claim a horse the first day of the meet. Isn't that just wonderful? Great rule, guys, chalk another one up for the homeboy network.

"Hold on," my voice was getting loud now, "we raced Honey's Best here three nights ago and she won. We *have* raced here."

She looked back up at me and said, "Oh yes, I see you did."

I was vindicated. They could take that rule and collectively stick it up all of their asses. It didn't work this time. But she wasn't done speaking.

"But Honey's Best was raced under Doug Mitchell and the claim was made under Harry Mitchell."

I heard nothing else she said after that. There was a ringing in my ears and I was getting tunnel vision. My mind hit rewind, as if I was watching my life in an instant replay but backwards at high speed. The truck ride up in reverse, the viewing of the overnight sheet with Hardwood Bret's name on it, the changing of the ownership process, and then I pictured walking backwards with E.T. Vic into the paddock to where I should have taken that right to the spit box. I started rolling tape in my head in forward from there.

I take the right. We go to the spit box. No suspension. No ownership change and I'm loading Hardwood Bret into the trailer and heading home.

I was hoping Clarence the angel from *It's a Wonderful Life* was about to speak in that squeaky voice of his and say, "You never got Hardwood Bret because your father never raced a horse at Skowhegan. Your father didn't race at Skowhegan because you never went to the spit box."

We would somehow then be transformed back to the barn where Bret would be safely back home in our stable. I *had* gone to the spit box. We never changed the paperwork over from Harry to Doug. Clarence spoke up again, "You see, Marc, you really have had a wonderful life."

But he didn't. It wasn't some fantasy of what could have been if just one little instance in my life had changed. It was actually happening.

My mind was clearing and I heard my nemesis speaking again.

"You see, if you had raced Honey's Best under *Harry* Mitchell, the claim would be valid. But since it was under *Doug* Mitchell, and *Harry* hasn't had a horse race here yet, it isn't."

Each time she spoke a name, she emphasized it, to ensure she was making her point clear. And for the first time, I saw her smile.

I could feel the pulses in my neck getting stronger and stronger. I felt an anger that I had never felt in my life. It was scaring me. I had to leave the office or there likely would have been a need for a new secretary to the secretary. She had no idea how much I wanted to smash her wrinkled little face in. My heart was pounding through my chest. I felt as if I could have run through a wall.

In the paddock, Hardwood Bret had already given his urine and was being walked out. The owners looked over at me and were laughing to themselves and pointing over at me. Bret was no more than ten feet from me as he made his way past and left the paddock. I was standing at the gate of the paddock and holding onto the chain link fence. I was grabbing it with my hands and shaking it back and forth, pulling it toward me and pushing it away as I tried to rip it down. I think I was screaming, but outside noises weren't really getting through. I was in a complete mental breakdown of anger. I thought for a moment that I could possibly start turning green and tearing away my clothes.

Tears were streaming down my face and the chirping in my head was my pulse crashing into my brain. My chest hurt and my hands were bleeding from my tantrum on the fence.

"I think I'm having a heart attack," I thought to myself.

My alter ego spoke up, "Don't be an idiot. You're seventeen years old, and seventeen-year-olds don't have heart attacks."

My chest was still pounding and the chirping was relentless.

"Maybe so," I chimed back, "but how many seventeen-year-olds have gone through this crap?"

"Good point," the alter ego answered, "you're probably having a heart attack."

I had to calm down. This was insane. It was only a horse. But this whole scenario was my fault.

"Take a right, go to the spit box," my words echoed in my head.

I became aware of my breathing and realized that I really wasn't. I made an effort to start taking some deep breaths, inhaling and exhaling. That's when I noticed a lot of people watching me. They looked like they were waiting for an alien to pop out of my chest. Mouths open, heads cocked, wondering what else this little Rumpelstiltskin was going to do. I thought it best to just walk away.

In the distance, I saw my father coming toward me. He was angry but noticeably calm. How was it possible that he wasn't out of his mind right now?

I don't think he was prepared for what he had to deal with. And I had calmed down by then. He hadn't seen me at my peak performance; he was only going to witness the aftershocks. Tears were still rolling down my face. I was having trouble speaking. I never hated racing in Maine more than at that moment. I wasn't paranoid, it really was a conspiracy.

It was the longest ride home of my life. And certainly for my father. It took four hours to get home, and I never stopped bitching. Looking back, I really don't how he put up with it. I think I would have smacked the crap out of me. Or pushed me out of the truck. Or both.

To this day, thankfully, I have never felt the same anger and anguish that I felt that late summer day in Skowhegan, Maine. As I reflected back on it over the next few weeks, I began to see a greater picture, one with acceptance, understanding, and objectivity. I had lost all perspective of what was really important in life. This would pass. No one died. We just didn't buy a $3,000 horse.

Hardwood Bret slipped into oblivion as I saw him race only two more times the rest of the year. After that, I never saw him again, but he will always be with me. He had given me the gift of temperance and self-control, and for that, I am truly grateful.

OUZO

uzo had just turned five months old when I broke my wrist in September 1992. Ouzo. What a great name for a horse. Too bad we wasted it on him. He was born out of a mare named Drift Along. His mom was a home-grown lower-classed pacer. She was what you might equate to the purple real estate in the Monopoly game (low income property). She wasn't much of a racehorse, but she had functioning ovaries, and we figured we would give her a chance. We bred her to a decent stallion on several occasions, but none of her foals ever really amounted to much. The apple doesn't fall far from the tree. Back in the early eighties, she produced a horse called Orcma M. He won a few stakes races back then, our first one ever actually, and that was enough for us to think she could produce another one. It never happened.

Drift Along was a fertile brood mare. She never failed to get pregnant. Trainers have had some of the nicest, most successful mares in the world that they were unable to get to drop a foal. Not Drift Along. In true Baltic Avenue style, she got pregnant just walking by a stud.

As she got older, she developed a condition called "heaves." It's an allergic condition much like asthma that makes horses cough, especially around dust. We would have to water down her hay and even her stall in order to lower the dust content for her. She was on antihistamines regularly to help, but for anyone who has ever been in a barn, dust is unavoidable. She would cough on a regular basis. And after each cough, she farted. Every single time. Although we shouldn't have laughed because she was plagued by the condition, it was still funny. Cough. Pause. Fart... Cough. Pause. Fart. It was like a thunderstorm. Lightning. Pause. Thunder. Except the timing was always the same. Poor Drift Along.

They say that you can tell the temperature at night in the country by listening to the crickets. They will chirp at exact intervals. If you plug those times into an equation, you can figure out what the temperature is outside. With Drift Along, we could tell you the pollen count by the intervals between her oral/rectal expulsion cycle. Spring was rough.

Her final gift to us was Ouzo. She stayed on the farm as a retiree for many years, until she passed away at the age of twenty-nine. Legend has it she coughed, farted, and then died.

In the fall of 1992, the dark little foal was growing fast. Too fast. His bones were outgrowing his tendons, especially on his left front foot. He was developing a condition called contracted tendons. The condition causes the heel to elevate and the hoof to become "clubbed." A clubfooted racehorse is almost useless. He would require surgery if we ever wanted him to race or do anything athletic. During my training at school, I had learned how to perform the surgery and had just received my license to do so. One major problem. My wrist was shattered during a training accident and my left arm looked like something out of a Frankenstein movie. Surgery with only one hand is fairly impractical.

All was not lost. During the summer of '91, I had the good fortune of doing an internship with a board certified equine surgeon. I worked the whole summer for no pay as his personal assistant in his surgical facility. It was a fantastic experience, but exhausting. We performed (well, he performed) all kinds of procedures like colic surgery (where you lay a horse down and open up the abdomen and repair what is wrong with the intestine), castrations, enucleations (removing a diseased eye), and as luck would have it, superior check ligament desmotomies (the surgery Ouzo needed).

I figured since I worked for the guy for a full summer, he might give me a break on the cost. You know, a professional discount or courtesy. Besides, we were colleagues and had developed a friendship. He was more than happy to do the procedure. At full price.

Needless to say, we respectfully declined his generous offer to help out. We weren't going to spend $1,800 on a colt out of mare that produced more flatulence than quality stock. Please don't be judgmental. In 1992, $1,800 was a small fortune, and my school debt was over $100,000. It just couldn't be done. If we didn't do the surgery, it was more than likely Ouzo's condition would deteriorate to the point where he would need to be euthanized.

We also couldn't wait three months for my wrist to heal. This condition needs to be corrected almost immediately for it to be successful. Plan B was initiated. My wife, Jen, had just graduated with me from Ohio State (excuse me, The Ohio State) and she was now also a veterinarian. Granted, she wasn't trained as an equine vet, but she knew how to work a scalpel. We decided that with me running anesthesia, and showing her the way, we would get the job done. Simple, right? Right. And if the surgery didn't go perfectly, at least he could make someone a nice little riding horse.

It was like the blind leading the blind. I had only watched the surgery twice before and it was not the easiest of procedures, especially in the field (not in a hospital setting). With us, it would be done literally in a field. Anesthesia time was limited since in this scenario we would use solely injectable drugs and no gas anesthesia. Second, Jen had *never* performed surgery on a horse in her life, with the exception that she had just sewed up Consonance and Frugy four days previously. Consonance and Frugy were two of our horses that my brother Doug and I were training at the fairgrounds. We were involved in an accident which resulted in breaking my wrist and causing some minor lacerations to both horses. Remarkably, she accepted the challenge.

We walked the colt to the side of the barn to the grassy area next to the faucet we used for washing the horses. This would serve as our surgery room. A surgery room without the amenities of lights, a table, and gas anesthesia. You know, the unimportant stuff.

One-handed, I gave Ouzo his medications to lay him on the ground. He went down easily and we went to work. With the textbook of *Equine Surgery* opened to page 981, we clipped and prepped the area. I made the initial incision, and then let Jen take over. We had no more than eighteen minutes to perform, as the anesthetic would wear out and we would have a little colt scrambling to get up with his tendon exposed to the world. Dirt and tendon sheaths equal disaster. The irreparable kind. It was not an option.

For those veterinarians reading this, saying that we could have used this or that drug to keep the colt down longer...I want you to think back to when you just graduated and tell me if you would have even tried something like this given the conditions. For argument's sake then, we had eighteen minutes, according to my calculations. I had a contingency plan with a second round of drugs for emergency use if necessary, but didn't want to use it for reasons that would compromise the colt's health.

As we made our way to the tendon, deep into the tissue of the leg, we were having difficulty determining which was nerve and which was the small tendon we needed to cut. To the relatively untrained eye, it can be difficult. Once you've done the procedure a few times it is obvious, but let me tell you, when you're under the gun like we were, everything looked the same. It was like we were trying to defuse a bomb and deciding which wire to cut without the proper training.

"It's that one, the blue one...I'm sure of it. No wait, the red one. Look in the book; does this look like the red one or the blue one?"

You would think they would make a surgery book in color. Black and white. Please. That's no help at all.

More dissection and the tendon we were looking for became obvious. Phew. Good thing we didn't cut the blue one. That was his palmer digital nerve. Pretty sure he needs that one. Jen cut the red one. No kaboom. Very nice. She closed the incision, and at sixteen minutes, little Ouzo was lifting his neck and looking around. At twenty minutes, he was standing, his tendon sealed off to the outside world. For a small animal vet and a guy with one arm, I was proud of us. We had spent forty dollars.

The next day, his leg was already looking better. In a week he was standing normally. My wrist was still broken.

A year and a half went by and Ouzo was finally in training as a two-year-old and showing only minimal promise. He was a spunky little guy. We had to geld him early, because he was becoming unruly before he turned a year old. Usually you try and wait for them to mature a bit before castration, but with Ouzo, those things needed to come off. He was obnoxious. His lineage was not something where saving his testicles for future use would become necessary.

Most colts are gelded to keep them manageable. There are two reasons you don't castrate a colt. One, he's a perfect gentleman and he does everything right (except around a mare in heat, but that's understandable), or two, he's bred to the hilt and you will likely want to use him as a stud somewhere down the road. Some trainers decide that every colt should be gelded to make their lives easier and safer. We were a little more liberal. We always gave them a chance. If they could handle being a stud, they would be spared. If they were cantankerous little bastards like Ouzo, well…the decision was easy.

Somehow, in the summer of 1994, Ouzo qualified to race. He barely made the required time, but he did it. We brought him to Scarboro Downs in Maine where he was going to make his first start. We had raced Honey earlier in the night. He was in the tenth race and had drawn the six-hole.

After paddocking Honey and putting her up for the rest of the evening, I left my father (also known as Harryman, because he was "the man") and my brother Doug (whose nickname is Gooch, a name that came about through a serpentine evolution as I will explain later) with Ouzo. I figured I would go up into the grandstand and keep my mother company. She too was nicknamed along the way, two of them being Mama Pajama and St Elaine.

The grandstand at Scarboro was completely made of wood. No chairs. No padding. Just wood. The steps were ordinary wood steps, and for every three steps, there was seating made of plywood. They didn't call them grand*stands* for nothing. The last thing you wanted to do was sit in those "seats" for any length of time. I think I may be able to attribute my current back problems to those conditions.

We sat there in our misery, waiting for the race, knowing it would be awhile. The sixth race was on the track racing and we were bored. As those horses rounded the final turn, a loose horse entered the fray, coming toward the field from the end of the homestretch from the mile track. Scarboro was a half-mile track, with a mile track that surrounded it. The two tracks had the homestretch in common with each other. So basically the racetrack was a track within a track. The mile track was used for jogging purposes, and years ago, they raced Thoroughbreds on it.

The renegade beast was heading in the opposite direction of the field as the horses made their way down the homestretch. There was a cacophony of groans from the crowd as he entered the picture. The sight of a driverless horse galloping recklessly into a field of eight heading for the wire was disturbing. Surely the drivers in the race weren't immediately aware of his presence, nor should they have been. In a race, you aren't often checking the real estate ahead to make sure it's clear of, say, an oncoming horse.

In this case, it was Ouzo. And he was closing in on the field at sixty miles an hour. At that point, we didn't know whose horse it was, but part of me just knew it was him. You know, it's the part of you that just knows stuff. Like when you just gossiped about your friend's sister and you suddenly realize she's standing right behind you. You don't want to believe it. She couldn't have been standing there the whole time. You don't want to look, but you have to. And there she is. That part.

Behind him was what was left of a sulky. On his right side, still attached to the harness, was the stub of a shaft. On his left side was an intact shaft dragging a wheel that was completely bent in half. There was no sign of the seat...or the driver. He was galloping wildly as he paraded in front of the stands, and the crowd that had at first gasped now watched silently in a collective inhalation. He was closing in on the horses finishing the race. After five or six seconds of waiting, he cleared the field along the outside fence, somehow dodging eight very large bullets. For now, the danger had passed.

My mother is endlessly sympathetic to other people's plight and turned to me and said, "Oh, those poor people."

I half laughed and quipped back nervously as that part of me had a bad feeling, "Yeah, that sucks. They'll have to scratch that one."

I knew Ouzo was in the tenth, and I also knew he had the six-hole that night. When the mystery horse entered the raceway in the middle of the race, I desperately hoped it wasn't him. I was clinging to the idea that some other six horse was warming up four races out. Not likely. Searching for the race color on the tenth race, I was praying that it would read blue, or orange, or pink. Not yellow. Please. Don't be yellow.

It was yellow indeed. Like a shot of Tequila. It was Ouzo alright.

"Hey, Mom. That was Ouzo."

She gasped. It was one of those gasps that makes you think someone just died. That was her thing. When something went wrong, she was good for a gasp. It could have been that someone spilled a glass of milk. You never knew how significant a problem had arisen when you heard it. There were no variations of it. The Mama Pajama gasp. This time it was justified.

I ran down to the paddock. It was about a half-mile run. When I got there, there was no sign of Harryman, Gooch, or the little colt. Someone told me they went out back, onto the backstretch of the mile track. Already winded, I kept running...another quarter mile. The backside of the mile track at Scarboro is not where you want to be at night. It is absolutely pitch black and the mosquitoes are in numbers that are frightening. Without protection from them, you could become anemic in ten minutes. It was no joke out there.

They weren't on the backstretch. I could hear my father calling for the colt from way off in the distance. "Come oooooooonnnnnnn! Come oooooooonnnnnnnn!" It was how we called the horses in at night from the turnout area back at the farm. They would almost always come. Ouzo was either deaf, or ignoring them.

There had to be five hundred acres of woodland behind Scarboro. No lie. This wasn't just Maine. It was backwoods Maine. It was trees, highway, and a couple houses. If we thought the backside was dark, the forest was even darker.

After meeting up with my dad and my brother somewhere in the blackness, we broke up and were going to try to surround him like wolves. The problem was we had no idea where he was. We stopped, listened, held our breath, and waited.

A twig snapped.

"Shhhhhh."

Another twig. Trying to triangulate the sound in a blind environment wasn't easy. He was *out* there. No telling how far out he was.

We searched for hours before we located him. He was still dragging one wheel behind him. How could we not hear that? He should have sounded like a stampede. Stealth Ouzo. Just like the drink. It'll sneak up on you if you're not careful.

It took twenty minutes just to find our way out of the woods. The spotlights for the track had long been turned off. Fortunately there was still a single small light on in the grandstand that gave us some assistance. Honey was waiting patiently in a dark and quiet paddock when we finally got there. She had to be wondering where we went. From the number of mosquito bites we had on us, she might have guessed.

We were sure that I was going to be suturing up countless lacerations when we got back to the farm, but as we inspected Ouzo before loading him up to go home, he didn't have a scratch on him. I know it sounds cliché, but it's the truth. Not a scratch. The three of us were bleeding from random twigs and vines that we encountered. Not Ouzo. He was unharmed. A nice horse would have broken a leg. A nice horse would have had a piece of flesh the size of a large salmon hanging from his side. But a nice horse wouldn't have broken a bike and run loose like a maniac through the woods. It was as if he were running away. Away from the life of a racehorse. This was Ouzo. We never should have wasted the name on him.

After we got the horses loaded into the trailer, I got the account of what actually happened. Harrymann and Gooch had hooked him up in the bike and were taking him out to warm up. As a rule, horses that race will warm up about an hour before a race. Throughout the years, we had stuck to a game plan. We warmed up horses four races out. This almost never wavered. If the horse was in the sixth race, we would go out after the second. With only twelve or so minutes between races, we couldn't take our time getting them out. At Scarboro, the paddock was at least a half-mile away from the main track, so when the race we were going to follow was at the quarter pole, we would have to be checking the horse up in the paddock and sending him out. By the time the race was almost over, Doug would be just about entering the head of the stretch to warm up. The timing had to be fairly precise.

As they checked him up, he decided to rear up and act like the ornery colt that he was. He did this a lot. Rearing up was nothing new for Ouzo. It was one of those qualities in a young horse that will drive you crazy. He would throw himself up in the air like "Hi Ho, Silver" and then come back down with an expression that said, "Look what I can do!"

This time, he had been showing off a little too much. Much like a child learning to do a wheelie on his bicycle, he went too far past vertical and flipped over backwards. Doug was still seated in the bike. He had to move quickly to keep himself from getting crushed. Doug did a reverse somersault off of the seat just as Ouzo slammed the crest of his neck onto the vacated area. Ouzo then scrambled to his feet and started up the backside into the darkness of the mile track.

It was a few minutes later when he entered the raceway heading the wrong way as the horses were coming down the lane to finish the sixth race. I then recounted to the others that luckily he stayed on the outside of the track, or it could have been one of the biggest catastrophes in harness racing history. With the splintered bike bouncing behind him, he continued to run down the track toward the paddock. Doug and Harryman were there waiting for him to return.

A loose horse is very difficult to slow down. Men have tried to stop them for years by waving their arms to try and distract them. In theory, this would cause them to slow down in fear of what was ahead of them. (I stress that *men* have been doing this for years, because most women are smart enough to avoid this stupidity). This technique almost always fails. It only works when the horse is finally too tired to continue running. At that point, however, the horse is going to stop anyway. The waving of the arms is not necessary.

In order to perform this act, you start by standing directly in front of the charging equine. Then you can start waving your arms above your head like you're on the jumbo screen at a baseball game. These acts are strikingly similar. In both cases, you not only look foolish, but you're being ignored. When the horse decides not to stop, you step out of the way and let him continue on.

At Lewiston Raceway one night, a groom did this maneuver right in front of the grandstand and got freight trained to the ground. It wasn't pretty. Four broken ribs, one lost tooth, and a pair of shattered eyeglasses was what the horse left in his wake. The last part of the instructions is very important. Step out of the way.

After our two matadors ducked the Ouzo Express, he continued on his course along the outside fence. There was a problem with that particular route at Scarboro. It was where they kept the metal drag that was used for smoothing out the track. A "drag" can be many different shapes and forms. Some places use I-beams. Some use a piece of machinery called a York Rake. In Maine, the drag was a diamond-shaped piece of metal that was pulled by a tractor. Each side of the diamond was about six feet long and there were a few hundred railroad spikes that stuck down off the metal in order to make the track softer by somewhat turning up the soil. To get a better mental picture of what this is, imagine a king-sized bed with just the metal frame on it with large spikes jutting off the bottom of the metal runners. Now turn the bed forty-five degrees and hook the corner of it to a tractor via a chain.

Ouzo was heading directly for it at a dead run. They could only watch helplessly and wait for the carnage. His front legs clipped it head on and he did a complete forward somersault over the drag, clearing it entirely. He was traveling so quickly that he actually landed feet down and slid to a stop on his belly. He wasn't done. Unscathed by his brush with death, he got back up and took a left turn into the woods.

As Doug recalls, the shaft of the bike dragging the wheel was smashing into trees as Ouzo flashed by them in the darkness. He said it sounded like someone was taking full swings at the trees with a baseball bat. As he skirted through the thicket, the echoing sounds of wood on wood became a distant thud, as the little horse delved deeper and deeper until he was nearly out of earshot.

Wise men would have quit with him that day. But we are stubborn Greeks. He was born to be a racehorse. His mother was a racehorse. His father was a racehorse, and it didn't matter what Ouzo wanted, he was going to race. His speed from the gate was wickedly fast. That speed teased us to give him another chance. We had waited two years to get him this far, and we weren't ready to give in just yet.

We put Scarboro behind us and decided to try and qualify him at Foxboro in Massachusetts. This is the same venue that the New England Patriots play their NFL games. The track was just a stone's throw away.

It was a gorgeous Saturday morning in June when we shipped him almost two hours south to try one more time to get him to the races. Qualifying races were such a waste of time. There was no purse, and if you failed to make the time necessary, the horse would have to wait a week to try again. If the horse broke stride or didn't run fast enough, he then failed to qualify to race.

There was an awful lot riding on those two minutes. Four hours on the highway for two minutes on the track. I wasn't getting a good vibe that Ouzo was ready for this. Even if he didn't do anything silly, like flip over backwards, he hadn't harnessed the stamina to carry his speed for a full mile. His three-quarter times were outstanding, but like so many young horses before him, he still hadn't been able to bring it home.

We stopped for breakfast just before getting to the track at the Red Wing Restaurant just outside the entrance to Foxboro. They served a reasonable meal, and it was so close to the track that we could keep close watch on the time so we knew we wouldn't be late if our server was slow. That day turned out to be only the third time in our career that Doug did not join us at the track. It was just me and Harryman... and Ouzo, of course. My mother was driving down from a friend's house in Massachusetts and was supposed to meet us there. So far, she was a no show.

The stools at the counter of the Red Wing were the typical throwback stools of the old-time diners. The bases were made of a silver cylinder with two little foot stirrups on either side, and the cushions were a thick red, round vinyl. Most of the seats had tears in them with some sort of colored tape holding them together. All of the food items were on a marquee board whose letters could be replaced if the menu or price of an item changed.

Both my father and I laughed as we recounted the story of when Greg Moretti (a wannabe trainer-driver that helped out at the farm) last came to Foxboro with us and stopped for food on the way home. If I hadn't witnessed the events that I am about to tell you myself, I would call myself a liar. No human could possibly do what he did. But then again, if he *didn't* do it, it wouldn't make such a good story.

* * *

It was sometime in the winter of 1988, and Greg was still trying to get all of his qualifying races in. One of the strangest observations about Greg's behavior during this learning experience was his resistance to watching races. Ask any professional in any sport, and they will tell you that you can learn volumes by just watching a pro perform. Self-help videos from countless sports are based on this fact. You watch, you learn. Apparently Greg never got the memo.

If he did ever go to the races, which was rare, he would just sit at one of the horse's stalls. He perched himself up on an upside-down five-gallon bucket that would later be used to wash the horse and stare out into the aisle. Just fifty feet away, there was a television with the races being shown. He never even so much as looked up at the TV. When the races would go off, nearly everyone in the paddock gathered around the little television set in the corner and watched the race...except Greg. All alone, on his bucket. People were yelling as the horses thundered for home, the excitement rising to a crescendo in the paddock as they crossed the wire. Greg sat quietly, staring into the distance, eating a hotdog.

This particular night, we had asked him to come with us because we were in back-to-back-to-back races. Although we may have been able to swing it, it would be infinitely easier if he came along to help. The horses did well that night, and we stopped in at the Red Wing for a bite to eat on the way out.

My father and I split a cheese pizza (they made a pretty good pie for a greasy spoon), Doug got a clam roll, and Greg got a cheeseburger. We loaded up our food and headed home, as we almost always ate as we drove to save time. The smell of Doug's clam roll had piqued Greg's interest and he asked if he could try a taste. I'm pretty sure Doug knew what he was doing when he said he would let him have the *last* bite. We had seen Greg do some strange things and you never knew where or what his mouth had been in contact with lately. On more than one occasion, we had witnessed him sucking the blood out of a bleeding insect bite of a horse. I'm sure visions of that disturbing sight were fresh in Doug's mind when he handed him the last of his clam roll.

It was then that Greg began his week-long crusade to get himself one of those clam rolls. Off of one bite, he was in ecstasy. It was a little embarrassing, to be honest, the way he carried on about it.

"Relax, Greg, it's just a clam roll," I told him. He just kept raving.

"That's the best clam roll I have *ever* had. That was unbelievable! When are you guys racing next?" he asked.

He would have to wait a week. I'm not sure who it was longer for, us or him. We endured a week of him ranting on about a stupid clam roll. He would constantly want confirmation that we in fact were going to the races on the weekend and that we would stop at the Red Wing. Each time he asked, we assured him that we were going and we would be sure to stop. Six days of this. Clam Roll. Clam Roll. Clam Roll. Saturday couldn't come quick enough.

On the way down that night, he was eerily quiet, like he was in some sort of meditative state as his quest was almost complete. He only asked once in the paddock if we were stopping at the Red Wing on the way home.

"What do you mean, Greg? What Red Wing?" I sarcastically answered him.

"Don't bust my balls," he snapped back with a little smile.

I think he was starting to see the absurdity in all of this. He turned back to the stall and plunked down on his bucket as the next race was going off on the television.

As we left the racetrack, he was beaming like a kid at Christmas. It was only a minute's drive to clam roll heaven. We all climbed out and stretched out four across at the counter. A young, good-looking waitress approached us from behind the counter and started off with my father's order. He ordered a meatball sub. Doug was next and got the clam roll. He apparently thought it was good too. I followed with a pepperoni pizza, and we all turned to Greg.

The little waitress stood in front of him and asked him for his order. Greg paused and had the look of a kid who was asked the answer to a calculus problem that he had no idea what the answer was. His mouth was agape and his stare was distant as the words came out of his mouth.

"I'll have a roast beef sandwich," he said softly.

The waitress thanked us for the order and quickly went out back. Now all of our mouths were agape. Did we just hear that right? Are you kidding me? Roast beef?

My brother broke the silence. "Greg, what the hell was that? Call her back, get the clam roll, you idiot."

"It's too late, she's gone," he meekly answered.

"Why didn't you order the clam roll?" my brother pressed. And the next two words he spoke were priceless.

"I choked," and that was all Greg had to say for the rest of the ride home.

It was a ride that included him watching Doug eat his very own clam roll right in front of him. In his defense, Doug did offer it to him, but Greg just shook his head and accepted his defeat.

To this day in our family, when someone chokes or screws up, we refer to it as "getting the roast beef."

* * *

Ouzo was acting in his usual ornery fashion that morning. To be honest, he was a pain in the ass. He never stood still in the stall, was constantly pawing (digging a hole to China as horsemen often call it), and was nippy when you walked by him. Nothing aggressive, but enough to give you a decent blood blister if he caught his incisors on your flesh.

Harryman checked him up as I got on the seat and headed out of the paddock for the qualifier. He had drawn the eight-hole, but in a qualifying race it really didn't matter. The horse just had to stay on stride and go for time. Winning was unimportant. There is very little warm-up time for these races. You get on the track and go to the gate. No post parade, no fanfare.

The track at Foxboro was banked much like a NASCAR track. The difference here was that after the six path, the tracked domed and was reverse-banked from the seven-hole out to the outside fence. This was done for water drainage purposes as no horses ever raced that wide in a mile to necessitate continuing the banking that far out. It did, however, make it a bit tricky on the turn before the start if you had an outside post and wanted to rush the gate with momentum. Most drivers would stay in the sixth path or lower on the turn and then swing wide down the quarter-mile stretch to avoid the reverse bank with any speed. If you were at the gate early enough, it didn't make much difference as it didn't travel that fast around the turn.

A classic eight horse starting gate.

The starter called us to the gate and I turned Ouzo to face it. Up in the air he went again. He was almost perfectly vertical when I jumped off the bike, having flashbacks of what I had envisioned him doing to Doug the week before. I swear I could hear my mother gasp as he went up. I looked over my right shoulder and, sure enough, I had. She was standing at the fence of the grandstand after just making it for the race. Apparently she had been stopped for speeding en route to watch this debacle. It was the only ticket she has ever received. Mama Pajama shouldn't have rolled out of bed.

Thankfully he didn't flip over. But when he did go up in the air, he broke a piece of equipment called a headpole that would have made steering him a little easier. Without it, he would be less controllable. The field was approaching the gate, and I was still trying to put the headpole back on. I yelled up to the starter that I had broken equipment, but in qualifying races they don't like to wait. He told me that they were rolling and to get my horse going.

I threw the headpole aside on the outside of the track, hopped on the bike, and cracked the whip over the wheel disc to wake up Ouzo. He woke up alright. In a matter of seconds, he was at top speed.

"Man," I thought, "this colt really does have crazy speed."

That's when I started to get nervous. We were doing thirty-five miles an hour and the gate was going about twenty. As we hit the turn, I kept him in the five path to avoid the banking and started angling him outward on the tangent where the track straightened out. So far so good. I was bent over backwards trying to slow him down but he was in a frenzy. For those of you that don't know horses, the word "whoa" in these scenarios is nearly useless. As a matter of fact, it is useless.

We were closing in on the gate at a reckless pace. On the backstretch before the start at Foxboro, because the track is still sloped downward in the eight-hole, the arm of the gate is fairly high off the ground way out there. With Ouzo's modest height, it was fairly obvious we were going under it if he kept his speed up.

My hands were numb from pulling so hard and I gave a final surge of strength to slow him down. He would have nothing of it. He wasn't going to slow down. There was nothing that was going to stop him at this point. At least that's what I thought.

As the backstretch extends, the slope of the track flattens out. The arm of the gate on the right side was coming down like a drawbridge. If his head made it through, the rest of us would clear it. The timing had to be perfect.

The gate slammed down on the top of his head, dropping him to his knees. As he hit the ground, I pulled back on the reins with everything I had, trying to right him back onto his feet by giving him some support and prevent him from losing his balance completely.

It worked. He popped back up and started galloping out of control. This, in the minds of the judges, if you haven't figured it out by now, is not acceptable for qualifying. After I got him back pacing, he was exhausted from his shenanigans. Down the stretch for the finish, I seriously could have run faster than he was going. I was disgusted with him. He had nearly killed my brother the week before, and now he almost had an encore performance with me. His days as a racehorse were numbered. One to be exact.

I had a few moments to reflect on the events that had taken place over the last week. He had flipped over and destroyed a bike, ran into the woods and got lost, nearly flipped over again, and then Kamikazied himself into a starting gate. It was becoming clear that this horse was talking to us, and none of us were listening. He didn't want this life. He wasn't like his mom and dad. Like the son of the army colonel who is pushed his whole life to be a military man, Ouzo was finally rebelling against it.

When we got back to the paddock, I was both angry and shaken from the experience I had just been through. As I hung the reins up on the harness, I emphatically spoke to both my father and the colt.

"This horse will never see another racetrack."

And he never did.

He was sold to a friend named Paula who kept him on the farm as a riding horse for the next fifteen years. He had found his calling. His new owner loved him. She would take him through town on a grassy strip through the center of town known as the Plains, and he would be a perfect gentleman. He never reared up. And when anyone challenged him to a race across the Plains, he would flash that brilliant quarter-mile speed, and no one came close to him. After he was retired, his attitude changed. He was calmer, sweeter, and happier. Paula and Ouzo were a perfect fit.

I have to think back on that day at Foxboro when he pulled his final stunt on the track. We finally realized what he was trying to tell us. He never was a racehorse. It wasn't in him. If he understood what I said when I hung the reins up on him for that last time, his heart must have smiled. He was free. Ouzo. What a great name for a horse. I'm glad we didn't waste it.

MOHAWK KNIGHT

The soothing sound of twenty-two horses quietly munching on their morning grain filled the spacious barn. It was the most peaceful time of our day. The calm before the chaos. With three horses racing that night and two having raced the previous evening, that left about twelve racehorses that needed to go out and jog. The others were either broodmares, horses on the injured reserve, or boarders.

The deep guttural grumblings of Mohawk Night broke the serenity. He was finished eating and wanted out. Might as well get him done first and get him out of the way. He was one tough son of a bitch.

In the early eighties, before Honey made us some working capital, we had a lot of cheap claimers. We were racing on the premise of quantity rather than quality. Most of it was done out of necessity. There wasn't a lot of money floating around that we could use to go out and buy a $4,000 or $5,000 horse. Instead, when we had just enough to afford a lower-tiered animal, we went out and claimed one. Usually they were in the range of $1,000 to $1,500. Strength in numbers.

It made for a serious logistical problem, having so many equally valued animals. There were only so many races a night and each week for that class of horse. We had to juggle where we put each one. Sometimes we would have to race certain cheaper claimers in a higher class than we would have liked because some of the other horses we had simply had to race at the bottom of the barrel. It wasn't optimal as the competition was often times much steeper than we wanted a horse to race in.

Races were drawn three days out. Friday night's race card was drawn at nine o'clock in the morning on Tuesdays. Saturday night's were drawn on Wednesdays, and so on. The whole family lived together back then in the farmhouse. Our parents had a bedroom downstairs, and Doug and I had bedrooms down the hall from each other upstairs. Each morning of a draw, Doug would have to call the track before nine o'clock and enter whatever we had ready to go. The old adage "early to rise and early to bed" did not pertain to the Mitchell Farm. When John Denver sang the words "it's early to rise, early in the sack, thank God I'm a country boy," he wasn't referring to a racing stable. We would almost never get to bed before one a.m. on any given night. We raced almost five nights a week, and the closest track was over an hour and a half away. On most nights, we never left the track until after midnight.

If we were lucky, we got up at ten 'til nine in the morning. That's when the shouting started. Doug would yell down the hall from his bed, wake me up, and ask who we should put in the box. I was sleeping, of course, and had to clear my head. What day was it? Who raced last night? Who hadn't raced this week?

You would have thought that we could have planned ahead and wrote this stuff down the night before, but we never did. In all the years of racing, we never planned it out. We winged it.

"Hey, Cope," he would echo down the corridor.

He was referring to me by my nickname. We had given each other many nicknames as we grew up, but Gooch and Cope would stick forever. Doug would make fun of the way I dressed. He said I was a "preppy." I wore button-down shirts and the latest style of pants that were in, but only if I went out with my friends on the weekend. At the time, they were likely the white painter's pants. Don't laugh; they were what everyone was wearing.

When we raced, I was in full farm boy attire. Doug then modified my first name to an Italian-sounding pronunciation. I'm not sure why he used an Italian accent with us being Greek and all, but that's what he did. My full nickname became Preppy Marcopio, spoken by rolling the first "r" in Preppy and accenting the first "o" in Marcopio. It later evolved into the abbreviated "Cope."

I couldn't just sit back and let him tease me like that. I needed to create one for him. Whereas I was somewhat trendy, Doug was the complete opposite. He wore the same clothes they wore in the sixties. Jeans, a lettered T-shirt of some sort, and sneakers worked just fine for him. If he wore a peace sign around his neck you could have shipped him back to the summer of '69. I started calling him Flashback, and since he gave me an Italian sounding name, I thought I would copy that and add it to the mix. His full name became Flashback Dougoochi. In a matter of months, "Gooch" had caught on. I haven't addressed my brother as "Doug" in years.

He called back to me again. "Hey, Cope. Who should we put in for Saturday?"

"How about Kid Eagle and C.C. Beauty?" I quipped back quickly, knowing we only had about six minutes to make a decision.

"We can put in Kid Eagle, but there's a race for C.C. on Sunday for fillies and mares," Doug replied.

"That race was going to be for Good Time Foxie," I explained, "she needs the cheap class, we really should race C.C. on Saturday. Or you can put in To Ri Harry with Kid because they ship together well."

"Mohawk needs to race before To Ri Harry since Mohawk hasn't raced in ten days," he answered back.

"Yeah, but Mohawk doesn't like Kid Eagle, we shouldn't ship them up together," I reminded him as time ticked away.

"Yeah, I know. I gotta put him in, though. We'll figure it out. I gotta call the track."

This type of conversation went on every single morning of a draw during the racing season at almost the same exact time each day. It was comical to listen to us. Both half asleep, both unsure of what we wanted to do, but somehow we got it to work. There were only a handful of instances that we completely gaffed and missed entering a horse. When Honey was racing in the stakes program, we usually called it in the day before.

The Maine Sire Stakes were state-funded races for two- and three-year-olds with purses that were up to ten times what we normally raced for. The Sire Stakes were created to stimulate the breeding program in the state of Maine to perpetuate the harness racing industry. We couldn't take a chance of screwing that one up. If she missed just one race, it could cost us thousands of dollars. If we overslept or the phones didn't work, it would have been disastrous.

We were racing anywhere from twelve to fifteen head during the Mohawk Knight era. We were in our heyday. My friends Scott and Jim had become like surrogate brothers to the family. They ate dinner with us. They went haying with us. They would come over and just hang out in the afternoons after school. There was so much to do at the farm. We would work for a few hours doing chores and then be free to do whatever we wanted. With over sixty acres of land, the options were limitless.

We would swim in the pond, fish in the pond, ride dirt bikes on the track, drive go-carts, play wiffle ball, play Frisbee, a game of H-O-R-S-E (how appropriate for a racing stable) at the basketball net on the front of the barn, street hockey when there wasn't snow on the ground, ice hockey in the winter, AFX cars in one of the rooms upstairs in the house, board games when it rained, walks through the woods, target practice with the .22 rifle, and countless other activities. The work we did was well worth the pay-off. It was outstanding.

When they came over to the house, they didn't even knock, they just walked in. Food was never a question; it was how much. They started going to the races with us and became quite proficient at grooming the Standardbred. Being a groom requires an intricate knowledge of all the equipment a horse wears and knowing how to put it on properly. Both of them caught on quickly. To watch the three of us strip down a fully harnessed horse and wash him was breathtaking. We were quite the equine pit crew.

Without their help, however, we might not have been able to race as many as we did. It wasn't in any of our plans to use them (us) for cheap child labor, it just worked out that way, and the stable grew as a result. Besides, to us, it wasn't really work. We were having the time of our lives.

We should have known better. Mohawk couldn't ship with Kid Eagle. They were arch enemies. It was odd, really, to see two horses that really didn't like each other. It probably didn't help that they were stalled diagonally across the aisle in the barn so that they could eyeball each other for hours at a time.

Mohawk was an intimidating horse, your prototypical black stallion. He wasn't tall, but what he lacked in height, he had in strength and girth. Most unruly colts are castrated at an early age to prevent people from getting hurt. If his adult life was any reflection on his adolescent one, he should have lost them long ago. Someone in their infinite wisdom while he was a yearling thought his testicles should be spared. I wish that person could have seen what kind of a monster he or she produced.

In his prime, he was a real nice race horse. As he got older, he slowed like most of them do, and at the end of his career he became a bottom feeder, but a good one. We feared that castrating him at that point would likely eliminate his desire to race enough to make him non-competitive in the lower echelon, so we dealt with him. He was a pain in the ass. He struck out with his front feet without warning. He reared up if a mare was in heat within a hundred feet of him. He bit other horses as they walked by. He didn't just bite them, he would lunge at them, nearly breaking through the stall. We quickly realized that he needed a gate over the door to prevent passersby (horse or human) from being shark attacked. To Mohawk, every horse was chum, and he wanted to sink his teeth into them, especially little Kid Eagle.

Most horses don't really know how strong they are. They are gifted with strength that humans can only marvel over, yet they can be as gentle as a puppy in a child's arms. Mohawk was a thug. He was big and tough, and he knew it. He was the classic high school bully that never went to college or ever wanted to. He didn't like punks like Kid Eagle or any other pretty horse out there. Mares were the only thing he cared about, and they too were afraid of him. He was like an inmate in a prison that no one went near. He was in his little stall with his cage in front of him. He went out only to exercise. He had to be turned out in a paddock of solitary confinement because he was such a threat to others.

When he was led around, a chain had to be placed over his nose to keep him under control. Even then, you never really had control. You tried to give him the illusion that you had some sort of authority over him. Use a gruff voice, snap the chain down over his nose a few times, random expletives to sound tough, and hope like hell he didn't call your bluff. More often than not, he had to be spun around in circles on the way to his destination. Turning his head toward you and making him do a three-sixty was the only way to slow him down as he pressed forward.

He didn't have a whinny or a nicker. He had a war cry. It was as loud as any horse I have ever heard, and it literally sent chills through your body. He let every horse on the grounds know that he was the Alpha male. He certainly had my vote. There have been many horses over the years that we respected the strength and stature of, but this guy was different. We actually feared him.

Kid was the antithesis of Mohawk. He was a gentleman horse. Very slight in build, yet tall, he would have looked right at home holding a martini glass and smoking a pipe. He had a beautiful white blaze that went all the way down his forehead to the tip of his nose that stood out starkly against his dark face. If horses went to school, Kid would have been an Ivy Leaguer. But he also had a mean streak. Comically, he only used his toughness on any small animals that happened to find their way into his stall. He killed more rats than any barn cat we ever had there.

To watch him in action was remarkable. When something entered his lair, and they did quite often since his stall was directly across from the grain room, he would wait and watch. That was the local hang-out for rats, mice, and even the cats that lived in the barn. As a rodent unsuspectingly walked in, Kid would cock his head to the side and fixate on him. With his one eye locked in, he would track him by only moving his neck and holding his head perfectly still. Then, like a snake, he struck with his right front hoof. Wham. Over and over and over he slammed down on the little guy until he knew it was dead. He was brutal.

Kid Eagle paces to victory flaunting his beautiful blaze on his forehead.

Cats stayed away from his stall. He nailed a calico named Bingo once, but fortunately she got away with just a firm hoofprint on her side. She must have told her friends to stay away, because they avoided him. Mice weren't as smart. They strolled through there on a regular basis. There were some horrific crime scenes some days when only pieces and parts of some mammalian tissue were recovered. He didn't just strike once. He just kept driving them into the dirt.

We were still racing at Scarboro back then, and we had our four-horse gooseneck trailer doing runs to the track four and five nights a week. We never wrote it down, but we all knew which horses rode with each other well and where in the trailer they preferred to be. Some liked to have an open stall beside them, like Hardwood Bret. Some didn't like to ride on the right side of the trailer, like Synek. Others would rather ride in the back where the breeze was.

There were some odd exceptions. One horse by the name of Keithy J. had to ride in the back, facing the traffic. I'm not sure how we figured that one out, but that's how he liked it. We got a lot of honks and panicked looks from people trying to tell us something was wrong in the back. We would smile and wave back at them like they were crazy.

Doug entered four horses that morning, and they all got programmed. He often entered more than we expected to race because sometimes races didn't fill or one of the horses got bumped out of a race because there were too many entries for an eight-horse field. You would then have to wait for the next available race. There were some draws where we would enter four and only one horse got in. It was almost not worth shipping just one animal up, but we did it anyway. We didn't have much choice in the matter.

The logistics on where to ship these four started an hour before we had to leave. We had D.M.'s Honey, C.C. Beauty, Mohawk Knight, and Kid Eagle. D.M.'s Honey was a half-brother to Honey's Best. That meant he was out of the same dam (or mom). If they had the same sire (father), then he wouldn't be called a half-brother. He would be referred to as having the same sire as Honey's Best. This vernacular helps distinguish which parent they have in common without having to actually say it. This also sheds light on how important the dam is to pedigree. Yearlings at sales bring much higher money if a half-sibling has performed well in the past when compared to a foal that has the same sire as a horse that has done well.

D.M.'s Honey was the foal that hit the ground a year before Honey's Best entered our world out of Honey Sparkle Way. He was fast and could pace cleanly. He had an odd smoothness to his gait. He had the look of those speed walkers back in the seventies that waddled when they were going. Their heads didn't bob up and down like a runner's, and they shifted back and forth as they went. That was how D.M.'s Honey paced. Smooth as silk but somehow it seemed like he never extended himself or was restricted from really hitting top speed. He barely picked his feet up off the ground. In horse circles, he was known as a daisy cutter. He won his share of races but never amounted to all that much, but he was racing that night.

The ride up to the track was uneventful. We figured if there was going to be a problem that this would be when it would happen. There was no way we could put C.C. Beauty next to Mohawk. It was bad enough that he could smell her behind him. Putting him next to her would have been a mistake. We might as well ask a monkey to guard the bananas. We certainly couldn't put him in the back stalls, because she would have been in direct eye and scent line in front of him. At this point in their storied rivalry, we really didn't know how much Mohawk had a problem with Kid, so we placed the two of them up in the front stalls, while D.M. and C.C. traveled in coach in the back.

There were so many strikes against the stocky stud that should have made us hate him, but when all was said and done, he won races. Losing breeds contempt, but winning breeds admiration. Although he was racing in $1,500 claimers (one step above the bottom rung), he got the job done week after week. He was a steady paycheck. In twenty-five starts that year, he had seven wins, six seconds, and nine thirds. He made us like him despite being a problem child.

Besides his bad attitude, his equipment card was a nightmare. If there was a piece of equipment that could be worn by a pacer, Mohawk wore it. He had to wear a hood, which covered his ears and partially blinded his eyes. He needed that to keep his mind on business. Without it, he would often get excited by the mares at the track, and you would have to deal with his baseball bat-sized penis flailing about. It was quite embarrassing, and distracting for a racehorse. He had trouble walking with that thing swinging in the breeze, let alone try to race with it. The hood stayed on. On top of that, he wore a shadow roll on his nose. For most horses, it was there to block out shadows on the track so they wouldn't get scared in the lights. For Mohawk, we wanted him to just focus on what was in front of him. The racetrack was not a nightclub for him to look all over the place trying to pick up dates. He also wore a tongue tie. They all did.

That was just his head. During the race, he had a tendency to bear out in the straight-aways, and then bear in on the turns. When horses do this, it causes a driver to have to pull on the opposite rein to keep the horse traveling straight. There are many reasons horses bear in or out, but for Mohawk, he was just a bull. He did it because he could.

When a horse has his head turned while racing, it dramatically reduces air intake. In order to keep his head from turning in the mile and maximize oxygen flow, headpoles were used on either side of his neck to hold his head straight. They went from the bridle to the harness and were hooked into the same place that the head check was clipped to (the check, or overcheck, is a strap that runs from the top of the horse's head to the center of the back to keep the head elevated). The anchor point is called the water hook. It should have been called a check hook, but I didn't name it. I guess in cart and buggy days, there were water hooks. I don't know.

Mohawk Knight in the winner's circle in all his armor.

In any event, the double headpole scenario made checking him up extremely difficult. To make it even trickier, the left headpole, which faced me, was wrapped with small rubber burrs. They were there because when he felt the burrs on his skin, he would be less likely to fight the headpole. Like I said, he was a bull. To him, the burrs were no more than a nuisance, but to my human skin, they hurt like hell and bored into my arm as I tried to put on the check.

The two leather straps that held the headpoles onto the harness took up a good amount of the stem of the water hook that the clasp of the overcheck snapped onto. This was located at the very top of the harness over his back. I had to push down on the leather straps and try to clip on the snap while he threw his head up and down. His head was considerably heavy and much stronger than my one left arm. I swear he knew exactly when I was just about to snap it on, because at that precise moment he would lower his head swiftly and prevent me from doing it. To make it even more challenging, it all had to be done at a brisk jog.

Most horses just walk off and let you check them up. Easy process. Not with Mohawk. It was an event. One that I dreaded the whole night. If you tried to check him up at a walk, he would try to flip over backwards. It wasn't a safe option. Doug would get on the bike while I led him out of the paddock. There was at least a quarter-mile stretch from the paddock to the grandstand for me to accomplish my task. I had to sidestep next to him like in a defensive basketball drill. Meanwhile my right hand had to press down on his double headpole straps as my left hand tried to elevate his head enough to snap on the overcheck.

Doug would have him rolling right along so that he didn't try to stop or flip over, but sometimes he got him going faster than he needed to. I think he enjoyed watching me suffer. Scratch that. I know he enjoyed it. He would be laughing at me as we made our way up the stretch. I'd be screaming at him to slow him down, and he'd be chuckling saying, "I can't, hee hee hee."

I was actually traveling faster than I could run, using my right hand on the harness to brace my body and just flick myself back up in the air with my feet to keep up with him doing the sidestep. It usually took me at least an eighth of a mile to get it done, but there were instances that it took me a lot longer. One time, I was actually in the post parade in front of the grandstand. Thanks, Gooch. I appreciate you slowing him down back there. We had a running joke that one day I would still be trying to check him up as he crossed the wire at the finish.

Doug would make the call as if he were the announcer at the end of the mile and say, "And at the wire, it's Mohawk Knight closing on the outside and here they arrrrrrrrrrre! Click." And the head check was finally on.

We mused that I would be there in the photo between two horses at the finish, smiling at the camera as I mercifully got that stupid snap on the hook and of course looking like a complete idiot.

As the months went by, we finally figured out a better way to check him up. It had to be well orchestrated, but in the end, our new plan worked out much nicer.

The paddock at Scarboro was a long barn with a single aisle running up the middle. The aisle was about thirty feet wide and separated the stalls on either side. The even numbered races were on the right side, and the odds were on the left. There were fifty stalls on either side. The roof was made of tin, and when a New England thunderstorm rolled through, the noise of the rain off the metal was deafening. The floor was dirt, unlike the one at Lewiston that was made of cement. It was much more comfortable to walk on, but the dust was unbearable if they didn't water it down. There were two nineteen-inch television sets on either end of the three hundred-foot expanse. If you wanted to watch the races and were located in the center, you were going to get your exercise.

In the paddock, with Mohawk still on the crossties, we would have the sulky already on him in the stall. Then, with him standing there, we would check him up. He couldn't flip over backwards because he was essentially tethered to the ground by the crossties on either side of his head. He was like a bull in the chute at a rodeo. At that point, he was angry. He wanted out. Doug got on the bike and I unhooked the two crossties simultaneously and pointed him down the aisle of the paddock.

Before this was done, I had to make an announcement that Mohawk Knight was about to be sprung loose. He was well known at Scarboro. People ducked for cover. I always waited for the last horse of his race to be outside of the paddock before releasing him. He traveled at a good clip down the aisle. Most horses walked. He was crazy. If he was in one of the later races, he had a good bit of runway before the exit. There were a few nights he was just a blur when he went past the paddock judge's office at the end of the barn on the way out.

The new technique certainly put more people at risk, but it was better for me, and that was good. No more running beside him and having Gooch laugh at me. No more stomach cramps from sprinting a half-mile at top speed. No more headpole burrs digging into my arm. Yup, this new technique suited me just fine.

His equipment card didn't stop at the neck. He wore hopples, of course, since he was a pacer, although there a few horses out there that don't require them. They are called free-legged pacers and are beautiful to watch. Mohawk wasn't one of them. He also wore knee boots, tendon boots, bell boots, back brace bandages, a tail tie, and a jock strap. His testicles were bigger than most studs his size. We had to keep those boys from jostling around or he might get more irritable than he already was.

When we sent him out to the track, he looked like one of those horses in King Richard's Faire getting ready to joust. If Doug's whip was a lance, they would have fit right in.

Even carrying the extra twenty pounds of equipment, he won again that night. He was a machine. Meanwhile, Kid Eagle was second as was C.C. Beauty, and D.M.'s Honey got a third. They all hit the board. What a great night. We wished they all could be like that. Since the ride up worked out so well, we loaded them up in the exact configuration that we had earlier. We stopped at Lisa's Pizza for a celebratory slice and headed home. That's the way it was supposed to be. That was why we raced.

We were about halfway down Route 95 South when the ruckus started. Doug and I were in the tack room of the gooseneck trailer, talking about the night and how well the horses had done, lying on our backs with our legs facing forward. We could tell right away that the two horses up front were having major issues. Harryman was driving the truck and could feel the weight of the two animals shifting back and forth and knew something was wrong and pulled over. We both jumped down off the mattress and scooted through the little half-door to gain access to the horses' quarters.

It was a war zone.

Mohawk had ripped down the four-by-eight piece of plywood that separated him and Kid at their heads. He had also ripped out the strap that held his head secured to the opposite wall. He was attacking Kid on the left side of the trailer. He had the whole center partition pressed up against him, forcing Kid to the ground. His legs were under Mohawk and the stud was kicking him while he was down and at the same time biting him from the top.

Doug and I both grabbed Mohawk's head and pulled him away, yelling at him to stop. If horses don't understand a simple command like "whoa," a crazed stallion in a fight isn't going to understand anything we were going to shout at him. But the adrenaline we all had running through us prevented us from doing anything but scream out loud.

After stopping the rig, my father and mother were unloading C.C. Beauty and D.M.'s Honey off the back of the trailer. Once Doug and I separated the two up front, we could then unload at least one of the two that were fighting through the vacated stalls. On the side of a busy highway at midnight is not the optimal place to be unloading horseflesh. Eighteen wheelers rushed past them, inches from the side of the road. They didn't even slow down a little bit.

Trailers are a dangerous place for us humans. Years ago, my mother was helping to unload a horse by the name of Em Press Walter. I never liked the name, and I never liked the horse. He was a typical ornery stud and didn't have much of a personality or manners. When he backed off the trailer, he liked to back off the ramp to the left instead of walking off straight like a gentleman. Someone needed to push him to the right to straighten him out.

One night at Scarboro, my mother reached in on the left side to coax him over to the middle of the trailer when the stallion leaned hard against the center partition and slammed her hand against the left wall. Her ring finger was smashed. Living on a farm and getting hurt routinely, you learn about injuries and swelling. Her broken finger started to swell quickly, and realizing that her ring may get stuck from the edema, she ripped the wedding band off her finger and inadvertently flung it into the darkness.

She lost the ring but saved her finger. Self-preservation is the key when you work with the horse. Material items can always be replaced. We looked for the ring for over an hour. Finally, it was my mother who called off the futile search.

"It's just a ring, it's not my finger," she said definitively.

I had to respect her grasp of perspective. In the big picture, she was right. It was only a ring. I'm not convinced there are a lot of women that would have walked away that night. She let it go. It wasn't what was really important. She had been hurt, but not as severely as she could have. It was a lesson learned in dealing with horses on trailers.

That night it was my turn to go to school. Once I had Mohawk's head fairly secured and he couldn't keep Kid Eagle pinned down, Kid scrambled to his feet. He was one pissed-off horse. Doug saw that I had Mohawk under control and went behind him to unhook the back gate and let him out. Like a referee trying to break up a hockey fight, I was positioned in the middle of the trailer trying to keep the two of them apart.

As Doug was trying to get the bar behind Mohawk released, Kid retaliated. He lashed out and sunk his teeth into my back. Apparently he didn't get the memo from the commissioner about the etiquette of fighting. Once the ref steps in, you stop throwing punches.

The pain ripped through me as he tore my flesh and the sweatshirt I was wearing. More screaming. He was coming back for a second attack as I ducked left. Thankfully Doug had opened the gate and I pushed Mohawk back down the aisle. I could hear Kid still scrambling around up front, trying to fight back. It's over dude, let it go. Besides, he'd kick your ass. Just relax up there.

We had three horses on the side of the highway at that point and now had no idea what to do from there. We were in quite a dilemma. The partition we had set up was shredded and it was clear that Mohawk wasn't going to work and play well with others. There was no possible way we could ship him with another horse.

It was eerily quiet for a moment as cars had cleared away and none us were talking. It was a group brainstorm. It couldn't be done. The thought of just cutting Mohawk loose and parting ways with him crossed my mind.

After an agonizing minute of silence, Harryman had an idea. We could try to put one of the horses in the tack room. But which horse? The door into the room was no bigger than a door to a house, in fact a little smaller. Would it even be possible to get a horse in there? And if so, which one would be willing to actually do it? We all looked around trying to answer those questions and all of our eyes collectively landed on D.M.'s Honey. He had a look on his face as if to say, "Whoa whoa whoa, don't look at me, I'm not going in there."

Like in a sitcom, after the character just gets done emphatically saying he won't do it, D.M. was crammed into the little tack room with a blank stare on his face. He had an expression that said, "You have got to be kidding me." No, we're not kidding. He rode quietly in the little tack room all the way home with his head up on the mattress where Doug and I were located. He traveled like he belonged there. Not many horses would have gone through that little door. He got an extra flake of hay and pat on the forehead at the end of the night.

After we unloaded the rest of them, we tended to Kid Eagle's wounds. None of them were as bad as the day Hardwood Bret went down, but there was a fairly significant amount of blood on the floor of the trailer where he was. Almost all of his wounds were superficial. Luckily, while he was on his side and Mohawk was dancing on his exposed legs, no real damage was done to any tendons or ligaments. He just had dozens of little scrapes and a few good-sized cuts on his shoulder and hip. The old-timers had an expression for wounds like this. They'd say, "It's superficial; it's a long way from his heart."

I wasn't sure about that one. The one on his shoulder was pretty bad and there was a deep laceration on his chest that was fairly close to his heart. What a silly expression, I thought to myself. So let's see, if the trailer floor gave out on the highway, and all four feet got scraped off in a horrific accident, wouldn't *that* be a long way from his heart? Stupid old-timers. Tell Kid that his wounds weren't significant. I'm sure he would tell you otherwise. He was covered in cuts, bites, and scrapes. He was a mess.

In a couple weeks, Kid had just about fully recovered from his fracas with Mohawk and was fine. We were back to jogging him on the track and preparing him for the races. He still had one wound over his right shoulder that wasn't healed completely, and part of the harness would rub on it when he went out to exercise. It would be more prudent to tow him on the truck. This way, he didn't have to wear any equipment and the wound could heal faster.

The tow truck was just a modified pickup truck. A ten-foot two-by-twelve board was placed over the wheel wells on top of the rails of the pickup. Large half-inch bolts held the boards in place to the truck body. Three feet of board stuck out on either side for the horses to be held safely away from the tires of the vehicle. Two horses could be hooked up and they would jog right alongside the truck. Remember, this is not a very big deal to a Standardbred. They are trained to follow inches from a starting gate that is traveling in excess of thirty miles an hour. Jogging at ten to twelve miles an hour next to a truck is of little concern to them.

If we had three horses to jog and the chemistry between them was good, a third horse could be hooked on the very back on the trailer hitch with a five-foot lead chain. This saved tremendously on time and effort, because one person could essentially jog three horses all at one time. You needed help putting them on and taking them off, as most horses got anxious when they were just standing there. The first horse got put on the right side of the truck, and then traveled one lap, then the next horse got hooked up on the left side, and then the two of them jogged a lap together. Finally, the third one got put on the back and they kept going. The driver of the truck stayed seated the whole time. On the last time around for the first horse, the driver would honk the horn indicating the white flag lap. The first horse that was hooked up came off and so on until they were all safely removed.

The standard jog distance was four miles, or twelve times around our track. The whole process took about twenty minutes. By doing three at once, it saved at least forty minutes of work each time. Since no harnessing or un-harnessing was needed, the time saved was even more significant. It was worth it.

We had blamed ourselves for the incident between Mohawk and Kid a few weeks back. The only reason it happened was because we put a crazy stud too close to another horse. We should have known better. But we didn't have a huge choice after they had been pro-grammed to race. The real mistake was made the day of the draw when all four horses got entered. After that, it was just a matter of fate. We had taken precautions by putting up a large wooden partition between the two, and a blanket. We even chose the easy-going Kid Eagle to ride next to him. We couldn't have pre-dicted Mohawk throwing a nutty and trying to kill the poor horse.

It did teach us never to ship Mohawk with anyone next to him ever again. It also taught us that a horse *can* in fact fit in the tack room of a trailer. Who-da thunk it?

There are horse people out there calling me a liar right now. But then again, they were never stuck on the side of a highway with a lunatic stal-lion and no other reasonable options to get all of their horses home safely. Necessity is the mother of invention.

If we should have known better about the shipping incident, we certainly should have known not to do what we did next. Kid was already on the right side of the truck, and there was only one more horse to jog. It was Mohawk, of course. Because Mohawk didn't like to be checked up, it was not fun to hook him up to jog either. We almost always towed him on the truck except when he was in need of a training trip (a mile at near top speed to prepare for an upcoming race). We had a choice. Tow Kid by himself and then do Mohawk after that, or just don't bother towing Mohawk at all. It was getting late in the day, and we needed to get ready to ship out for the track. A decision needed to be made. It was the wrong one.

After Harryman took Kid for a lap, I brought Mohawk out of the barn and hooked him to the outside clip on the fly. I was used to clipping things with Mohawk jogging so it was no big deal. We figured keeping him moving would keep his mind to task, and we were right. He hollered and carried on like he always did, but things went smoothly. The two adversaries were out there together, ten feet apart, with a pickup truck in between them. Seemed safe enough at the time.

It was just a half lap or so, and the two of them were talking trash. They were jogging sideways, facing each other from either side of the truck. They were both angry. The conversation was becoming quite heated. I don't speak horse, but I'm sure it was not fit for a yearling's ears.

It was obvious now that the incident on the trailer was not just an accident or poor judgment on our part. There was real bad blood between these two. But now what? We were in it at this point. Trying to grab Mohawk off the truck would have been suicidal. He was frenetic, yanking on his chain and trying to snap it off, rearing up in the air. Kid wasn't any calmer, but he didn't look half as mean as the stud. Wow, he was scary when he was like this.

How to get them off the truck was quickly answered. With one huge yank of his head, Mohawk ripped the bolt clean through the board that held it to the truck. Uh oh. The velociraptor just figured out how to get out of the electrified fence.

No sooner did he do that, but he swung around the back of the truck and then yanked out the other side as well. The two horses were completely removed from the truck but were held together by a ten-foot board and two pieces of chain that had the board hanging between them like a child's swing.

They were crazed. They wanted to kill each other, but fortunately the board was keeping them apart. As they faced each other, Mohawk was charging at Kid and pushing him backward even though Kid was trying to hold his ground. The stud was too strong. They danced like this across the track and through a paddock, destroying fences along the way with the board that hung between them. We couldn't get close to them. It was too dangerous. We would have to wait for them to figure out that nothing was going to come of this fight, and they would eventually settle down.

It was a good thought until the board broke in half. The sheer force of the two horses facing off and pressing it into one another splintered it exactly in two, with the ends that broke becoming giant wooden stakes. Before the board broke, Kid was

acting brave enough, pushing toward Mohawk as if
to say, "Come on, big fella, come get some." When
the board snapped, both horses backed up two steps
and froze. They were assessing the situation. Kid no
longer looked confident and cocky. His eyes changed
expressions and he had a look of horror on his face.

Mohawk's look was just the opposite. He looked
triumphant, and his eyes flashed at Kid as if to tell
him, "That's right, boy, it's on now."

Kid turned tail and ran away as fast as he could
with a splintered board hanging by his head, banging
against his chest and legs. Mohawk didn't hesitate. He
followed him with the other half smashing away at his
front end. He didn't care, he wanted Kid and that was
all that mattered.

He cornered him in a paddock and the real fight
started. It was out of control. Not only were these two
fighting head to head, just like in the days of their an-
cestors, but they had brought weapons into the ring.
As they threw their heads about, the boards were
flung at each other, smashing into their muscles and
skin. The splintered ends were five feet long and easily could have penetrated through the heart if they
were unlucky. Now *that* would not be superficial.

Doug, Harryman, and I could only stand and
watch. And yell, of course. We tried several times
to get between them, but it was so perilous that we
bailed out. Finally, Doug got a long whip used for
longeing (trotting in a large circle with a person at
the center) horses and snapped it a few times in front
of Mohawk. It backed him off just enough for Kid
to escape out of the paddock, dragging his wooden
dagger with him. I'm not sure if it was the whip that
did it, or just exhaustion that made him stop momen-

tarily, but it was finally over. Mohawk was lathered up with white foamy sweat and was blowing fiercely.

Doug crept up to him slowly, unhooked the board from his head, and clipped on a lead shank. Now it was really over.

It was official. These two could never be together again. We were fortunate that Kid wasn't killed that day. The board got in the way enough to prevent Mohawk from getting on top of him and finishing him off. They both were hurt but nothing so serious that they wouldn't be able to race in the next few weeks.

After that experience, Mohawk had to be jogged by himself for the rest of his days with us. We knew he was powerful, but that display of raw strength and determination was something none of us wanted to see unleashed again. It was terrifying.

The summer dragged on, and Mohawk kept finishing in the top three. We raced him all the way up to $2,000 claimers by mid-September and he was still doing well. The fights seemed to make him even braver than he already was. His menacing screams as he paraded down the aisle of the paddock with his grotesquely large phallus rocking back and forth like a gigantic metronome led us to believe that we might just own him forever. His Kamikaze actions checking him up didn't help any either. Who in their right mind would ever want to claim this horse? He was a freak.

Believe it or not, someone claimed him the very next week for the inflated price of $2,000. It was a bittersweet parting. Part of us celebrated his leaving because we were free of his obnoxious behavior. The other part of us would miss the income. He was our little ATM machine.

The barn was quiet without him around. It was nice. Everyone breathed a little easier. Winter was coming, and dealing with him on the ice was always even more difficult than usual because the footing was so poor. It was a relief. It was late November when Doug saw that Mohawk was racing up north at Lewiston Raceway. He was in for $1,000.

It was almost the end of the winter meet. Just a week more and the tracks would close for Christmas and New Year's and reopen sometime in February. We had all but shut down the stable for the year. We usually gave the horses forty-five days off and started them back in mid-February.

We sat in the family room having dinner when Doug suggested we might claim him back. There was a dead silence that followed. Was he joking? He couldn't be serious. "Please let him be joking," I thought.

"You're out of your mind," my father spoke up. "Why would you want that crazy son of a bitch back? He's going to hurt somebody one day."

"Yeah, but he's in for a thousand bucks. He'll make that back in two weeks for us," Doug replied.

"Two weeks, right, but not until February. You're crazier than *he* is," I said.

We had had bad experiences claiming horses back. There was, of course, the Hardwood Bret fiasco. Then there was the Denza Gait debacle at Foxboro. We had wanted to claim this classy claimer back after we had lost him the previous week, but we were racing up at Scarboro. We had to ask a friend to pick him up for us. His name was Mike Sherr. He was an ex-football coach at Central Catholic High School who was habitually late to everything he did. We referred to him as the Late Mike Sherr. It made me nervous that he was going to go get him for us. I was right. He blew it. Apparently there was a Monkees concert at Foxboro Stadium the same day of his race, and the traffic was backed up for miles. He was running late as it was and didn't even come close to getting the claim in on time.

After that, we decided it was a bad omen to claim horses back. Now, we not only were considering claiming a horse back, we were getting the equine version of Genghis Kahn. My father and I were not thrilled. We discussed the pros and cons and cons and cons for quite a while. Doug won the argument. Much to my disbelief, we were claiming him back. I had nightmares that night of running down the track trying to check him up again. There was Gooch, sitting in the sulky, laughing an evil laugh, not even trying to slow him down.

There were no issues with the claim whatsoever. It went through just like it was supposed to. No Hardwood Bret technicalities, no Monkees concert. Of all the times for something to go wrong, I wished it was this one. It couldn't have gone smoother. I couldn't tell if the people we took him from were happy or not. Something told me that they weren't going to lose any sleep over it.

When we got him home, he strutted down the aisle and gave out a yell to all the horses that were sleeping just to let them know he was coming home to roost. Kid must have woken up in a cold sweat thinking he was having a bad dream. Looking diagonally across at Mohawk's vacant stall certainly would have given him some relief that he was in fact just dreaming. As we made our way past him in the barn, he became aware that it was all too real. The bully was back.

We had all but shut it down for the season. With only one week left in the meet at Lewiston, we decided to race Mohawk on closing night to try to recoup some of the claim money. If he won, we could recoup half of what we bought him back for. Lewiston was a good two-hour drive, and we would only be taking the one horse up there. He needed to win for it to be worthwhile.

We entered him in a $1,500 claimer, which was a pretty big step up from the $1,000 class we took him from. The purse was significantly higher, as was the competition, but we knew he could handle it. Besides, we really didn't want someone to take him back the following week after we just got him. Well, Doug didn't want to lose him, I really didn't care.

It was December 4, 1989. The weather was calling for the first real snowfall of the season. Perfect. This would be an ideal time to drive two hours north up Route 95 into the teeth of a Nor'easter and race a horse that was certifiably insane. I was excited about this plan.

We tried to talk Gooch into scratching him to avoid driving in bad conditions. Negative. He wanted to race him. If we didn't go with him, he was going up there by himself. Sitting next to the woodstove, sipping hot chocolate and watching old movies was certainly tempting. We couldn't let him go alone. The three of us got in the truck and headed north. The only sane person of the family was my mother. She stayed home.

Halfway up to Lewiston, the snow started to fly. It was going to be a long night. When the race went off, it was an absolute white-out. I saw the horses only when they were directly in front of the grandstand on the television in the paddock. When they left the gate, Mohawk was pressing for the lead, and then disappeared into the turn. The announcer went quiet. At the half he was third. I had no idea what had transpired in the first part of the mile. I'm not sure Doug did either. The visibility was the worst he said he had ever raced in. I picked up the field again at the head of the stretch. Mohawk's hood and double headpoles led the way. The lunatic had won the race. He did what we asked of him once again.

We loaded him up and started for home at around 10:30 at night. We had outrun the storm somewhat heading north, but it had caught up to us and then some by the time we got in the truck and headed homeward. Lewiston Raceway was twenty minutes north off of mile seventy-one of the Maine Turnpike. When we hit mile marker sixty passing through Gray, the visibility was near zero. Doug wasn't saying much because he knew how we all felt. There was a giant elephant in the cab of the truck that no one wanted to acknowledge. It was whispering the words, "I told you so." In the trailer, there was a thousand-pound beast of a horse reveling in the fact that he was spending the winter in a barn that could give him the chance to beat up Kid Eagle again.

It was midnight when we crept through Kennebunkport doing twenty-five miles an hour. The conditions were becoming treacherous. The snowplows hadn't done much of anything yet and the storm was intensifying.

It was nearing one in the morning when we hit Greenland at the New Hampshire border. Passing by the previous off ramps, it was becoming clear that it was possible we might not get home that night. They hadn't yet plowed them and there was almost a foot of snow on the ground. If we had any chance of making it up the incline of our exit, we needed more speed.

Two miles out, Doug started to accelerate slowly. The tires were spinning badly as he tried, but after a while he was up to about fifty miles an hour. Heading toward the exit, Doug drifted two lanes left and then started angling right to get a more direct shot up the ramp. The main highway was packed down somewhat from the traffic. When we hit the ramp with a wall of snow on the road, it felt like he slammed on the brakes. We could feel Mohawk lurch forward as we slowed down abruptly. The trailer started fishtailing to the left. Doug laid off the accelerator and let the inertia of the truck take us up the hill. I looked back and could see the trailer catching up to us on the left. By some stroke of luck, the trailer wheels caught the edge of an even larger swath of snow and stopped sliding. It kicked back behind us and straightened out.

We were slowing down quickly and were not quite at the top of the off ramp. Doug was feathering the accelerator to get as much traction as he could. The rig was slowing down as we neared the top of the hill. He had no choice but to lay on the gas pedal as we came to a stop. The tires spun violently under the truck. The speedometer was reading fifty-five but we were doing about eight miles an hour. If we didn't make the crest, we were spending the night right there.

The front end of the truck leveled out as we inched forward. The little short-bed Chevy broke the crest of the hill and started to ever so slowly creep down the other side. We made it in one piece. We all exhaled at the same time. Wow, that was close. But it wasn't over. We were still twenty-five miles from home and we were in the heart of a blizzard.

Almost two hours later, we limped into the driveway at the farm. It was nearly three in the morning. We barely got the back end of the trailer off the road as we got stuck pulling in.

The snow muffled almost every noise in our little universe. It was beautifully quiet when we got him off of the trailer. Then Mohawk let out one of his blood-curdling screams that only he could. He had won his race, and he was letting everyone know it. Normally we brought the horses in through the side door when we got home. There was too much snow on the ground to go that route. We had to enter through the front, under the basketball net. This meant we would have to pass in front of Kid Eagle's stall on the way by.

The first part of the barn was cement and the clip-clop of his shoes echoed down the aisle. We clambered down the shed-row and I could see the blaze of Kid's face lurking in the darkness of his stall to my left. He was not impressed with the entrance of the thug. I was sure to keep the stallion's head away from Kid's stall as we made our way through.

With stunning quickness, Kid lunged out and nailed Mohawk in the left flank with a well-timed bite.

Welcome home, jerk. Mohawk kicked back at him with double-barrel action but we were already too far past for him to connect. It was extraordinary. These two horses loathed each other.

We owned Mohawk for another two years until he got to be thirteen years old and he was sold to the Amish folk in Pennsylvania. He was too crazy to sell as a riding horse, but the Amish liked his size and really liked his black coat. They took him for breeding purposes and he was actually turned out as stud with a harem of mares. Although public perception is that all stallions eventually get put out to pasture, the reality is that most studs aren't of breeding quality and are gelded when they are done racing. This allows them to be used in everyday situations without the increased risk of hurting someone, which is common when working with stallions. His bad behavior was rewarded. Of course it was, nice guys finish last.

He did extremely well for us. We put up with his nonsense, and we collected the purse checks. We treated him better than I suspect anyone else would have or really should have based on his attitude. I gained a lot of respect for Kid Eagle that night when we came home. He already had two run-ins with an obviously stronger foe, but he was still willing to stand his ground. He didn't care if Mohawk ultimately would beat him up. He wasn't going to lay down for anyone, not even for him.

In life, there are people that for some reason or another you just can't get along with. Some people are just ugly. If possible, it's best to just alienate yourself from them and go on with life. Sometimes you can't, and you have to deal with them. Even the most passive and peaceful person has his limits. As gentle an animal as Kid was, he recognized evil when he saw it and stood up to it when he needed to. Every once in a while you need to make a stand. Bad people can bring out the worst in good people. Occasionally you have to fight back against the bully, whether it be an abusive classmate, a harassing boss, or a deceitful establishment. The world is full of them. Avoid them if you can, but if you can't, sometimes you need to take off the gloves. Even if it means getting your ass kicked.

Rochester Fair

The Rochester Fair has been around for over a hundred years. When people imagine a country fair with tractor pulls, greased pig contests, and vegetables on display for the right to win a ribbon, they are imagining this fair. Although I wasn't around when it first started, I get the feeling that the atmosphere and texture of the fair itself has remained constant throughout the years.

The only thing missing that year from the midway was the tent with "Lobster Boy" and the "Rubber Man." They almost always showed up on the Maine circuit at fairs like Fryeburg, Cumberland and Skowhegan. For some reason, they hadn't made it to Rochester this time.

As a kid, I can remember walking by the tent hearing the same call over and over again…"Come see Lobster Boy, instead of having hands like you and me, he has the claws of a lobster!" I never did pay to see him and often wondered if his hands were webbed or if they were red. Maybe they were both.

I passed through the main gate, making my way by the agricultural barns, past the chickens and the pigs, and then by the sheep and ponies, the smell of cotton candy mixing with the straw of the bedding and the wafting of manure. It was sweet and pungent all at once. The young kids and their parents loved that last barn. Surprisingly, I never heard of any child losing a finger to an omnivorous goat or an ornery pony.

With the smell of the barns behind me, the true flavor of the fair came to aromatic life. The lure of Pat's Apple Crisp and the giant slabs of fried dough with honey and powdered sugar poured on top, drifted invitingly through the air. Jim's French Fries, made from fresh peeled potatoes topped with a sprinkling of vinegar that made your mouth water without even tasting it. The candy apples, the steaming hot homemade chili with extra Tabasco sauce, and of course the authentic New England clam chowder all seducing me to stop. It was an orgasmic journey of olfactory pleasure. Some newcomers would race through the fair tasting as many things as they could. I was a seasoned veteran. I had learned to walk and try them all.

The last three barns were located just before the grandstand and were there for the horsemen that had racehorses. Most guys shipped in, but a few of the locals actually kept their horses there almost year round. The track didn't charge them for the stalls as long as they raced at the fair. It was a pretty nice set-up for them.

Between the last barn and the stands was the pulling ring. Most of the time I had to weave around the draft horses and oxen as I made my way through the horsemen's entrance along the back fence of the grounds. The general public had to stay on the outskirts of the fair to park, or was shuttled to the infield of the track. Ironically, I would often wonder what would make someone want to have pulling horses and waste their time with such nonsense. As I peered back at them in my rearview mirror, it's likely they were thinking the same about me.

It was the fall of 1987. We were preparing for the Rochester Fair once again. The little track to the north of us was a break from the monotony of the summer schedule in Maine. It was a considerably shorter trip for us since it was in our home state and only about a half-hour drive up Route 125. Each year, the fair fell on the third week in September and ran from Thursday to the following Saturday. Ten race cards in all. They held double headers on each Saturday to get them all in. There were days we would race three or four in the afternoon, go home, and then pick up three or four more for the evening card. It got hectic at times, but it was fun.

We didn't need a farmer's almanac to tell us what the weather would be like that week. It was going to rain. It rained every Rochester Fair. It was a given. If you ever visit New England in the fall for the foliage, don't come here on the third week in September. Trust me. It will rain.

The track was made of stone dust and clay. When it rained, the surface became a wet, sticky, muddy mess. In all the years of racing, I've only seen them cancel the races once due to weather. It was the year the starting gate drove clear through the outside fence on a particularly slippery track surface. There was no other car available to start the races. On the nights the track was listed as sloppy, and at Rochester it seemed like it was all the time, the drivers would come back to the paddock looking like little gray gumby dudes. The only untouched human part of them that was recognizable was the whites of their eyes and their teeth if they could muster up a smile.

Doug was at the pinnacle of his racing career. For the past three years, his number of drives had increased consistently as more and more owners and trainers used his services. The run we had with Honey's Best and the rest of our improving stable through the mid-eighties had opened up the eyes of a lot of people. He had made the top ten drivers' list at Scarboro over the long summer, and at one point was ranked number three. It was now time for Doug to try to win the Rochester Fair driving title in earnest. For many years, he was no more than a long shot to win it, since he never had enough drives to have a legitimate chance. For the first time, we felt this could be his year.

I was in my third year at the University of New Hampshire in the Life Sciences and Agriculture program. I was just starting to apply to veterinary schools and had no idea if I would be accepted. Along the road, there had been many people that told me it was only a pipedream, including my own guidance counselor in high school. At that point, although my childhood ambition was to become a vet, I hadn't ever worried about what would happen if I didn't get in. We had a strong family unit, and what the future held for me would never change that, so worrying about potential failure wasn't the focus of my thoughts.

As a senior at UNH, I lived at the fraternity house of Lambda Chi Alpha on Madbury Lane, which was known as fraternity row. The house has long since been condemned and our chapter was revoked. The Greek system generally gets bad press, and probably for good reason, but those years at UNH were arguably the best of my life. It was a simpler time. No cell phones, no lap tops, and no Blackberries. When I got in my car and drove to the races from UNH, I felt a beautiful peacefulness.

I drove a gold 1981 Datsun 710 hatchback. My father bought it used two years previously for $3,100 when Honey was winning in the stakes program. At the time, it was the most we had ever spent on a passenger vehicle. As it got older, and I went off to college, he gave it to me. Man, I loved that car.

It may seem odd that he would just give me the car like that. In reality, our family was based on a more socialist way of functioning. There was no real mine, his, or yours. Everything was ours. I don't care what it was. Bikes, fishing rods, cars, and even money. We never got allowances when we were kids. If money was available, we got it. If it wasn't, we made do. Even though he gave me the car, it was still *our* car. I called it mine, but if for any reason anyone else wanted to use it, it was fair game.

During school, I got a work study job in the biochemistry department making $4.10 an hour. I made enough money to buy an Alpine stereo and some Bose speakers and installed them myself. At the time, it was the bomb. By today's standards, it would likely be low-end crap, but you never could have told me that. Each night of the fair, when all the students would either go study or party, I would drive to Rochester by myself to meet the family in the paddock and groom whatever horses we had in that night. The brothers at the house thought I was crazy. Maybe I was.

I made a routine of the drive. Back then, we had cassette tapes. We were just hearing about the CDs for the home, but for now it was just cassettes. Although I had a fairly decent collection of various artists neatly strewn about the entire floor of the car, the only tape I played on my way to the track was Bob Seger's *Night Moves* album. There was no particular reason that I started playing that album, but it all started on opening night. When I pulled into the grounds, the song "Sunburst" was playing. That night, Doug had three wins, three seconds, and a third. I didn't want to change anything. When I was about four minutes away, I would start the song "Sunburst" and ritualistically play it as I neared the racetrack. Karma. Don't mess with Karma.

The song was quite fitting for the mood and landscape of what we were going through. Sunburst describes the type of guitar the character in the song plays. He uses it like a weapon on stage in his performance. Doug, who is an excellent guitarist, had just recently purchased a beautiful sunburst guitar himself. The lyrics were echoing the story of what was unfolding at the fair with my brother. As one line in the song goes…*"He's stepping proud and bold, and everything he touches turns to gold."*

Some of the horses Doug led to the winner's circle that week had absolutely no right winning. If he wanted to claim the title and win the Jesse Brown Memorial Driver's Trophy, he would have to have the Midas touch for ten straight days. Most of his drives were for people that had only one or two horses. He drove for the smaller stables and most of them didn't have the preferred stock. He took the extra time with those trainers who really just wanted an ear to talk to. Doug was a great listener, and trainers trusted him with their horses. While the other big name drivers relied on the larger stables to fill their dance card, Doug had started a grass roots campaign and was filling his card one horse at a time.

My little gold car was what you would call a sub-compact and could fit into some fairly tight spaces. To finalize my ceremonious arrival, there was always the same parking spot waiting for me. It's not like I had a V.I.P. spot or anything like that, it's just that no one had figured out how to use this one particular piece of real estate to park. I would squeeze the car between a telephone pole and the guide wire that came down alongside of it. There was very little room to spare on either side, and in order to get out, I would have to make sure the doorjamb was clear of the pole to allow the door to open.

It was an ideal spot, as most nights when I got there all of the spaces within a mile of the paddock were taken. The fair was quite popular back then, and it was not unheard of to park well outside the facility and walk in. Not me and my little 710. I owned that spot for two years after I discovered it. Later on, other little parasites with tiny little parasitic cars saw me there and started using it themselves. I guess nothing lasts forever.

After wedging fifty-two inches of car into my fifty-four-inch spot, I would pull out the program and see what we had in store for the evening. The little car was getting older, and starting to show signs of age. In order to turn the dome light on to read the program, it was necessary do three things. 1) The car had to be car running or the ignition had to be on, 2) the driver's door had to be open, and 3) the car had to be in reverse. No lie. That part of the car I hated. But it always made me laugh. For several months before the winter of '86, the dome light stopped working. Serendipitously, I figured out how it could turn on when I was stuck in a snow bank during a blizzard. With the car running, I had to open my door to look behind me while I backed the car up...Eureka!

To make the scene even more humorous, when the car was in reverse, it would make a repetitive ding-dong noise to let you know that you were backing up. As the dinging took place, the dome light would get dimmer and brighter as the dinging started and stopped. I didn't spend a lot of time perusing the program. The purpose of looking was to count the drives Doug had for the night. It gave me a pulse as to what to expect.

The Driver's Title at Rochester was a highly coveted award. Every driver that set foot on the track wanted to win it. Not most of them. All of them. Winning was a matter of prestige. The trophy and the small $500 check that came with it was nothing more than a formality. It was the winning that mattered. The odd thing about the quest for the title was that no one talked about it. No one. I suppose it's similar to actors who wish to win an Oscar. They don't go around talking about how they hope to win a little gold statue of a man, or how nice it would be just to get nominated for it. No. They go about their business and if they so happen to be in position to win it, they cherish it forever.

It was no different to these guys. Since it was only once a year, and a very short ten-day meet, if they were lucky, there may be only one opportunity in a driver's career when all the stars would line up and the time was right for it to happen. So many things had to go perfectly, but so many things could go wrong. Realistically, a driver needed at least five drives a night out of the ten races slated. Of those five drives, he had to have some sort of stock. Not just any horse in the race would do. He needed quality stock. Even good drivers can't win with a rat (another name for a nag). He also needed some luck with drawing post positions.

Rochester was notorious for its "rail bias." An extraordinarily high number of the races were won by horses from the one- or two-hole. The turns were so tight that coming from behind or being on the outside was a major disadvantage. If he didn't have a superior animal in the fight, the driver didn't have much of a chance from the outside posts. Finally, he needed some racing luck. Wins don't come easy, and they weren't going to come without a little help from the racing gods. With all those factors in place, a driver then simply had to drive flawlessly. No mental errors would be acceptable. The races you were supposed to win, you absolutely had to win. There were no do-overs at Rochester.

The point system for keeping tally on the standings was simple. You got three points for a win, two points for second, and a single point for third. Nothing else mattered. A strong fourth-place finish got you a pat on the back and a big goose egg in the point's column.

Many years ago, it was much different. Every place got a point. The winner was awarded eight points, second place was given seven points, and so on, down to a single point for eighth. Back in those days, if a driver was popular enough to be programmed in every race, he could simply win by default. That would be like awarding an Oscar to the *Ernest goes to Camp* actor because he made six films that year. It didn't make sense. The new scoring system made it much more difficult to win than just being on the track. It was now quality-based rather than quantity-based.

When this change was made, the pursuit of the title was on. It brought out some ugly qualities in a lot of drivers. There were no friends on the track at Rochester. The same guy that let a competitor in a hole at Scarboro the week before would hang his own mother out to dry in the first turn if he thought it would benefit himself or be detrimental to his opponent. These guys were no longer out to win races for their owners; they were out to win races for themselves.

It got dangerous as well. Guys would be squeezing their horses out of holes that didn't exist and driving more aggressively than ever. No one was going to hand you a championship. At Rochester, it was earned.

Most of the drivers knew Doug was a threat. Some didn't want to believe it, because in their minds he was still a kid and hadn't earned the right to join their fraternity of the elites. Guys like Leigh Fitch, Paul Battis, and John Nason had all won the title before and were not keen on letting anyone else in their club. During that summer, Doug had run-ins with all of them. It was a form of hazing. It didn't matter that he hadn't done anything wrong, they just didn't like him winning and they would go out of their way to make it known.

Shipping in as we did certainly didn't help. Doug wasn't part of the track scene during the day. He didn't hang out at the track kitchen shooting the breeze. He didn't walk around the stable area in the mornings after a training trip. He simply showed up and won races. From their point of view, he hadn't earned it. They didn't see the hours we put in. We worked just has hard as everyone else and drove an hour and a half both ways to race.

In the years leading up to that week, Doug was finally gaining recognition he deserved from the judges. When he first started driving, if a driver put an objection in on him because they claimed he interfered somewhere in the race, more often than not, he got taken down. The judges can place a horse from where they finished to behind the horse they interfered with. If you won the race but the horse you allegedly impeded finished last, then your horse would be placed last, moving everyone else up one position. The horse that was affected only moved up one spot.

Vindictive drivers that finished out of the money could put objections in just to take him down from the win even though they knew it wouldn't have a real effect on their place in the race. Early on, drivers had a vendetta for this young driver with great hands and high track I.Q. Most judges would take the veteran's word on it and literally not even listen to Doug's side of the story. At times, it was maddening.

But times were changing. They were not only listening to Doug's side, they were asking for his input. Even if he wasn't directly involved in the incident in a race, he would often get called into the paddock office and asked for his account of what had happened.

He had gained the respect of the officials with his style of driving and integrity. Yes, times were changing.

After the first night, Doug already had sixteen points and a five-point cushion over the next driver in second. He drove in seven races and hit the board with all of them. Some of the stock he had was just pathetic, but somehow he got them home. It felt like it was destiny and we were only one night into it. As I looked at the program on Friday night, he needed to have that great prelude, because it wasn't looking promising for him. He was down to drive only three horses.

One of them was none other than the great Honey's Best and she was in the ninth race, the feature race of the night. She had drawn the seven-hole, but at Rochester, the track is so narrow that the starting gate only carries the horses six across at the start, and the seven and eight horses trail behind the one and two respectively. The six hole at Rochester was like having the Grim Reaper himself riding shotgun. Those two trailing horses caused chaos leaving the gate as everyone on the outside was either looking to make the top or find a spot along the rail (so as not to get "parked-out") in order to save ground.

Traveling on the outside the whole mile at Rochester and subsequently win was nearly impossible to do. Getting caught on the outside was actually simple; it was the finishing part that was difficult. With the gate set up the way it was, many horses and their drivers found themselves in the unenviable position of just that, parked out. If you were stuck on the outside at the quarter pole, you might as well go back to the paddock. The race was essentially over for you.

Honey was coming off of her sensational three-year-old campaign where she had won eleven races and set the world on fire. We had soaring expectations for her as she matured from a filly to a mare. Although she had a decent season, it wasn't quite what we had expected. In late August, she was stricken with a puzzling muscle disorder that made her unable to clear the toxins that were being produced while racing. Her muscle enzymes were off the charts. (Muscle enzymes are values that measure the damage to muscles. The most reliable one that we use in veterinary medicine is called an SGOT count.) She was experiencing what people might call muscle cramps, but over her entire body. It's a condition that horse people call "tying up."

There are many reasons for this phenomenon to occur, and most of them are treatable. Try as we did, with the help of an excellent and well-respected veterinarian, we could not figure out why this was happening or how to treat it effectively. To this day, I still haven't figured it out, other than to theorize that it was some sort of virus. It would take a year for her to fully recover from it.

Knowing now what we didn't know then, we would have quit with her for the year. Hindsight is twenty-twenty. We had measured her muscle enzymes that morning to get an indication of how bad off she was and the numbers weren't good. Her SGOT count was over five thousand. Normal values were somewhere in the three hundred range. There was no way we could race her. For a stable that was bringing a full arsenal of weapons to do battle at Rochester, our biggest gun was no longer available. It was extremely disheartening.

Furthermore, this was only day two of the fair, and we would have to think long and hard about her realistic chances of being able to race there at the end of the week. And even if she could race, we couldn't be sure she would have had any real chance of winning given her condition. Her name alone was a strong indicator that she would be up against the iron. No race secretary would put her in an easy class just because we told him she was sick. He had to go by past performance and earnings. Her racing season for 1987 was likely over and, along with it, Doug's chances at the title.

Needless to say, we scratched her. Without her racing that night, Doug would have to rely on whatever catch drives he had to stay in the hunt. He had two remaining drives. One horse had drawn the five-hole and the other had the six. It just kept getting worse. Making it more dire was that these horses were just plain bad. Jesus Christ himself couldn't get these horses to win. Well, maybe if Jesus had drawn the rail.

The other drivers that had a hat in the title ring like John Nason, Paul Battis, Bruce Mattison, Leigh Fitch, Rick Flanders, Tommy McNamara, Greg Annaloro, and even Kelly Case must have been thankful for what they saw. They knew Doug was a primary threat that year, although no one would admit it. He had their attention. He had quickly stepped out to an early lead over just one night, but with his current lack of drives, the door was now wide open.

As disappointing as the night had started, things quickly got better. The presiding judge at the time was Roger Smith. He was a straight shooter and liked the way Doug went about his business. He knew that

Doug was an honest driver and could count on him when an owner was in need of someone to drive a horse that for one reason or another needed a pilot. At the fairs, this need arose on a regular basis as many owners that shipped in didn't have a regular driver at the meet. When they entered their horse, they would have to name someone for the job, but often times the driver they picked was no longer available because he had chosen another horse in the race that they were also listed to drive.

For most catch drivers, the obvious choice was to take the best horse available out of the ones they were listed on. Some of the top drivers could have as many as four or five horses to choose from. Roger started naming Doug on a lot of the horses that had no driver programmed. Although he was picking up drives, they were obviously horses that other drivers had passed on. On the second night, Doug was put on four more horses after we had arrived.

It was an uncommonly warm and dry night at Rochester. Instead of the typical muddy conditions that dulled the colors and diminished the crowds, it was a perfect fall day. The race numbers and the drivers' colors were vivid and crisp. The lights that illuminated the track made the blues, oranges, and yellows jump out and dance as the horses post-paraded in from the grandstand. The rides in the distance were equally dazzling with their brilliant lights and sounds through the clear night air and added to the festive, circus-like tapestry of the fair. The feeling in the paddock was nothing short of magical as day two got underway.

Despite having less than optimal stock, Doug once again improved those horses and won two more races.

He was hot. The public was taking notice. Almost every horse he was on was going off the favorite. It was getting absurd. Even the complete rats that he got on were going off short money. To make it even more improbable, he was hitting the board with them. It was as if he was sending some otherworldly signals to these animals and they were responding. I know that sounds ridiculous, but to see the past performances of some of the horses he was bringing home, you would have to agree. There was a sense of destiny after that second night.

Coming off the track, the mutterings were already starting. The other drivers were clearly upset. They didn't like what they were seeing. The threat was real. A couple of the bigwigs would skulk off to the side and make off-color comments that were just loud enough to be heard like, "next time he tries that shit, I'm putting him over the hubrail." It was meant to intimidate him. The ironic part was that he hadn't done anything to justify that kind of retaliatory action. He was just out-driving them. That kind of talk and the hostile stares from the good old boys continued the whole ten days. Doug never backed down.

On Saturday, we had three horses racing. One of them was the half sister to Honey; a three-year-old chestnut filly named Sparkle Road. She was coming into top form as the season was ending. She had won just one race all year because of a late start due to some lameness issues. For the most part, we had her the soundest she had ever been. We had entered her in a condition race that was for horses that hadn't won two races all year. It was mid-September and horses that hadn't had two wins the whole season weren't much to talk about. We had the huge advantage of having a horse that hadn't raced all year but still fit the condition. She outclassed the field by a large margin. She was a strong three-year-old filly in peak form, racing against horses that couldn't find the winner's circle with a GPS system. It would take an act of God for her to lose this one.

The bettors knew it. When they turned for the gate, she was going off at 2:5. That's about as prohibitive a favorite as you're going to see in a horse race, unless of course the horse is barred from wagering, which we know never happens. Well, almost never. Sparkle was still green and Doug was having some trouble turning her the "right way" of the track (the "right way" is considered the direction of racing, which is counterclockwise, the same as NASCAR). He was off the bike and had grabbed the reins by her neck and was guiding her in a circle to face the gate. The carnival rides and lights of the fair were giving her a scare and she was balking at them. After he got back on the bike, facing her in the right direction, she panicked and turned around again. The starting gate began rolling.

In the starting gate, there is an appropriately named official named the starter. At the fair, Dale Childs had the honors. She sat in the car facing the horses and controlled both the speed of the vehicle with hand levers and the arms of the gate. The actual driver of the car simply steered it. He or she was in no way responsible for anything else. Many times, if the need arose, the starter would declare a recall for which there are several reasons. Broken equipment, interference between two horses, a horse that is galloping instead of being "on stride" before the head of the stretch, or in this case, a horse that has refused to go can trigger a recall.

Doug was yelling for her to wait, but the gate kept accelerating around the turn. He had finally gotten her righted and pacing but was still on the back-stretch when the starting gate was midway through the turn. She was nearly a quarter-mile away. I really wasn't worried at the time. More often than not, the starter would announce the recall at any point before the sixteenth pole (just a short way down the home-stretch), which was done by turning on flashing lights on the car, much like those on an ambulance.

The horses reached the head of the stretch, and Sparkle was just entering the turn. No flashing lights. Halfway down the stretch and the gate was accelerating as if nothing was wrong. The crowd was sensing that the race was indeed going to start and reacted with a cascade of boos and profanities. Still no lights. The race started, and Sparkle was just turning into the straightaway. It was surreal. Not even Sparkle, with her fresh legs and gifted speed, could overcome spotting a field that much distance. Dale Childs had started the race without her.

By the end of the mile, Sparkle had caught the last horse in the field but couldn't go any further, clearly exhausted from the energy she spent chasing them down. She would have won by twenty lengths if she started the way they were supposed to. All of us were in shock. Adding insult to injury, Doug's primary threat for the championship, John Nason, went on to win the race. It was a six-point swing and he had lost possession of first place.

As Doug got back to the paddock he was furious. He jumped off the bike with Sparkle still moving and threw me the reins. My father was already approaching the starting gate as Dale Childs was getting out of the car. She had parked at the edge of the track where the grandstands and the paddock were adjoined at the end of the stretch. I saw Doug running toward them but couldn't hear the heated exchange as I took the filly back to her stall. If Dale were a man, I am almost certain there would have been a fistfight. A crowd of twenty or thirty patrons were hanging over the fence throwing some fairly ugly profanities in her direction. *That* I did hear. One of the bettors from the stands had hopped the fence and had to be physically restrained as he made his way over.

The paddock judge made an announcement. "Number two, Sparkle Road, to the urine stall."

"You have to be joking," I thought. "After what you guys just did to us, you now have the audacity to call us to the test barn?" I was already angry, but now I was as angry as my brother and father.

This couldn't really be happening to us. I had never seen a race where a starter wasn't aware of one of the horses. And this wasn't just any horse, she was the favorite.

I washed Sparkle, took her to the spit box, and threw a cooler over her. It was about twenty minutes later when I was able to hook up with Doug and Harryman. They were still talking with Dale. Things had calmed down, but it wasn't over. She was claiming that she saw Doug and his horse when they were on the turn, and that she saw Sparkle pacing and heading toward the gate, so that there was no need for a recall. She was obviously lying and couldn't admit that she had just screwed up and didn't see them.

After the two men had settled down, it was actually Dale who seemed irritated. She was quite adamant with her story and didn't want to discuss the matter any further. I felt as if I was in one of those films that when you're watching it at the theatre you say, "That wouldn't happen in real life, that's so unrealistic." Nothing was being done about it. No apologies. No sympathy. And no three points. Not to mention the lost purse money. It was devastating. The feeling that destiny was on our side was washing away from me. I could feel it all slipping away.

It would be nearly ten years before Dale Childs approached us and formally said she was sorry for what she had done. Ten years. Although it was still a painful memory of what could have been, we accepted her admission and have stayed friendly with her since then.

I wasn't sure how this would affect Doug's psyche. He was in a zone before this disaster. Stuff like this can have a profound influence on a professional. It can take him out of that athletic, cognizant, zen-like state, and put him into a completely cerebral state of mind. He was down to drive a horse in the very next race. It didn't faze him at all. He won it going away.

Fortunately Doug has an uncanny ability of turning it off and on as he needs to. Over the years, Doug and I have given each other numerous nicknames. One of those that he was appointed was "Lub Dub." This aptly describes his almost always steady heart rate given any stressful scenario. That trait served him very well at Rochester. Ironically, I am quite sure the whole Sparkle Road disaster had his heart rate up a few notches, but he was able to recover quickly and get back to the task at hand.

It didn't change the fact that Sparkle hadn't won. As it turned out, another race for her wasn't available the rest of the meet. That was her only chance at Rochester to help, and it had been taken away. It was up to the rest of our troops to finish the job.

Going into night three, Doug only had four drives on the program and didn't pick up any over the course of the card. We had two of our own, and he had two catch drives. Our stock that night was pathetic. If Honey and Sparkle were our big guns, these two guys were peashooters. Benny Jo and Jiffy Doodle were going to have to pull off a coup. The names alone were weak. Jiffy Doodle? Come on. That doesn't put the fear of anything in you. It sounds more like something you get caught doing as an adolescent boy in the bathroom.

Benny Jo was a four-year-old gelding that was an experiment of sorts. We had bought him for cheap money in the middle of August to take up space in the barn and give Doug a couple of drives at the fair that we knew could be pivotal in a tight race for the driving title. My father had qualified him at Scarboro, where he barely made the necessary time and was on his hands and knees coming home. In his first official start at Scarboro the following week, they put me down to drive him to sharpen him up. He made a break at the gate and finished fifty lengths off the lead. The final start before he got to Rochester, Harryman got back on him, and once again he made a break, then broke a hopple and didn't even finish the race.

As a somewhat humorous sidebar, my father drove only three horses that whole summer. Not one of them finished a race. They were all DNF (Did Not Finish). To give you an idea of how outlandish that statistic is, Doug drove over five hundred horses that year and finished the race with *all* of them. To have only three starts in a season and have every one of them officially listed as DNF's has to be some sort of record.

Benny Jo was a tiny little bay gelding that was better suited carrying children around in the pony barn. It was just a matter of weeks before that fate would actually befall him. Benny Jo had drawn the two-hole and to be honest, I didn't think he had a chance. Even as hot as Doug was, there was no way he was going to win with him. The public didn't care, they made him the favorite. I was quite amused. Back in the paddock, I told Benny Jo to enjoy his fifteen minutes of fame, because it was the last time he would ever be the favorite in a race. We liked the little horse alright, but he wasn't much, and shortly after Rochester he was converted into a riding horse due to his lack of performance.

In what I can only describe as outrageously implausible, the little horse won the race. It was one of the slowest times of the meet, perhaps of the year. He needed it to be as he won by a nose. The muses were mocking me. They snuff out Sparkle Road at the gate, and then they carry Benny Jo home. It was crazy.

In the next race, Doug won with a horse called Keystone Salvo and kept the kismet rolling. Two more drives to go for the night, but one of them was the aforementioned Jiffy Doodle which gave us little hope for a strong finish for the evening. His next drive was a horse named Raintrees JR in the sixth. He was coming off a five-month layoff and had two wins over the

last two years. He really should have been the long
shot. Once again, the public made him the favorite.
Doug paid them off. Three drives. Three wins. It was
bordering on the absurd.

Jiffy Doodle was in the eighth and had the cursed
six-hole. In a shocker, he lost by a neck and finished
second. The rollercoaster was back at the top again.
It made me almost completely forget about what had
happened just twenty-four hours ago with poor Sparkle. I got in my car, cranked up my Bob Seger's *Night
Moves* cassette, and headed back to UNH. The week
was three days old and I was emotionally drained.
Seven more nights of this. I didn't think I would
make it.

The race for the title was still tight amongst five
drivers. Doug had his three wins and a second, but
the others had eight and nine drives a night. Their
second and third place finishes were adding up,
keeping them close. Night four was moving day in
the standings, and Doug only had three drives. He
made the best of it with another win and a second,
but despite having a freakish batting average, he had
dropped to third.

We had only one of our own racing on day five
and that was Chelsea Lad. He was a strapping dark
black gelding with tremendous power. But he was
a crazy horse and racing him at the fair could be
dangerous. There were times that he just decided he
wanted to go over the hubrail and he would veer to
the left sharply with no real warning. There was no
explanation for his actions. One night at Foxboro, he
nearly took out the entire field when he pulled that
stunt leaving the gate out of the eight-hole. Doug sent
him out for the lead but as they entered the first turn,

he sliced across all seven horses, creating pandemonium. The wheels of Doug's sulky clipped multiple hooves as they knifed across. He wound up winning the race but was placed last for the interference and mayhem he left in his wake.

For that reason, Doug could never ask Chelsea Lad to go for the top ever again. It was way too dangerous. After that, he had to consistently take him back at the start of each race, making it difficult to win races with him. He had finished fifth on opening day, and he would finish fifth again that night. No points from Laddie, but more importantly, he didn't kill anyone. Shortly after the meet, he too was retired from racing as a safety precaution.

There are times in your life when you go through certain experiences and only upon reflection can you grasp the gravity and scope of what you're going through. It's like when the rookie quarterback wins the Super Bowl but never gets another chance the rest of his career to do it again. In the moment, he doesn't realize how big the stage is until he can one day look back on his life and appreciate that one mystical run he had.

For us, this wasn't one of them. We knew exactly what the stakes were. The events and scenarios that were unfolding during the madness of the week became magnified and more meaningful as the days passed. Each race became a battleground.

Since I can remember, we had been going to the Rochester Fair. When I was a kid, all my friends would pile into the truck to watch the races while my father drove the horses. We didn't have many back then, but we had more fun in one week than most kids I knew had in a whole summer. Jim Streeter, Scott Ouellette,

Jay Borin, and I would race through the crowds of the midway in order to make it back to the grandstand to watch one of our horses perform. We would be clear across the fair and realize that we had spent way too much time in the arcade and have to make a run for it. We made a game out of it, dodging people and weaving in and out of human traffic at a dead run.

It was a like real live game of Frogger. You had to look three moves ahead. Girl and guy holding hands, weave left. Old man just in front of them, diagonal dash through the gap, avoid the woman with the baby carriage, two skips to the right, full speed ahead for six strides, stop, bounce out right, sneak through the basketball toss, and keep on going. We were good at it. We knew we were in the zone when no one yelled at us. It was a time of great innocence. Making it back to the grandstand as the horses reached the head of the lane for the start, we high fived each other and enjoyed another night in adolescent paradise.

I laughed to myself thinking back on those days in the midst of this championship run. I found myself unable to even go out and get a slice of my favorite pizza from Andrea's Pizza trailer. It was too risky to be away that long. I might miss something. Doug might pick up a drive at any point and I was chronicling every race. Even if Doug wasn't in a race, I had to watch to see what the other guys had done and keep the score. I wasn't going to entrust it to the powers that be. Someone had to watchdog this situation.

Sam, Joe and Ed's Sausages, famous for piling on heaping loads of peppers and onions, was located just outside the entrance of the grandstand and it was just about as far as I could allow myself to wander to get something to eat. And I hate peppers and onions. It has been the source of great insults all of my life from my whole family. They jokingly wonder if I am actually related to them with my quirky taste in foods. They often poke fun at me in a broken Greek accent when I order my food without peppers and onions, "You are not a true Greek!" Whatever, just make it plain and leave me alone.

At Sam, Joe and Ed's, I couldn't go for the sausage sub since they cooked everything together, making it nearly impossible to pick out the stuff I didn't like. Besides, even if I did manage to painstakingly remove every bit of disgusting pepper and nauseating onion, the smell of them remained permeated through the sandwich anyway. The safest move was the meatball sub. Quick, easy, and simple. But I'll be damned if a rogue onion wasn't somewhere in the sauce every time. That would be good for a *huge* laugh at my expense.

As my family had their little fun, I would sarcastically think to myself, "I'm so glad you guys are amused. Would you like some dog shit in your sandwich so I can have a little chuckle as well?"

With each passing day, the pressure got more intense. It was the seventh night of the meet, and I had a mammalian physiology test the next day. I really needed to study. Right. Study. It would have to wait until I got back to the house. There was no way I was missing this.

We had Jiffy Doodle back in to go, but more importantly, Doug was on a horse called That Cat and another called Eustis. That Cat was a medium-built black stallion out of a sire named Skunk. I never figured out why he was named that, but hypothesized it had something to do with the character Pepe Le

Pew and how he fell in love with a cat in the cartoon. Who knows? Strange name for a horse. He was owned by a character in his own right named Ted LaFleur. He was a portly man shaped like a teardrop that everyone I knew referred to as Mookie. Except Doug. He always called him Teddy.

I don't think he was tied to the mob, but I'm sure he wanted people to think he was. It seemed like he had at least a quarter bottle of aftershave on, even late in the evening. I can't imagine what he smelled like first thing in the morning. His hair was always greased back, and the top two buttons of his shirt were left undone, showing off a few gold chains. When he smiled, his outside incisor teeth were a little too long on the upper jaw, making him look like a distant relative of Dracula.

Mookie was notorious for holding horses back (stiffing) for a few weeks and then laying the money in to make a nice score when the odds were in his favor. He knew Doug very well and almost never used him to drive his horses because he respected Doug's integrity for never stiffing a horse. Early on, he had asked him to drive for him, and when Doug politely refused to lose with his horses, it became obvious the relationship wasn't going to work out professionally.

Even though Mookie was somewhat dishonest in his approach to the game, he was a trustworthy guy in other respects. He liked Doug and realized that he had a chance to win the title that year. For the first time in a long time, he asked him to drive his horse. But only this one. I'm not sure why it was just That Cat, but that was that. It couldn't have been that this was the week he wanted the horse to win, or he wouldn't have picked Doug to drive. He was way too hot and the bettors were making him the favorite on donkeys. Mookie couldn't have wanted him to be the favorite or he wouldn't have been able to make any money with him. I can only assume he was doing it to help Doug out.

On paper for the season, That Cat had only one win all year racing in lower claiming races. At the fair, Doug had already won twice with him that week. He was looking for the hat trick. He was in the first race of the night. The last thing on my mind when the gate opened up was mammalian physiology. That Cat cruised to his third victory in the opener. Twilight crept over the fair as the sun's heat drifted away. The crisp cool night air replaced the warmth of the afternoon. The photographer's flash captured the moment as That Cat took his place in the winner's circle. The words from the song "Sunburst" played in my head as the darkness of evening staked its claim over the track. *"A blinding flash of light, a single strobe ignites the night...bring on the night"*. And night seven was officially underway.

In years past, the drivers' title was watched closely by the announcer. Each night, at various times during the card, he would give the public an update as to who was in the hunt. In 1986, just the year before, Doug made a serious run for it late in the week. At one point he actually was within one point of the leader. His name was never called as a contender. Not once. When he slipped back into third, the announcer came on and told us that Leigh Fitch and John Nason were in a heavyweight bout for the crown. It was obvious that they weren't going to give Doug his props.

As I followed the points as the week wore on, it was killing me that he wasn't getting any attention.

Some owners are swayed by hot drivers and end up putting them on their horses as the meet progresses. That lack of publicity did not help the cause. He ended up finishing a very close and respectable third, and nobody knew about it. Nobody but us.

Things were no different in 1987. During the first eight days, while Doug had the lead, not a word was spoken through the loudspeakers about the driver's title. It wasn't until John took the lead midway through the ninth card that it was brought up. What a surprise. My pulse was pounding. The announcer was acting like he was the great wizard hidden from sight up in the crow's nest of the grandstand, insulated from accountability. He was concealing the statistics of what was actually happening. Doug was in the Land of Oz, in search of a title, but the "eye in the sky" was trying to somehow deny him the credit he deserved.

They really didn't want us to win. I was being too dramatic. It was really only the announcer and the other drivers. The crowd was rallying for him. After he won with That Cat, people were cheering and wishing him well.

The favorable energy was feeding him. The announcer couldn't play the Wizard of Oz anymore. The public was savvy. They knew he had become the points leader, despite the lack of a spotlight. The curtain had been ripped down exposing the truth, not by a little dog named Toto, but by a horse named That Cat.

Dallas Knight, racing his third time in seven days, followed with an encore second place finish in the fifth race, capping off the Bridesmaid hat trick, finishing second for a third straight start. The focus, however, was on the eighth race. It was the feature, and a most unlikely horse named Eustis was in it.

Eustis was in way over his head. He was owned by a gentleman named Al Therrian who was a Rochester, N.H., native. Doug and he had become friends over the summer as they both had common interests in music and horses. Al had owned a few lower echelon racehorses before and was interested in getting better stock than he was used to having. He had about $3,000 to spend and asked us to find him a horse.

My father, brother, and I took pride in our ability to pick out horses to claim that we could likely improve on. There was a myriad of criteria we used to find a claim worthy of taking a shot at. Our job was very much like that of a professional scout, looking for the young player that can make it into the big leagues. You search for something that other people might overlook. We looked for horses that may have been driven poorly, had bad racing luck, or maybe even if we suspected someone was cheating with them. This practice of cheating with an animal is not done quite as much as most skeptical bettors would think, but it would be naïve to think it doesn't happen at all, especially at the smaller tracks where the purses are poor.

These are just a few of the rationales we used to pick out a horse. We were good at it. Very good. There were only a handful of horses we didn't make better. Less than that. Perhaps it was just one and her name was Pixie Frost. Ouch. We would all really like to forget that one. She was an embarrassment to the stable. There are some mares that just don't want to race, and we refer to them as being sour. There's nothing worse than a sour mare. Pixie Frost was a ten on the pucker factor meter.

Unbeknownst to us, the previous owner never jogged her on the racetrack because she disliked the workouts so much. We found out later that he was an avid runner and would take her jogging with him through the stable area each day to keep her fit. This kept her just sweet enough to race her once a week. When we took her home and started jogging her on the track pulling a sulky, things went south in a hurry. We raced her four times before she decided that she wasn't going to race for us anymore. We sold her back to her original owner for half of what we bought her for.

We had been clocking Eustis for several weeks. We considered getting him for ourselves, but our stable was fairly full, and we knew Al needed a horse. We told him that we liked the little black gelding and he agreed to put a claim in on him. He was racing in $2,500 claimers when Al took him home. He really liked the little horse. So much so that he didn't want to put him back in a claiming race, not even for a higher amount that would likely deter people from re-claiming him back.

Al didn't want to take a chance of losing him. He put him in a conditioned race for non-winners of $200 a start. It was steep competition for him and a much higher class than he was used to racing in. In his first start for Al, Doug had to drive one of our horses that was in the same race. Eustis went off a 25:1 long shot and finished third to the horse we had in the race. The next week, Doug was able to drive him at Scarboro. The six-year-old gelding paced the fastest race of his life and missed winning by a nose. He dropped a full three seconds off of his regular racing time. That's the equivalent to fifteen lengths of horseflesh. He apparently liked his new home.

The following week at Scarboro, Doug won with him handily in a gutty performance that had him on the outside the whole last half, head to head with the front horse, until Eustis opened up down the lane to win, setting a new lifetime mark as the fastest win in his life (something that very few six-year-olds ever do). Most lifetime marks are set in the three- and four-year-old campaigns.

Al Therrian was feeling pretty good about little Eustis. At Rochester, he entered him in the Invitational Race on opening night. Even the race secretary asked him if he was sure he wanted to race him there. After all, he would be up against the best horses on the grounds, and Eustis was just a low-level claimer. Al entered him anyway. There were more than a few giggles and snickers from the railbirds when he put him in the box. This guy couldn't be serious. Eustis didn't belong there.

To make it even tougher on him, Eustis had drawn the three-hole against the track record holder, Armbro Blaze, who had landed the rail. The track record at the time was 200.2. It had been set by the good-looking chestnut stallion just one year ago. He was aptly named for the majestic white blaze he donned on his forehead. Eustis was unaware of the class he was facing. He was just out doing his job.

He got away second and followed Armbro Blaze and driver Freeman Parker. The half-mile time was slow, and Freeman was backing down the pace to ensure that when he cut his horse loose during the last quarter, no one could catch him. No one but Eustis, that is. He had followed him for seven-eighths of a mile until Doug swung him out for the short stretch run at Rochester, perhaps one of the shortest straight-aways in the nation. Eustis nailed him at the wire by a whisker. It was one of those "hold your breath" finishes that called for a print.

Back then, when the photo was extremely tight, the judges called for a print, which was a black-and-white snapshot of the finish exactly at the wire to determine the winner. Today it's done digitally so it takes a fraction of the time. It was so close that they needed a magnifying glass to call it. The cheap claimer had beaten the track record holder. Funny, I didn't hear any of those railbirds laughing when his picture was taken in the winner's circle. Cinderella had showed up at the ball.

A week later and Cinderella was still at the ball. Eustis had been assigned the three-hole again, and ironically enough, Armbro Blaze had drawn the rail again. It was setting up to be a repeat of the first race they had together. In the first match-up on opening night Eustis was going off 9:1. This time, the crowd wasn't going to get fooled. They didn't care that he was just a lower-priced claimer. They didn't care that he was facing the track record holder.

When they left the gate it wasn't going to be as easy as it was the first time, and that was hardly a walk in the park. Armbro Blaze got the front effortlessly. Lauxmont Yoga, who had the two-hole, settled in right behind Armbro Blaze, forcing Eustis to tuck in third. Going past the half-mile marker, Doug pulled Eustis first over and would have to go the long way home, racing uncovered the rest of the mile.

Freeman Parker, apparently learning his lesson from the week before, didn't back down the half this time. He had Armbro Blaze breezing on the front

end. They froze the teletimer past the half in one
minute even.

Doug tipped Eustis out and locked Lauxmont
Yoga inside and rushed up alongside Armbro Blaze.
Three quarters was rifled off in a minute and thirty
seconds flat. They were on pace to break the track record. The top two horses drew away from the field. It
became a match race on the last turn. The classy veteran dug down deep on the inside while Doug asked
Eustis for just a little bit more coming for home.

As they headed down the stretch, Eustis got a nose
in front but was getting leg weary. As is the case with
tired horses, many of them will drift wide down the
stretch as they fatigue. The clock was striking midnight as the Cinderella horse was desperately trying
to finish off an impossible performance.

Midway down the stretch Eustis was drifting badly,
so much so that the wheels of Doug's sulky were nearly rubbing up against the outside chain-link fence
that protected the crowd. Armbro Blaze meanwhile
was hugging the rail. In all my years of watching racing, I had never seen two horses finishing so far apart
from each other yet so close at the wire. Doug knew
that if he pulled on the left rein it would likely act as
a brake and slow the horse down so he let him drift
wide. With the horses fifty feet apart from each other
across the width of the track it was another photo
finish.

Once again, Eustis had won by a nose. I looked
at the teletimer as Doug snapped the horse's head
to the left to avoid crashing into the fence. They had
stopped it in 200.1, setting a new track record. In
three weeks time, the little black gelding had gone
from cheap claimer to open invitational pacer and

new track record holder, winning two races by a total of an inch.

One day left. It was a double header on Saturday. In the afternoon session, Doug was programmed to drive three horses and got two wins and a third. The magic continued and he was tied for second. We had seven trips to the winner's circle of our own and going into the last day of the meet, Doug had a total of sixteen wins over nine cards. He had driven in only forty-one races. Although there were several drivers within twenty points of the lead, there were really only two left with a real chance at the title, and that was Doug and John Nason.

The wave of support Doug was getting from the patrons must have risen up to the crow's nest. The announcer had changed his tune and had jumped on to the Doug Mitchell bandwagon. Suddenly he was mentioning him after every race. More cheers erupted when he stated Doug had taken the lead in points.

One night left. We had just about used up all of our weapons and they had given us everything we could have asked for. Even Sparkle, who had the race stolen from her, tried hard despite having no chance to win after the starting gate debacle. We were running out of ammunition entering the last day of racing. We would have to get help from the last two horses we had to send to the frontline for the evening card.

Night settled over the track. The flashing lights of the rides and games of the midway flashed in my rearview mirror as I drove in. With my door open the dome light got dimmer, then brighter as I flipped through the program, counting the number of drives each man had. Doug had five and John had eight, but

Doug held the lead by seven points. This was going to be close. I shut my stereo off, took a deep breath, softly closed the door behind me, and headed for the paddock to do battle.

We had two of our own in that night: Dallas Knight and Honey's Best. Both horses had been the center of a much heated debate at the farm three days before the race when they had drawn for post positions. Neither horse should have been entered. If it were any other week, in any other year, they wouldn't have been put in to go. But this was different. The heat of the fight had consumed us and we were sliding into territory none of us found comfortable, and that was asking an animal to do more than it was either willing or capable of doing.

Over the first seven days, Dallas Knight had already raced three times. He had raced great. He had picked up three seconds, worth six points in the standings. He had done his job in the trenches. And for his troubles, because he had raced three times in a week, he was developing skin sores over his legs where the hopples wrapped around. Three starts in seven days is not overwhelming to a Standardbred athlete. There are horses that can do that without missing a beat, but with Dallas Knight it was his skin that was the issue. He had what we refer to as "hopple burns." This ailment is very much like blisters that runners get when competing in a marathon.

We didn't want to race him, but knew that if we didn't, the title would likely be in jeopardy. We all wondered if it was worth it. It wasn't how we operated. The final word on it came from Doug, and Dallas was entered in to go. We all decided that we would give him at least two weeks off after the meet was over.

The other ethical dilemma we faced was with Honey. She clearly wasn't right. Her SGOT counts were still above 1500, and she hadn't trained for three weeks. She was sick and not physically prepared to compete at a high level. In a cheap class, she would probably hold her own, but Honey never got in cheap. Her reputation preceded her. She likely would draw the feature race, which was almost always the second to last race of the meet.

Truth be told, most trainers probably wouldn't have hesitated to race her that night. She wasn't visibly sick, and she certainly wasn't in any pain, but this was our Honey. She was more than just a racehorse. We all asked ourselves a simple question. If we were asked to perform in a race like this as humans, would we be willing to do it? The answer was easy. We were unanimous in our response. Absolutely. We wouldn't be asking her to do anything we weren't ourselves willing to do. The moral issue then was that Honey didn't have a choice. We were choosing for her. That's what was making it so difficult.

We all agreed it could easily become the pivotal race for the championship. I thought back to that fateful day in Lewiston when she fought through sickness only to finish second in the finals. Not once then, but twice, we would be compromising our principles and entering her in to go. Earlier in the week, under similar conditions, we had scratched her. In our defense, her muscle enzymes had dropped considerably from the beginning part of the week, but none of us felt good about this. Karma has a way of evening things out, I thought. This could end badly.

Things certainly started poorly for us after the first race, when John Nason won with a horse called

Sadie Ho. The bad vibes were creeping in. I could feel it coming. In the second race, Nason finished third and was within three of the lead. It got ridiculous trying to follow the points after that. Doug had wins in the fourth and eighth races while John won the sixth and finished second in the seventh. After the eighth, Doug was clinging to a four-point lead.

They both had drives in the ninth and tenth races and neither had one in the finale. John was on the favorite in both late races. Both of his horses were much the best, but Doug was at least in there with him.

To the ninth race it went. Dallas Knight had the four-hole and Goombay Girl had the six-hole for John. I threw nearly a whole bottle of Gold Bond powder on Dallas' blisters and sent him out to the track. It really didn't matter what John's horse did if Dallas could just get a second. After that, the worst that could happen would be a tie for the title. If Dallas beat John's horse, it was officially over. On paper, Dallas was easily the second best, and with a good trip, he could win. We were hoping he could pull it off, even with some hopple chafe. If he did, we could then subsequently scratch Honey from the tenth. With the title in the bag, she wouldn't have to go to war. Dallas Knight strapped on his armor and went out to the post parade.

The race started exactly as it read on the program. Goombay Girl got the top and was clear on the lead at the quarter pole. Doug settled Dallas back to fifth and rested him. Up the backside for three quarters, Doug caught live cover (followed another horse and in essence was drafting) and was third gaining on the leader. Dallas was a big, strong horse with huge strides. Those strides asked for extra long hop-

ples, which ironically caused more slapping to occur
and therefore the peeling of skin. Dallas was hitting
top speed as he pulled three wide and was closing in
on John's horse. He had the speed and enough real
estate ahead to catch him. I had seen thousands of
races before and could just tell he had the horsepower to win it. Dallas Knight was reeling in a title.

I knew he had to be uncomfortable. He had traveled three and three-quarter miles in nine days of
racing. He just needed to gut out one more quarter
mile and the championship was ours. But the superficial pain of the blisters was affecting him. He
got rough-gaited heading toward the last turn as he
knocked on the door of destiny.

"Keep him together, Gooch," I said softly, hoping
that somehow he would hear me.

They passed over the area where the cars cross the
track to park in the infield where some horses even
without blisters have a hard time staying on stride.
The fatigue and stinging was too much for the big
horse. The change in footing over the tire tracks dis-
tracted him. He broke stride just as he headed the
leader. Not even Doug's soft hands could keep him
pacing.

I squatted down to the ground in disbelief, held
my head in my hands, and yelled out loud, "No!"

A wave of warmth caressed over my body as my
heart pumped too much blood through my veins. It
was followed by a sudden chill.

"Someone tell me that didn't just happen," I
thought to myself.

As Doug eased into him and slowed him down (as
the rules of racing dictate you do when your horse
breaks stride), the other horses passed him on the

inside. The hopes and dreams of a championship were fading with Dallas Knight. He ended up finishing last as Goombay Girl with John Nason won. There was almost nothing said between the three of us as we unharnessed Dallas and got ready for whatever fate lay ahead.

I was back in Lewiston in my mind, the day Honey lost the three-year-old stakes race. It was happening all over again.

"How can people that are so blessed be so cursed?" I thought.

The same empty feeling. The same empathy for a horse that probably shouldn't have been asked to do this. Did this title mean that much? Apparently it did. It justified everything we had worked for. It validated us. And now it was slipping away.

Honey was our last hope. I didn't tend to Dallas' wounds right away because Honey was in the very next race. Besides, the wounds were really not a big deal. They would heal in a week's time and he would be just fine. We didn't have time to think about what had just happened or wonder if we were putting our pride above our animals. We were now asking Honey to do exactly what we asked her to do last September...give us a great performance at less than top form. But all of us knew what we were doing. We had come too far.

Sadly, it seemed now that John was within a single point of Doug in the standings, it was essentially over. John was on the favorite in a six-horse race, and Honey would likely finish second to him on her best day. In order for Doug to win the title, she would have to either win the race, or keep John's horse from hitting the board (finishing first, second, or third). It was unrealistic to say the least. I checked Honey up and sent her off to the track.

As they glided away, I softly told Doug, "Good luck."

The grandstand was packed. It was a nice night for what historically was a cool and rainy evening. It was the second to the last race of the meet, and the crowd was eager to see the feature. In a quiet moment I had to myself, I could hear the noise from the midway carrying across the length of the stretch to the paddock. The whooshing of the "Zipper," the soft screams of people stuck hanging upside down in the "Pirate Ship," and the faint drift of music coming from the "Flying Bobs" carried across the track. I couldn't make out what song was playing as I mindfully placed myself in my little gold car and could hear Bob Seger singing "Sunburst"…*"The crowd without a face, begins to fill the space, in the arena. His weapon at his side, he flashes it with pride, before his legions."*

The public knew exactly what was riding on this one as the announcer finally gave Doug his due and explained the situation. It was clear that Doug had become the crowd favorite. Even though John Nason's horse was unmistakably the better horse on paper, Honey was still the public's choice. They knew who she was. Most of the patrons had followed her story over the last two years and knew how tough she was, no matter what company she was up against. They were pulling for both Doug and Honey. It felt good to have that positive energy aimed at us instead of what we were used to over the last decade.

I was feeling anything was possible and started looking for other reasons why Honey had an outside chance in the race. I knew I was fooling myself but needed affirmation that winning was not unimaginable. She had drawn the rail. At least she wouldn't get parked out and gutted. John's horse had the two-hole and as ironic as it sounds, his horse's name was Doctor Mark. I also knew that Honey was a racehorse and she had a heart the size of Texas. She would give him a run, no matter what her physical condition was.

In the paddock sometime before Honey's race, the three of us discussed the strategy going into this one. Realistically, the only way Doug could win the title would be to try to park John's horse out for at least a half mile and get him tired so the rest of the field could go after him. It was extremely unlikely that Honey could actually beat him outright even if she were in top form.

The gate in the feature races traveled just a little faster than in the others. Dale Childs had it rolling strong when it opened up and the race was underway. It was clear that John wanted the top, but Doug knew that if he gave it to him (by holding Honey back and relinquishing the top), he would easily be able to control the mile, and the race, in essence, would be over.

He asked Honey for her renowned gate speed and got it. She slipped underneath (forced her way through along the inside) Doctor Mark as John tried to cut across in front of her in the turn and refused to give him the wood. A gap was opening up behind the two of them and the rest of the field as they made their way to the quarter pole, but John stubbornly wanted the top. He had no intention of settling in behind Honey. He knew he had the best horse in the race and if he cleared her, the title was his.

Had John known that Honey was ailing, he most certainly would have settled in behind her and taken her on later in the mile when Honey faded from muscle fatigue. John's horse was clearly better even if Honey were at her best. It would have been a done deal. Leaving the gate, Honey gave him no reason to believe she was anything but a hundred percent. She had put on her game face and was giving Doug all the horsepower he asked for.

Up the backside to the quarter pole, Honey had cranked it out in 29.3. They were cruising. Doctor Mark almost got the top as they went into the second turn that lined the midway with all the rides, but Honey would have nothing of it. She shifted gears and strung him out through the turn. There was no turning back for John now, he had committed to the top and was going to live or die by it. The rest of the field was seven lengths back as the two drivers going for the championship were in a slugfest speed duel going to the half. Doctor Mark was tiring a bit and was head to head with Honey when they stopped the teletimer in a blazing 59.1.

She had just thrown down the gauntlet. It was the fastest half of the meet by far. Honey had just snapped it off even after a three-week layoff. Up the backside they rambled and Honey was holding strong. Nason was all out on Doctor Mark to try one last time to get by her. Both horses were feeling it.

When they hit the three-quarter pole in 1:29.1, Honey was out of bullets. That pace would have shattered the record Eustis just set if she could have kept it up. She had laid her heart on the line and had given Doug everything she could give him and then some. We could only hope that the winged pace they had set early on had also taken its toll on Doctor Mark.

Going past the three-quarter pole, Doug completely stopped driving Honey. He knew she had nothing left. Doctor Mark finally cleared her and saw the rail for the first time, but the early fractions and the long trip on the outside were finally catching up to him. As they turned for home, he was hitting the wall but had ten lengths on the field. We could only watch and wait to see if he would hold on. Midway down the stretch, he had nothing left. The whole field passed him as they crossed the wire. He had finished fifth, and was awarded no points. Honey was sixth, well behind the pack. It was over. Doug had won the title.

In the paddock after the race, we were all standing at the chainlink fence on the outside of the track watching the last race go off. Neither John nor Doug had a drive in the finale. As we stood there in the calm after the storm, John Nason came over and approached Doug. He had his helmet off exposing his fiery red hair. He had a slight grin on his face as he came over.

"That was a pretty dirty move you pulled out there," he said bitterly.

"Yeah, I know," Doug answered back.

"I would have done the same thing," John answered him with a wink and a wry smile that showed the small gap between his front teeth. "Congratulations."

He shook Doug's hand and gave him a pat on the shoulder. Doug was finally in the fraternity.

"Thanks, John. It was quite a week."

"It sure was," and John turned back to watch the race.

Having listened to the song "Sunburst" at least a dozen times during the meet, the words echoed in my mind again after it was over. *"He makes his great escape, leaves them in his wake, without a warning."*

The legacy of Honey's Best continued. She had done it again. When Doug stopped driving her, she responded in kind and stopped trying. Doug eased back into the reins to let her know it was okay to stop pressing. She had gone against the odds and taken one for the team. This time it was in her defeat that she had brought us home again.

We never drew a blood to see how high her SGOT counts were after that race. None of us wanted to know. She got the next five months completely off. Dallas Knight also got the rest of the year off and recovered from his wounds. He never raced more than once a week after that. We never pushed that hard for the title again. Although Doug gave it an honest effort and we had just enough stock over the next ten years to help in the cause, we never put *us* first again. We had compromised our ethics in the pursuit of our own self-gratification. It would have been a much harder lesson to learn if we had lost.

Honey's Best. She certainly was. We have had over two hundred horses in our stable over the years. If there was one horse that we wouldn't have wanted to ask to run in that race that day, it would have been her. But if we had to choose which soldier to go to battle for us given the same circumstances, we would choose her again. And if we could have asked her if she wanted to race that day, she most likely would have answered "yes," just like the injured athlete that still wants to get in the game. She was all racehorse.

As I headed back to UNH, the rest of the family went back to the farm. It was a good night. It was ten days of the most hectic, fantastic, frustrating, exhausting, and satisfying racing we had ever been a part of. On my way back, I could sense that this would likely never happen again. The fact that it happened once is still hard to believe. I stayed up late that night and savored the moment of what had just transpired. I'm sure Doug must have been wide awake when they got home in the early hours of the morning. After something like that, falling asleep is often impossible.

As I pulled into the fraternity house parking lot, for the last time I ritualistically played the song "Sunburst" in my car to let the memories of the week cascade over me. The end of the song played, *"The ritual is done, a night no longer young, fades into morning."* As I listened to the last lyrics of the song before going to bed, I thought of my brother…*"The sun begins to rise, as he begins to close his eyes."* The war was over. We were at peace.

The window of opportunity for a small stable like ours to battle against the big guns had opened up for just over a week. And in a time of year in New England that that normally brought endless rain for most of the meet, we experienced a ten day sun burst that shone down on us. We basked in it for as long as we could until the fall colors faded into the Rochester evening and the sun collapsed over the horizon.

Although we came very close in the years that followed, Doug never won the title again. The improbable run that ended with Honey's heroic efforts is permanently etched in history as Doug's name hangs in the Hall of Fame at Rochester Fair with the rest of the driving elite.

It's been over twenty years since that week in September, and somewhere in the old farmhouse, Doug has the Jesse Brown Memorial Trophy on a mantle.

Not far away, the great mare was laid to rest in a simply marked grave with no epitaph, as we haven't yet decided what words will truly capture her legend. Perhaps there aren't any. The trophy that he won during that incredible week belongs as much to Honey as it does to the rest of us. It may just as well be her headstone. She certainly earned it.

MIRACLE MILE

Honey's Best was now an eight-year-old. Her resume to this point was impressive, but like most horses after the age of four, her best racing years were behind her. Historically speaking, most horses will peak at age three or four, and then they start to decline a bit as they get older. There are a few exceptions, of course, where some horses don't really mature until they are five or six, but as a rule, it isn't much different than human athletes. Humans usually peak in their twenties, and once we hit our thirties, the decline starts to show. Don't tell that to Gordie Howe or Brett Favre, but they are the exceptions. In human years, an eight-year-old race horse is arguably about forty.

It was the end of the summer of 1990, and she had a decent year going. She was racing in the Fillies and Mares Open condition and holding her own. It seemed as the summer rolled on that she was racing better and better. The week I was down to drive her, she was entered in a condition race with colts and geldings, as there weren't enough mares good enough to make a race go that week. We could either hold out for the following weekend or race her against the boys. She was sharp, so it didn't make sense not to put her in the "box."

The "box" is literally a box. It is much like a suggestion box in an office where you write down the horse's name on a piece of paper with the race condition and date you wish to race. You then put the paper in for the race secretary to use later to make up the races. If enough people enter enough horses for that condition, then the race fills. Post positions are then drawn from a pill bottle like those found in a pool hall (they actually use a pill bottle from a pool hall), and the race is made.

It was a Friday night and Honey drew the rail. There was only one caveat. Doug was booked to sing that night at a gig that he once again couldn't get out of. He wouldn't be able to drive her. Years ago, our father (who we affectionately call Harryman) was our driver until Doug turned eighteen and literally took over the reins. No offense to my father, but Doug was younger and more talented. He had some of the softest hands in the business. My father had, for the most part, retired from driving apart from some cameo appearances in a father and son race here or there, or if he was driving a horse of our own in a race where Doug had another horse he regularly drove. It wasn't often.

I had just turned twenty-three and had my provisional license (called a "P" license) and was able to drive at most tracks, but on the program there was a "P" placed next to my name to let the public know that I really didn't know what I was doing. Most bettors steered clear of the inexperienced drivers.

By that time in my life, at twenty-three, I probably should have had my "A" license. This is achieved by driving in at least twenty-five races in a single meet, and if the judges think you performed at a high enough level at the end of the season, you could then apply for your "A" license. The stigma of the "P" was then forever removed from your name. On a program, there is no "A" listed next to professional drivers. The lack of a letter infers it. Doug had obtained his "A" license at just nineteen.

There have been exactly three instances where Doug did not go to the track with us over our thirty-three years of racing. The first was the night we didn't claim Hardwood Bret. This night would be the second. I was listed to drive Honey's Best. I was excited and nervous, and very apprehensive. None of us are very superstitious, but the last time Doug wasn't there, things went disastrously wrong. Not to mention the fact that I had only driven in a handful of races and still hadn't gotten to the winner's circle. If I were to break my maiden (that is actually what it's called), I would have to do it without Doug there, and on Honey's Best against the boys.

I probably should have had much more experience racing by this time in my life, but my quest to become a driver was impeded by two things. One was that we didn't really need another driver. Doug was better than I would ever be, and the relationship of Harryman as trainer, Doug as driver, and Marc as groom was a brilliant combination. Besides, I was studying to be a veterinarian, and driving harness horses for a living was highly unlikely. Second, when I was eighteen, we had a groom named Greg Moretti that desperately wanted to become a harness driver and we worked out a deal where if he worked on the farm, as compensation we would supply horses for him to drive so that he could get his license. I would have liked to think that I was making a huge sacrifice and being supremely altruistic in order for this to happen, but in all honesty, the desire to be a driver wasn't overpowering. I had my goals and that wasn't high on the list. I knew that one day I would get my license at some point; I just wasn't in any real hurry. As far as we were concerned, Doug was our driver, and that was that. Never once did I wish to compete against him for the position. Besides, there was no way he would ever be half the groom I was.

Greg Moretti was one of the strangest characters we ever had in our stable. He was in his late thirties when he drove up in his beat-up green, gray, and blue Nova to inquire about his life quest to become a harness driver. He was balding and he usually shaved his graying head to hide the fact that he was going bald. Once a year, often in the spring, he would shave his body completely. Yes, completely. Oddly, he paid someone to perform this act. I don't know how much he paid the poor woman who did this service, but it had to be substantial.

To say Greg was an oddball would be the understatement of the century. He still lived with his mother and collected government checks for some sort of undisclosed disability. Trust me, he wasn't milking the system. He had self-esteem issues and had difficulty dealing with pressure situations. Perhaps being a professional harness driver wasn't the best career choice given his psychological profile. He didn't care.

It's what he wanted to do. I guess you would have to throw in delusional when diagnosing his psychosis.

In order to get your "P" license, you first have to apply for a "Q" license, which stands for qualifying license. A written test is required as the first step. We helped him study for this every day. We taught him all the different kinds of equipment that you had to know about, including driving bits, overcheck bits, tendon boots, knee boots, all the different types of shoes a horse can wear, and so on. It was tedious. It took a whole summer to prepare him for the test, and somehow he passed. It was a shock to all of us. Now he had to start driving. This is where our deal really began in earnest. He needed to drive in twenty-five qualifying races in one year in order to be able to then request a "P" license from the judges. This was not an easy task for a relatively small stable.

Each spring, most horses have to enter a qualifying race in order to be eligible to race in an actual pari-mutuel event. If a horse has raced in the last ninety days, he doesn't need to do this, as he still remains eligible to race. This process is in place to protect the betting public. After a long layoff, many horses will not be ready to perform as the program's past performances indicated. The qualifying race acts as a gauge to the public to inform them of the readiness of the animal.

Many of our horses didn't need to qualify in the spring, but if we were going to uphold our end of the bargain, we would have to enter some horses into these races just to give Greg the drives he needed. It certainly was a sacrifice. Greg couldn't get horses to perform very well. After he drove them, we never knew whether any given horse was ready to race or not. Doug would often improve horses three and four seconds off of what Greg had been able to get out of them. He was *that* bad. And Doug was that good. But a deal was a deal.

To give you an idea of what Greg was like on the track, I must tell you the story of a training trip we had one day on the farm.

We had bred the old mare Honey Sparkle Way (Honey's mom) to a stallion named Middle Road. We were rolling the genetic dice once again in hopes of catching lightning in a bottle a second time. Middle Road was a powerful racehorse and seemingly a great fit for what we were looking for to match with Honey Sparkle Way's great desire and heart. The foal that followed their rendezvous was aptly named Sparkle Road. Sadly, Sparkle Road was the last foal out of Middle Road as the stud was killed in a freakish accident on the breeding farm when he got loose and impaled his neck on a fencepost.

Sparkle Road was a long-legged three-year-old filly who didn't quite make it to the races as a two-year-old. She was plagued by a puzzling hind end lameness that we couldn't quite pinpoint even with extensive testing. Ironically, now that we had the money to perform a potential surgery that could help, we didn't know what was ailing her to actually do it. Even with her chronic problem, we had managed her to a point where she was showing tremendous promise as a three-year-old. So much so that we thought she could surpass Honey. She had tremendous speed, power, and stamina. Looking back, if we could have kept her sound, she almost certainly would have been better than the indomitable Honey's Best. High praise indeed, but not unfounded. Unfortunately, her ailment prevented her from ever reaching her true potential.

She was in training that spring and was almost ready to qualify. She was young and spirited, and not an easy horse to drive. Lots of power and speed in a green horse equals trouble if not in experienced hands. Greg needed to prove he could drive her at the farm before we could let him on the racetrack with her.

Training trips at the farm consisted of a simulated race over our track, which was a third of a mile long. Three times around. It has to be emphasized that these training trips were not competitive races, but we often trained several horses together to give them a better feel for a live race, especially the young ones. As a matter of fact, the two- and three-year-olds were almost always "allowed" to win, to make them brave at the track. We never wanted to teach a horse to lose. A horse named E.T. Vic may have been a victim of this. He finished second in nearly half of his starts with us. Honey's Best was the exact opposite; we had taught her how to win.

We were now teaching Sparkle to win. She didn't need a lot of help. She was dominating everyone she faced with ease. Just the week before, I had swung her three wide on the last turn and blown away the two horses on the inside. She pulled away by open lengths at the end of the mile. Keep in mind this was a third of a mile track and winging it three wide was like being the outside skater on one of those ice capade shows that has a line of skaters spinning in a circle. The outside has to travel much, much faster than the inside.

On this day, roles were reversed. The same three horses would be training together. I had Kid Eagle, Doug had Mohawk Knight, and Greg had Sparkle Road. Doug and I secretly liked to beat Greg in these training trips just to bust his chops even though, as I said, they weren't competitive. And it wasn't hard to do. The guy had stone hands. He could stop a locomotive. We figured it best to give Greg the top (lead the way) and take the decision-making process out of his mind. Decision making was not his strength.

The training trip started like any other. Greg took the top, Doug sat second, and I followed third. Back then, Doug and I never wore helmets for these training trips. It wasn't until 1992, when we had a major accident that ended up breaking my wrist, that we started wearing them fairly regularly. To this day, I still can't believe we didn't wear them back then. We were traveling at speeds in excess of thirty miles an hour in an open carriage with wheels and flailing hooves all around us. For allegedly smart people... not smart. And as mentally cluttered as Greg's mind appeared to be, he always wore a helmet. I'm not sure how that thing stayed on at times, because his chin was nearly nonexistent. His bottom jaw sloped directly back to his neck. He wore more of a neck strap than a chinstrap when he put it on.

When we were heading to the half-mile pole, Doug was yelling at Greg to slow down. He was setting too fast a pace. Greg had zero sense of speed, whereas Doug didn't even need a stopwatch. He had this innate ability to know exactly how fast we were traveling. A typical mile for training on our track was about two minutes and twenty seconds. We often would try to set a slow pace for the half (say 1:15) and then

try to come home quickly, to teach horses late speed
and prepare them for the rigors of racing. If you told
Doug to go a half in 1:12, he could do it without a
stopwatch to the fifth of a second. It was scary. And
he did it every time.

We told Greg to get to the half in 1:14 or 1:15
and then we would cut them loose from there. He
always carried a stopwatch. We got to the half in 1:07.
"Where is he going?" I thought. He had Sparkle cruising and we both were having a tough time keeping
the gap closed.

Up until this point in Greg's training career,
he had never "won" a training trip. We're talking
about over the course of *hundreds* of miles. Whenever
we finished miles at home on the training track, invariably we would finish noses apart so that the horses
never learned to lose. Comically though, in all the
photo finishes that we had with Greg, Doug and I
made certain that one of our horses nailed him at the
wire and he would lose by inches. It was just in fun,
but we loved watching him talk to himself after those
losses. No matter how much Greg tried, he couldn't
seem to time a win at the wire. He always got nabbed
by one of us. Poor Greg.

Honestly though, it made the training trips so
much more interesting. Part of me feels just awful
about it, but most of me thinks it was hilarious. Doug
and I would never talk about it, but both of us knew
exactly what we were doing. After a close one at the
wire, we would just smile to each other and that was
the end of it. It really was a beautiful thing to watch.
Some of those finishes were just plain works of art.

This was going to be his first and he knew it. He
had the best horse, he had the top, and he was not

going to be denied. Coming around the final turn,
Greg's hands were working their black magic. Sparkle
was tiring some from the ridiculous pace, but she still
should have been able to carry him home without any
trouble over the stock we had. Smelling blood in the
water, Doug tipped Mohawk two wide on the last turn
as I followed his cover in a slip stream before I made a
stretch run.

The final turn on the farm track has a pond that
lines the inside of it. Although there used to be a
hubrail in the days of pony races, it had long been
removed for safety purposes. Now there was just
grass that demarcated the track from the inside rail.
From there, the ground sloped down at about thirty
degrees to the pond. It was fairly steep and not somewhere you wanted to go. Farther down the homestretch, the slope gradually was lost and it flattened
out to just grass and an inside jogging track.

Doug was gaining ground on Greg, and Mohawk
Knight was right outside of his wheel looking Greg
right in the eye. Greg seemed startled and looked
back to see where we were. We were bearing down on
him and he could sense the pressure. He started flailing the reins, asking Sparkle for more, and I'm sure
she had it; he just wasn't giving her the right signals
to tell her what he wanted. I was sweeping three wide
now and could see a bit of panic in Greg's eyes. He
was still facing to the right, watching us close in on
him.

Much like when you're driving a car and you reach
across for something in the seat next to you, the steering wheel gets yanked one way or another if you're
not paying attention. Greg was not paying attention.
His left hand was steadily pulling on the left rein as

he glanced over his right shoulder. As we straightened for home, Greg and the big filly disappeared. They were over the banking. Gone.

"Holy crap," I thought, "he's dead." In disbelief, I looked back over my left shoulder to see the wreckage. In what seemed an eternity, the rugged three-year-old filly pulled him out of the gully and was still pacing as she regained her footing on the track. Incredible. She stayed on her feet and didn't flip over. It defied physics.

In the mayhem, Doug and I had slowed our horses midway down the stretch to see how he was. If it weren't so serious a situation I would have laughed hysterically.

Both of Greg's feet had slipped through the stirrups of the bike and he was up to his knees hanging from them like he was on a monkey bar with his ass scraping the ground. His head was on the seat of the sulky and his helmet was hanging off the back of his neck with the chinstrap choking him. His glasses were skewed on his face with only the left ear piece hanging on by the very tip and he had caught the right lens in his mouth, completely fogging the glass. As he hung down in the swale of the bike, Sparkle was kicking dirt in his face. It was priceless. It was no wonder his helmet came off his chin, since he didn't have one, but how the horse didn't end up in the pond and upside down is still a mystery.

To state the obvious, he still didn't win.

It took Greg two years to get his "P" license. The judges were not impressed with his rookie year. I'm not sure what they saw in his sophomore season, but they let him drive. I'm just glad I never had to be in a race with him. He was dangerous. He'd come back to the paddock, and someone would ask him why he didn't pull out at the half, and he wouldn't even know where he was anywhere in the mile. It was as if he went into a fugue state out there. He couldn't recount anything that went on in the race. It was fairly obvious that this wasn't the right career choice for him.

By the time I was twenty, I was finally able to get my "Q" license and there was no hurry to get me starts since we didn't need another driver. We were only doing it for the sake of getting me a license. It seemed like the thing to do. I had some talent, knew the game as well as anyone, and if a situation came up where Doug got hurt or couldn't be there, I could be the backup.

That very need came to pass on September 4, 1990. My father and mother and I put Honey's Best into the trailer, loaded ourselves into the truck, and headed north to Maine. At the same time, Doug loaded his equipment into his van and was heading south to Massachusetts.

It just didn't feel right. This was Honey's Best we were talking about. She had never raced without Doug. He knew her better than anybody. They had a connection. I was getting more nervous as we made the trip, and I hoped that my nerves would steady for the race because Honey would certainly detect that through the reins.

In the paddock, I donned the team colors of blue, black, and orange. All drivers wear white pants and usually driving boots. I was twenty years old. I wore sneakers. I was finally growing, and stood about five feet six inches at this point (eventually topping out at a towering five feet nine inches by age twenty-four), and I could barely grow a mustache. I weighed in at a buck thirty five, and with the white pants, I looked like I didn't weigh more than a grain bag. My helmet was orange with black stripes emanating from the top center and cascading outward like fireworks. It was just about the time when the industry had adopted the new Marushin helmet (the ones motorcyclists wear today), and in comparison to the old style, they were huge. I felt like Gazoo from the Flintstones. I stayed away from any mirrors. Although I was twenty, I looked about sixteen, and I didn't need to be reminded of it before racing with a bunch of older men who had been racing for years.

The stirrups of the bike were too long. My brother is six feet tall and when he sat in the sulky he liked to stretch out and almost lay down in the seat. At his most relaxed state in the mile, he looked like he was in the sled of a luge race. Not good for my five-foot-six-inch frame. I had to sit forward at the edge of the seat (no, we weren't smart enough to bring tools to adjust the stirrups) and my toes stretched to reach a resting spot. First, I looked awkward, and now I felt awkward. It was like I was on a bad date. Check, please. I'd like to go home now. This isn't working out for me.

Harryman checked Honey up and I was heading out for the post parade. I didn't realize how big her hind end was in the sulky. I couldn't see around her even a little bit. In the jog carts at the farm, you are seated three feet farther back as the shafts are much longer. In a sulky, you can touch the horse just by leaning forward. Combine that with the fact that I was at the front of the seat, and all I could see was her huge rump. I torqued my body slightly to the side and

decided to look around her by changing my posture.
I was feeling a bit more confident. At least I could see
where I was going.

I had the rail, and the plan was to get to the top
since Honey had such great gate speed. I figured this
was best with my decreased vision. I wouldn't have to
worry about anyone in front of me. Just set the pace
and fend them off down the lane. She was in tough,
but I felt with the rail that she had a good shot. If I
were betting the race, there is no doubt I wouldn't
have viewed it with as much confidence. The scarlet
letter "P" was glaring on the program. It was a true
statement that Honey had a good shot; it was me that
didn't.

Harness horse races start with a rolling gate.
Horses follow the gate for a quarter mile, picking up
speed until the start when the gate flies open and
all eight horses are allowed to go where their drivers
ask them to. I had timed the gate a bit poorly. On
the turn before the start, the one-hole travels slowly
to allow the outside horses to keep up. When the car
straightens out, the gate on the rail accelerates faster
than you would expect. It's best to stay off the gate
on the turn and pick up speed so that when it does
straighten out, you are closing in on a gate that is suddenly moving faster.

This is not easy. Especially for an inexperienced
driver. Honey was revved up as we started to roll and
she pulled me flush to the gate on the turn. I couldn't
hold her. She was pulling too hard. One thousand
pounds vs. 135 pounds. You do the math. We straightened out for the start, and we lost contact with the
gate by a length and a half. When the gate finally
opened up, Honey had recovered but wasn't quite

snug with it. I tapped her with the whip once, the starter said "GO!", and we were off. The number four horse got to the front before we even got to the turn. We were left sitting in the two-hole.

"Ummmm. What just happened?" That wasn't how we drew it up at all. Fifty feet into the race, and I had already screwed up.

"Relax, Marc. You're sitting in the garden spot," as they called it in racing. The number six horse left as well and was trying to sneak in between us going to the quarter pole.

"I don't think so, pal," I thought as I pushed Honey on to close the gap. We were flying. We snapped off a brisk quarter as I leaned to the left to look around her and followed the cover of the horse in front of me. The horse that was parked outside remained there. For three-quarters of a mile, nothing changed. I was trapped. The horse on top was tired, the horse outside was tired, and they both were fading into me. I had Honey under a pretty good hold in the pocket, and as we rounded the last turn I started to wonder how the hell I was going to get out down the stretch.

For most good drivers, decisions on the track are made by a method of what I call athletic cognizance. This is when an athlete makes quick decisions without verbal thinking. There are thoughts being processed at a super high rate, but only in the mental periphery and not in the cognitive area. For instance, let's say you're driving to work and you wonder if you shut the oven off. You start thinking to yourself verbally, "Did I shut the oven off? I can't remember if I did, because the phone rang after I ate breakfast. I always shut it off but I can't be certain if..."

The process is verbal. You are discussing it in your head. The athlete is making these choices without verbiage. It just happens. There isn't enough time to be processing it this way. It has to be done in a split second. This is what separates the bad drivers from the good drivers. Soft hands separate the good ones from the great ones.

As we rounded the final turn, the discussion in my head was like a presidential debate. "Is this horse outside me going to fade in time for me to get out? Is the front horse going to drift out in the lane giving me a rail shot? What if I can't get out? I wonder if I left the oven on?"

There was a horse swinging three wide off the bend, and at this point I figured that even if the horse that had been outside me the whole mile died, the other horse was coming down to lock me in again. There was a symphony of voices in my head. Fifty feet into the stretch, the horse to my right packed it in and was giving me just enough room to squeeze out, and I started to think about pulling on the right rein, but not before my wheel was clear of his front legs. At that same instant, the horse on top drifted slightly off the rail.

In a moment of clarity, it just happened. Whether Honey made the decision or I did is still somewhat unclear. It was one of those moments like when you're driving down a dark highway at night and there is a heavy downpour smacking your windshield, making it difficult to even hear the radio. The wipers can't keep up with the rain. Your headlights aren't giving you much help. And suddenly you drive beneath an overpass, and for a brief instant, the sound of the rain stops, the pavement is dry, and your mind feels relaxed. It is brief, and you wish that the whole high-way was covered by a dome. You realize how tense your mind is and you didn't even know it until that single instant under the bridge.

At the head of the lane when the horse on top drifted wide, I was under that bridge. My left hand grabbed the left rein and I showed Honey the open-ing. She didn't hesitate. She may have been thinking about it even before I was and was reacting almost in unison with my hands. As she saw daylight, her hind-quarters dipped down as she drove forward, shift-ing gears. She dropped down so much that I could just see over her now. The power was awesome. She surged through the opening, and the driver on the front horse tried to cut us down to close off the rail.

I yelled at him, "Hey hey hey, I'm right here," and he realized it was too late and gently gave way. It was still tight as we drove into the hole as our wheels rubbed together on our way through. Clear sailing now. Just me, Honey, and the wire. We did it. She did it. My first lifetime win. I reached forward and patted her on the rump. I spoke to her out loud. "That a girl. We did it, Beast," addressing her by her nickname.

Oddly enough, I wasn't excited. It felt good, but it wasn't nearly as thrilling as when I watched races that Doug had won. I knew then that my real place wasn't *on* the track but *at* the track. We cruised to the win-ner's circle and got our picture taken. That win would account for half of my entire trips to the winner's circle. Fitting that my first was on the Beast.

She set a seasonal mark that night, which means it was her fastest win of the year. She was peaking. And she had more in the tank. I don't know what had got-ten into her, but she was razor sharp.

It was mid-September and Rochester Fair was once again opening up for a ten-day meet. Every year, we would pack up our stable and race at the local fair track rather than go to Scarboro, even though they sometimes were open at the same time. Rochester was closer and it was in New Hampshire. We felt welcome there. It was our home field. Doug had won the driver's title two years previously, and although we didn't have enough horses to make him a serious contender anymore, we still tried to give him a chance.

There weren't enough good fillies for Honey's Best to enter a fillies and mare race again, so we were forced to race her against the boys. The race secretary had buried us. The term "buried" is used to describe being entered in a race that has a much higher level of competition than your horse. This happens when there aren't a lot of horses to choose from (like at a fair meet) and the race secretary is begging to fill races. Like I've said before, sometimes you get buried and sometimes you jog. It depends on the day, and usually it all works out. Honey was buried.

She was once again in with "the boys" and had drawn the four-hole. The horses she faced were the "Open" colts and geldings. They were some of the best on the grounds. A tough spot, to say the least. I knew how well she had raced the week before, and I thought if she bounced back to that, she might finish third.

The track at the Rochester Fair was shaped a bit like an egg. It wasn't truly an oval. A birds-eye view showed that the first turn was tighter than the last turn and that the backstretch was just a bit longer. It was an engineering mistake for sure. The turns were flat making them very difficult to negotiate at high speeds. It had a grade of about two percent. Most tracks had some sort of banking to allow cornering to be facilitated and also for safety. Not Rochester; it was the prototypical "bull ring" racetrack, aptly named from the tightness of a rodeo ring.

It was September 10th, and it was cooling off. At race time, it was about fifty-five degrees and there was a light fog rolling in. She was in the ninth race, which was the feature. As the night eased toward the morning, the temperatures were still dropping. The speed of races is generally directly related to the climate. Hotter weather means faster miles. In the ninth race on this chilly night in Rochester, N.H., Honey was about to challenge that theory.

Honey left strong out of the four-hole, but the rail horse, D.C.R., was much too fast to even consider beating to the front. He was an elite horse in Maine and his gate speed was notorious. Besides, Kelly Case was driving him, and there wasn't a chance she would relinquish the lead. She was the sister of the great Walter Case Jr., who arguably had the softest hands in the business. He went on to be a world-class driver in New York until drugs and scandals stripped him of his fame.

Kelly Case was a hard woman, living in the shadows of perhaps one of the greatest harness drivers in history. She was constantly trying to prove herself, and although she wasn't necessarily a bad driver, she was a bit reckless at times and seemed to have little regard for the animals she drove. That's not to say that she was cruel to her animals. She drove them like they were machines rather than living flesh, often asking them for more than they were really capable of giving her. She stood about five feet two inches tall and weighed ninety-five pounds soaking wet. And I thought *I* couldn't see around a horse. She needed a periscope. Quite frankly, I don't know how she did it. There was no way Honey was getting the top. Kelly Case was determined to control the mile. The first quarter time was rifled off in 29.3. For Rochester, those fractions weren't shocking, but still quick. The track record up until 1981 had been 2:02.0. That was set by a horse called Strong Focus and the record that was held for over twenty-five years. The track just couldn't handle the speed. It was too tight, and the turns weren't banked. The laws of physics made it hard to consider a mile any faster than 1:58.0 on the best conditions with the top horse in the nation. The track record now stood at 1:59.3, set three years prior by an Invitational pacer that was world-class.

Doug sat in the two-hole, much like I had the previous week, but this time there was no one around them. They had skipped off by six lengths from the field. They rattled the half off in 59.3. At this pace, they would break the track record and stop the timer in 1:58.1. Not likely. Once a horse steps a half like that on that surface, the legs quickly tire, and the early pace takes its toll. I had seen plenty of these crazy halves at Rochester before, and they usually ended up coming home in 1:03 or 1:04. It was the classic case of the tortoise and the hare. It was best to pace yourself. This track was unforgiving for those kinds of early fractions.

Getting the pocket trip like Honey had was ideal. It allowed you to draft behind the leader the whole mile, take the short route by staying on the rail, and then tipping out down the stretch to take a run on what should by then be a tired horse. Doug was cagey.

He would always try to save ground and give himself the best chance at winning.

There were ten open lengths back to the horse in third when they entered the turn that was the "point of the egg" just past the half. There was no way Doug would pull yet. He had no one behind him to lock him in, and the front horse was still rolling.

Most drivers on the front end would take back a bit and try to rest the animal if not pressed in order to save something for the last part of the mile. Not Kelly Case. She kept D.C.R. fired up. I thought to myself as they passed by me in the paddock, "Stay right there, Gooch, you have live cover."

The paddock at Rochester was right at the end of the stretch, which was not customary for most tracks. As the horses came down the stretch, you got a head-on view of them, and it made it very difficult to get any kind of depth perception where your horse was relative to the others. You had to rely on shadows and the announcer to give you clues. The finish line was lit up at the end of the mile, so when they crossed the wire, the front horse would light up first, clearly indicating who won. It was the only way of visibly telling how your horse did from that vantage point.

When Doug tipped Honey two wide going into the paddock turn, I couldn't believe what I was seeing. They just went a half in 59.3, and he was pulling out on a horse (on the turn, no less) that was clearly superior on paper. It was one of the few times that I was upset with a move that Doug had made in a mile. There was no logical reason for him to pull at that moment. In fact, it was the exact wrong time to pull. He was using up any reserves Honey might have on the sharp paddock turn against a strong opponent. It didn't make any sense.

Honey drove up on his wheel and started pressing in on him around the turn. She didn't quite get up to his shoulder when Kelly Case cut him loose up the backside. Damn, she had given a good run at him, and he had put her away. Doug settled Honey back in behind them up the backside and was trying to give her a breather for perhaps another run down the lane.

Three-quarters of a mile in 1:29.3. They were on track record pace. I could hear the announcer, and he was getting excited. I'm not sure which I was more in disbelief of, the time of the mile or that Honey was still stalking D.C.R. She looked stronger than she should have for the fractions they were throwing down.

Going into the last turn, Doug pulled on D.C.R. one more time, and this time with purpose. They sling-shotted up to the big stallion and headed him. The two horses were eye to eye on the last turn. Honey was mentally locked in. Kelly Case was asking her horse for everything he had. Doug was doing the same. They spun off the last turn, knifing through the fog, and they were dead even. I could see the wheels of the sulkies' skidding off the tangent of the turn as they headed for home.

They weren't slowing down. So many things were going through my head. "Could this be a track record? How the hell is this horse still on top with Honey racing the race of her life? How is Honey still chasing him down?"

She had the momentum around the last turn and got a neck in front. I tuned into the announcer for the call to hear what the last sixteenth of a mile would give us. I was also gazing at the teletimer, then at the horses, back at the teletimer, back at the horses. This was going to be close. The time, the finish, everything.

The announcer was clear in my head. "Honey's Best is out in front by a neck."

I was screaming out loud, "Bring 'em home, Beast!! Don't let him take this one away!"

She had to be tiring. Her head was straight out and she was relentlessly driving home. The announcer came back to me; his voice was shrill from excitement as he sensed this was a historical race. "Honey's Best on the outside, D.C.R. coming back on the rail!"

Coming back on the rail? Absolutely no way. I couldn't believe what I was hearing. Not again. I couldn't take it. Too many heartaches. She has to fight this horse off. She's raced a monster mile. There's no way this could happen. I didn't think I could bear to lose by a nose in what could be the greatest mile in Rochester Fair history.

"Come on, Beast, don't let him do this to you. Not tonight."

I thought to myself, "What is this horse on that's allowing him to keep pressing like this? They had to have given him something. He's racing like he's possessed."

I suppose the owners of D.C.R. were echoing the same sentiment about Honey.

I got quiet with forty feet before the wire to go and felt myself holding my breath. I crouched down, put my hands to my head, and watched the tandem coming to the wire. I could see the light on the track.

Waiting for them to cross, I glanced at the teletimer...
1:56.2, 1:57.3. 158.1...then back at the horses coming
at me head-on. The announcer said the same thing
he said five seconds previously.

"Honey's Best is still driving, but D.C.R.'s fighting
back along the rail, and here they arrrrreeeee."

The light flashed on Honey's face first. In a blink,
D.C.R. lit up. I didn't need a photo. She had won. It
certainly would be a photo finish. It didn't matter.
I knew she had won. Doug gave me a thumbs up as
he passed by me in the paddock. He knew how close
it was and wanted me to be sure I knew they got it. I
knew. I could hear people talking about how tight it
was and that they didn't know who won it. I was calm.
I knew. The teletimer was frozen at 2:00.0.

She had just set the record for the fastest mile
ever posted at Rochester by a filly or mare. The previous mark was set in 1981 in 201.4. She had shattered
it. It was 1990. She missed the overall track record
by just two fifths of a second. In 2007, they stopped
harness racing at Rochester, and today the record
still stands.

My future wife, Jen, who was my classmate in vet
school, was visiting me just before we went back to
Ohio State for our sophomore year. As Honey passed
in front of us in the paddock, I turned to her and
said, "You might not know it, but you just witnessed a
miracle mile."

This horse never stopped amazing me. We made
the short trip to the winner's circle together. I was
on top of the world. It was an intangible feeling that
no amount of money can buy. This was just another
gift Honey had given us. Ask a parent to explain how

they feel when a child does something extraordinary. It can't be put into words.

Even though they had won the race, I couldn't help but ask Doug why he came out at the half. It was so out of character.

"Why did you pull her going into the turn?", I asked as the picture was taken.

He flashed a quick smile, "She felt good."

Apparently so. Wow, what a mile.

Honey never came back to that kind of performance ever again. Three weeks later, we got a letter in the mail that said D.C.R. was disqualified from the race because they found performance enhancing drugs in him. I didn't need the letter. It only confirmed what I suspected when Honey drove him down. And she was clean.

It was as if she was paying us back for that heartbreaking loss in Lewiston five years previously. That was when she lost the three-year-old Sire Stakes Final after winning eleven races in a row. She had come down with a respiratory infection that nearly caused us to scratch her. We reluctantly raced her and she finished a courageous second in what was the most devastating loss we have ever endured. She came back to the paddock with mucus pouring out of her nostrils and she was struggling to get air.

There was no reason for her to pay us back for anything. She had given us more in monetary and psychological income than we could have ever imagined. This time when she came back to the paddock, she was breathing freely. When we read the letter stating that D.C.R. was in fact on drugs that day, my first reaction was one of anger. As I thought about it more, the fact that they cheated gave us one of the most cherished memories we will ever have. If that horse didn't push Honey for more the way he did, the record never would have been set.

She had raced on seventeen different tracks over her storied life and went the fastest mile of her career that night on what was arguably a track with the lowest speed rating she had ever performed on. Add the fact that she raced on the outside for three-quarters of a mile, against a horse that was on performance enhancing drugs *and* on a cold September night makes the circumstances even more improbable and inspiring. She had taught us again that there are no certainties in racing, or in anything in life. When you think that the best times in your life have come and gone, fate has a way of surprising you.

It's never too late to do your absolute very best, even if logic tells you otherwise. To quote the words of John Mellencamp, "Life goes on, long after the thrill of living is gone." This is an anthem for many people after they reach a certain age that have lost their passion. It is a self-fulfilling prophecy. If you think there's nothing worth pushing for, it's likely you will never feel the rush of life's wonder again. Games you never play, you never win.

To Bad Honey

Our stable was substantially smaller than it ever had been. I was two years removed from veterinary school and was practicing equine medicine in southern New England. When we were younger, our lives revolved around racing. It was everything we did. We missed cousins' birthdays, weddings of friends, and other family obligations that almost all other families routinely attended. Racing came first. Everything else was a distraction.

During the summer, most of the bigger races landed on the weekends. It would have been almost impossible for us to forfeit a race just to go to an anniversary party. Racing was how we made a living, and although the people that were close to us knew what we did, they couldn't understand how we operated. We would never have asked anyone to give up a week's salary to celebrate a birthday, but that's exactly what we would have to do in order to accommodate these events. We had more fun racing anyway, at least most of the time.

As we all got older, during the mid-1990s, racing started to become a bit of a chore. Doug was performing more with his music, and I had a full-time job at a small animal hospital and was doing ambulatory equine work on the side. There wasn't much time left in the day for the horses anymore. But racing was in our blood. We couldn't just walk away. Not yet anyway.

As the racing industry changed around us, it was getting harder to win races. We ran a clean stable. Our horses didn't have the "benefit" of chemical help that some of the larger stables were turning to. It was frustrating to watch one or two big stables win all the races, knowing full well they were using drugs to get their horses to perform better.

The test barn was nothing more than a formality. The people that were winning knew what they could or couldn't get away with. Some didn't care. They were willing to take the risk. As a veterinarian, it was not an area that I wanted to get involved in. Nor did the rest of the family. Using or getting caught using illegal substances on our racehorses was not something we were ethically prepared to do. For me, it would have been professional suicide.

The idea of better racing through chemistry is not a new phenomenon. It is as old as the game and transcends all sports. If there is money to be made, someone is cheating. The baseball industry closed their eyes to it for decades before things got so out of control that something had to be done. In the harness racing business in small-time New England, there lacked a national stage to grab the attention of the general public or anyone else that might have taken notice and wanted to clean things up.

Back in the mid-seventies, we experienced first hand the real beginning of the drug scene and how discouraging it could be to race against chemically enhanced horses. Colen Mosher was the leading trainer at Foxboro. He had a huge stable with anywhere from thirty to forty head at any given time. He would race six and seven horses in a night. For a few years, nothing was amiss. Suddenly, in the summer of 1977, he started claiming mares and only mares.

In one week, these horses would drop three or four seconds off of their race times and be winning for fun. His win percentage was staggering. Our family didn't just suspect they were using something, we knew they were. A trainer can improve a horse by changing equipment or getting a better driver. Horses can also need better conditioning techniques to make them have more stamina. But when his horses were setting lifetime marks week in and week out after these claims, there had to be something else at play. To our amazement, the talk on the track didn't reflect this at all. Most observers were giving him credit for being good with mares and that's why he only claimed female horses.

At the time, we had a horse named Butler's Gal that was racing fairly decently. Harryman was our regular driver back then. This mare had some arthritis in her feet and had a procedure at some point in her life called a neurectomy. This procedure severs the nerve to the back of the horse's foot so that they could continue to race without pain. Because the nerve only affects the back half of the foot, the horse can still feel the ground and race without being at risk of falling down. This procedure is also known as "nerving" a horse. It is only legal when done at the very lowest portion of the foot, and horses that have had this done (and it is very rare, actually) are labeled as "low-nerved" horses. Many, many years ago, in the dark ages of racing, some people had their horses "high-nerved" for more serious arthritic conditions. This would deaden the entire foot.

It made situations dangerous on many levels. Horses with no feeling in their feet obviously can't feel the ground. On level surfaces, they seemed to manage just fine, but if they were to stumble, or land on an uneven area of the track (like a deep hoof-print), they would tend to fall down. These animals were brutally dangerous. Stories of entire fields of horses going down because of this practice were common in racing folklore. Thankfully, it was outlawed for obvious safety and ethical reasons long before we got into the business.

Even with the alleviating effects of the surgery that Butler's Gal had, she would always get rough-gaited in the turns. My theory was that pain wasn't the issue but that she may have felt awkward not having the full tactile ability to feel the ground when negotiating the turns. On the straight-aways she was smooth as glass. I can remember Harryman nursing her through the turns and then letting her open up when they straightened out. She was a gamer.

One night, after she had won her third in a row for us, the Mosher stable claimed her. She was in to go the very next week. They placed her up two classes and she won her debut with them by ten open lengths, going the fastest mile she had gone in three years. She didn't look like the same horse. On the turns, she never took a bad step. No trainer anywhere in the world could have done that with just an equipment change. It was all the proof we needed to know they were in fact using drugs. The only other question that we could ask was whether or not they had high-nerved her. We knew the stable was crooked, so nothing would have shocked us. It sickened us, but it didn't shock us.

It was clear that it was drugs. If she were the only horse that Mosher was improving on, we might have thought differently, but he was doing this across the board. "Mosher's Mares" they called them. He was being heralded by some as some sort of genius. Ridiculous. This scumbag epitomized everything that was wrong with racing. He was the reason certain factions believe that all forms of racing are cruel and should be outlawed. Based on this one individual, they had an argument.

There were many reasons we were upset by what was going on with Butler's Gal and the rest of the animals he had "kidnapped." She was a nice horse. Not knowing how they were treating her and what exactly they were giving her to make her race at that level was disturbing. These animals were racing at a level their bodies likely weren't capable of performing at, and it would surely take its toll on them. They couldn't last very long. And most of them didn't. It was like they were being claimed into a cult. They would race for a few months like they were possessed and then fall off the face of the earth.

It also made us and the rest of the trainers Mosher took animals from look like novices. He was showing everyone up. It certainly wasn't a jealously thing, but it was frustrating to say the least. No matter how much we told ourselves there was a chemical reason for these animals to be doing so well, it didn't help. We had lost a pretty good racehorse and had to watch her win with someone else week after week. Her price tag was twice what they had paid for her. There was no way we could get her back.

Mosher's Mares. Every time someone would say that, I would cringe. It was more like Mengele's Mares. He was capturing distaffers and doing chemical experiments on them. It was disgusting. Poor Butler's Gal. I wished she had never been taken from us. We just knew that eventually something would happen. They would have to catch him with whatever it was he was using at some point. But the weeks rolled on.

A year went by. He kept winning. Finally, a year and a half later, what we had suspected all along came to light. Three of his horses in one racing program tested positive for a drug called M-99. The generic name for it is Etorphine, an elephant tranquilizer. It is a super narcotic that is ten thousand times stronger than morphine. In the pachyderm it acts on the narcotic receptor sites to induce anesthesia. In the horse, it's different. The narcotic receptors in the equine have a different composition, and the effect is the opposite. It hops them up much like methamphetamine does people, except much more. It also blocks pain.

It was so sad. How could this have happened for so long? It made us think that maybe they should ban racing, but we knew in fact that this wasn't the answer. That type of thinking is backwards. That would be like making owning a dog illegal because some degenerate jerk kicks his poodle. They needed to ban guys like this and not allow this to ever happen.

In the weeks that followed, the investigation showed he had been using the substance for over two years. They discovered that some of his horses actually died from heart attacks after racing because of the excessive heart rate the drug induced. His license was taken away for thirty days for each offense and he was fined a hundred dollars for each count. The Massachusetts Racing Commission banned him from the state for the remainder of the meet but he was able to race again. It wasn't enough. He should have faced criminal and cruelty charges as well. The justice system is sometimes not just at all.

The only purse money he lost was for the races they caught him on. The two years of thievery from horsemen, deception of the public, and malevolence toward horses went unchecked. Countless trainers lost horses to him and just as many lost purses to horses that he won. None of that was going to change. He had tainted the sport in a way that was shameful to all horsemen and even to humanity. As trainers, we all know that horses are not humans and are obviously not treated the same way. They are kept in stalls. They are ridden for pleasure. They work for us. But this crossed the line. He had acted with a complete lack of compassion for the animal in a Machiavellian attempt to make money.

The question still remained in my mind, why only mares? Apparently it was all just a ruse. He figured if he took only mares, it would throw off the hunt for what chemical to test for. Etorphine works on all horses, regardless of sex. Scientists in the lab would perhaps be looking for a hormone or a drug specific for the female instead of a blanket drug that would affect all horses. I'm not sure that it mattered really. In the end, his greed caught up to him as he started using it on all of his stock and was claiming stallions and geldings and using it on them as well.

That was the early part of the 1980s. Things settled down after that. Random testing started to occur. No longer were just the winner and the second place horses tested. They now did the winner and one other arbitrary horse in the race, called the "special." We were able to compete again. The playing field had leveled off, at least for a while.

* * *

It was 1994. Our small stable was doing fairly well. Our run in the eighties was over and we were on the other side of the mountain coming down. The climb to the top had been as exhausting as it was exhilarating. Nothing lasts forever. Although we were descending from the summit, there were still plenty of breathtaking and beautiful things to see on the way down. We weren't going to just stop racing because we weren't winning as much. It was still fun, and it was what we did.

We were racing a few horses for a man named Ed Rohr. He owned a family-style restaurant in the next town over in Exeter, N.H. It was the classic sit-down family restaurant with standard American cuisine like spaghetti and meatballs, meatloaf, and lasagna. One of his specials was shepherd's pie. Not one of my favorites. Who thought of that dish anyway? Why anyone would want to lump meat, peas, corn, and mashed potatoes into a slop is beyond me. If I wanted my meal to look like leftovers from Thanksgiving, I wouldn't go pay for it, that's for sure. Besides, I want more meat than potatoes. And I want them separated on my plate so that I can decide which ones I want to eat and when I want to eat them. If you're going to cram them all together like that, you might as well throw it in a blender, make a frappe out of it, and be done.

Ed had two daughters that loved harness racing. They were really into it. One of them aspired to become a professional driver one day. For the time being, they had chosen us to train their horses and we were doing well with them. One of them was a black mare named Flawless Almahurst. She was a tough mare in her own right, and she raced mostly in conditioned races where no one could claim her. Early in the year she did well, but as she earned out of the cheaper classes, the going got tough. She held her own, but late summer held nothing more than a string of thirds and fourths for her until spring would roll around when she could drop back down in class.

The other horse they had was called To Bad Honey. No, that's not a typo. They either misspelled his name when they sent it in the U.S.T.A. (United States Trotting Association) or they wanted people to think they were stupid. Either way, it wasn't spelled Too Bad Honey, it was To Bad Honey. He was average size, had average speed, and was your standard bay color. For the most part, he was forgettable. Until that summer.

Things had come full circle again. There were two trainers that suddenly were winning more races than would have been statistically expected. Horses were improving after they would claim them in a way that only could be explained by outside help. There were rumors about what it was, but no one knew for sure. One of the theories was that these horses were being dosed with massive doses of baking soda before the race. The science behind the idea was that the lactic acid that built up during racing would be neutralized by high levels of a basic substance. Baking soda was cheap and safe to use. The problem in most people's eyes was the modality in which the animals received it. It was believed that in order to dose a horse with more than a pound of the stuff, they had to pass a tube into the horse's stomach and pump it in manually.

This process of passing a tube, in the right hands, is relatively simple. For many years, this was the only way veterinarians were able to de-worm horses as de-worming pastes were not invented until the 1980s. Most veterinarians were able to do this with ease.

It was also a practice that had to be done when horses had a condition called colic. A tube is almost always passed into the stomach of these sick animals to ascertain what kind of colic the horse has or to relieve pressure from excessive fluids that may be building in the stomach. It is carefully passed through one of the nostrils and then skillfully guided over the epiglottis (as the horse swallows), through the esophagus, and gently advanced into the stomach. This technique requires practice, a good working knowledge of the anatomy, and the ability to work with the equine. This is especially important for horses with blockages, as the equine anatomy is such that the animal cannot vomit. Increased pressure in the stomach and upper intestinal tract can become excruciatingly painful if it cannot be released. Even more horrifying is if the stomach were to rupture, leading to certain death.

In the wrong hands, the procedure can be disastrous. If the tube is mistakenly placed down the trachea and into the lungs, the result is usually a dead horse. The animal won't drown right there on the spot, but will end up getting severe pneumonia and die over a couple of days if not treated very aggressively and early on. The word on the backstretch was that some of these winning trainers had been killing horses doing just that. There was now a collective effort to ban baking soda from racing. Interestingly enough, the baking soda really wasn't the problem, as it truly can benefit an animal both during and after the race. It was the act of tubing that was being targeted.

We had been using baking soda for years, not by the pound, but a handful in all of the horses' feed every day twice a day. It was one of the treatments we used when Honey had her muscle enzyme issue. The daily dose of baking soda not only dropped her SGOT counts (one of the more accurate parameters in the blood when measuring muscle damage in a horse) after they were elevated, but it seemed to help in keeping them from actually spiking. We couldn't ever be sure if Honey had completely recovered from whatever ravaged her system back in 1987, but it was never an issue again after that. We weren't willing to stop using baking soda to see if she would get sick again.

Everyone who wasn't tubing their horses or using pounds of pre-race baking soda was happy with the new rule change. Every horse that was entered to race had to have a pre-race blood gas taken to check their bicarbonate level. The number they picked at the onset of the testing was twenty-eight. I'm not sure where they came up with that number, but it was the one everyone feared. Any animal that was caught with anything higher would be immediately scratched and the trainer would be suspended and fined.

There was only one problem that concerned all of us. It was a one-strike policy. First offense and you were gone. We knew they wanted to crack down on this practice, but the consequences for such a new testing procedure seemed a bit severe.

It didn't take long to notice the change in racing. Almost overnight, the competition was more even. Those trainers that were flying high because they were tubing their horses suddenly came crashing down to earth. It was extremely gratifying. Our horses were never close to the magic number twenty-eight. They hovered anywhere from fifteen to twenty-two, even with the baking soda we continued to feed. As a veterinarian, I assumed that the amount we gave in the food couldn't possibly have a profound effect on those pre-race levels. I was right, but just to be safe on race day, we cut back the morning ration by half.

The blood gas machine that Scarboro employed was housed in a little portable trailer, like the ones used at construction sites for offices. The instrument they used became infamously known as the "black box" by the horseman. It wasn't really black, and the shaped was an irregular rectangle at best, but for simplistic reasons, that's what we began referring to it as. The men running the test weren't laboratory technicians, but merely track workers that were shown how to insert the blood and subsequently read the number that came out. There were no controls run on a day-to-day basis, and the machine was rarely, if ever, calibrated. It was a disaster just waiting to happen.

As the dog days of summer came into full swing, the trainers who couldn't handle racing on the level started experimenting with the amount of baking soda they could get away with. The track would not just say if your horse was legal to race, they would actually give you the number. Not smart. This only gave information to the cheaters. They started with one ounce of treatment, then two, and so on. After a month, they knew exactly how much they could use and not be positive for high levels. The same trainers that were winning previous to the rule change slowly started to rise to the top again. If you give a rat in a hole a little daylight, he'll dig himself out.

To Bad Honey was in to go on a Sunday matinee. It was a summer day like all the rest of them at Scarboro. Hot, humid, and a slight breeze gently pushed dust across the track. I could hear the familiar horn of Chuck Mangione blowing in from the grandstand. They had one tape they played all summer long for at least three years. It had Frank Sinatra's "Summer Wind," John Rafferty's "Baker Street," and an instrumental by Chuck Mangione. That was it. They played it over and over and over in a loop. If there's a Hell for me, and music is playing there, that's what it will be.

They raced fifteen races on Sundays. If you happened to draw the first and last race, which I cannot tell you how many times happened to us, it made for a grueling afternoon. It just so happened that we had one in the second, and To Bad Honey was in the thirteenth. Bad enough, but it could have been worse. The main paddock had enough room for twelve races. The last three races would occupy the first, second, and third race stalls once they became available. Since we got there early, there was no place to put To Bad Honey. There were a few stalls in an auxiliary barn next to the paddock; two of those stalls were used for collecting urine, and the rest were vacant. Out of necessity, we put the bay gelding in a holding pattern out there until the first race cleared out.

Going into that race, things had been going poorly for To Bad Honey. He had developed some sort of breathing problem, which isn't all that uncommon in the equine athlete. Treatment for these problems is usually fairly simple; the difficult part was diagnosing it. Having me on retainer as a resident veterinarian at the farm was a huge bonus. There was never a reason to call a vet out and have to wait days or weeks to have a horse looked at. If there was a problem, we could address it immediately and move forward. In racing, time is money. The longer a horse is shelved with an ailment, the less he makes.

In the weeks leading up to that race, we had worked on To Bad Honey exhaustively trying to figure out what was wrong with him. He would race three-quarters of a mile like a giant, and then pack it in like someone punched him in the gut. He came back to the paddock blowing hard and fatigued. There was obviously an oxygen deprivation thing going on. I knew it had to be his respiratory system because when he started to fail in the mile, he would make a roaring sound in his throat, so turbulence in his airway was clearly the problem.

There are a handful of diagnoses that lead to turbulent air in the equine throat. The key is to identify it correctly and then make it go away. The first is the tongue. If a horse manages to get his tongue over the bit while playing with the metal in his mouth, the driving bit can then get caught under the tongue. As the driver pulls back on the bit to control the animal, it in essence drives the tongue into the back of the mouth, effectively shutting down the air passage. This is known as "choking down" a horse. It rarely happens if the horse is equipped with a tongue tie. Essentially it anchors the tongue down to the bottom jaw loosely to prevent the horse from being able to pull the tongue back and then over the bit.

All of our horses wore a tongue tie. It was a safety precaution. As a driver, having a horse choke down is devastating. It usually happens when your horse is in a spot where he wants to go faster but there are horses surrounding him, preventing his ability to get out of a hole and pass the slower traffic holding him up. The first half of the mile is notorious for this. The horse is hot, stuck in a hole, and wants to race. Meanwhile the driver on the front horse is trying to rate the mile and slow things down to save his horse's strength for the end. The horse trapped in the box usually starts roaring and the drivers around him know what's happening. Experienced drivers will often ask the other driver having trouble if he needs to get out for safety reasons. If so, the crisis is thwarted.

But sometimes it happens so fast nothing can be done. In less than fifteen seconds, the horse that's struggling for air can be dangerously close to blacking out. Even if the driver is able to release him and let him breathe again, the oxygen to the brain has sufficiently been cut off to a point of no return. The lag time for the horse to breathe freely and make up for the oxygen debt is too long. The horse staggers, slows down abruptly, and drops to the ground.

Good drivers alert others of their plight before this usually happens. They are allowed clearance and steer out of any danger. Although this occurrence is relatively rare, when it happens to you once, you never want it to happen again. It happened to Doug on a horse named Suzie Butler. Fortunately he got away from the field before she did a nosedive. Neither horse nor driver was hurt, but she wasn't wearing a tongue tie. That was the last horse to ever go without.

We knew To Bad Honey wasn't choking down. That would have been way too easy. We would have to explore further. An endoscopic exam of the throat was in order to rule out the three most likely reasons. What followed was nothing more than a frustrating series of exams that revealed next to nothing.

Of the big three conditions that can affect the horse's breathing apparatus, the first was ruled out quickly. He did not have a "flapper" problem, as horsemen call it. This is the layman's term for a condition called left laryngeal paralysis. The horse's voice box, or larynx, is very similar to ours in structure. They can't speak, of course, but they can talk. The two pieces of cartilage that make up the cords that come together to make sound are called the arytenoids. In a most bizarre evolutionary mistake, the nerve that feeds the left one is wrapped around the aorta and swings back up into the throat. Because the aorta is only on the left, the right side has a nerve that runs a straight course to its target.

The aorta in the equine is extremely large and undergoes great expansion and stress when it is used in the elite athletic horse. The constant pounding of this vessel on the intimately associated nerve can cause damage over time. Slowly and steadily, in some horses, it becomes permanently affected to where the left arytenoid cartilage is unable to move and allow proper airflow. As it hangs in the center of the pipeline, it causes great disruption of the airflow dynamics, and the resulting sound is similar to the aliens in the movie *Invasion of the Body Snatchers*. The noise is made repeatedly with each inspiration at high speeds. These horses are aptly referred to as "roarers." To Bad Honey's arytenoids were just fine. Strike one.

As I scoped him, looking for any possible reason he was having difficulty breathing, I was concentrating on his epiglottis. Even though he wasn't a true roarer, he was still roaring, so there had to be a reason. The epiglottis is at the source of the second and third causes. Ironically, To Bad Honey's owner's name was Ed Rohr. Only now can I truly appreciate the humor in that. Back then, it wasn't funny at all. Not one little bit.

His epiglottis looked fine. No help there. But the condition that affects it can be intermittent and sneaky. Often times there are lesions or some reddening on the tissue which helps suggest some sort of trauma during racing. Nothing. I was trying to identify either of two conditions: dorsal displacement of the soft palate or epiglottic entrapment. At the risk of becoming too tedious and boring, I will try to explain both of them. Besides, both conditions are quite interesting...but I'm a vet, and if I didn't find them compelling, I probably wouldn't have chosen this profession.

When a horse is examined endoscopically, it is done through the nostril. The view of the airway is then viewed from the top. As you peer into the laryngeal area, the epiglottis can be seen sitting right on top of the fleshy soft palate (this is the back part of the roof of your mouth). It is triangular in shape

with the tip of it pointing directly at you. It looks a lot
like a stubby little pink piece of soggy pizza that curls
slightly downward because the crust is too thin to
hold it up. In dorsal displacement of the soft palate,
it has simply vanished. If the soft palate is displaced
dorsally (or upward), there is no possible way you can
miss this diagnosis.

The problem is that when the horse is at rest and
swallows (and they usually do when you pass the
scope), it corrects the problem. The idea is to make
the horse swallow multiple times to see if you can induce the action. When you can get this to work, the
epiglottis suddenly disappears then reappears. It's like
watching a magician doing a coin trick with his hand.
Now you see it, now you don't. With To Bad Honey, it
was now I see it, now I see it, now I still see it. Strike
two.

I knew it had to be epiglottic entrapment at this
point, but had yet to be able to identify it. In another
evolutionary glitch, the fleshy little tongue that rests
on the soft palate has a hood-like structure that sup-
ports it. It can be described much like the hood of
a sweatshirt that has a drawstring. If it's loose, you
can flip it on and off your head easily. If the string is
cinched down somewhat, it can be difficult to get off
your head. When the horse swallows, this fleshy hood
can get stuck, enveloping our little friend the epiglottis and make it look more like a meatball than a slice
of pizza. Unlike in dorsal displacement, the gnarled
up epiglottis can be seen. The irregular shape it has
become during this transformation wreaks havoc with
the physics of airflow. The airway in the horse has
evolved over thousands of years to perfection, and
major changes like this are fine if the horse just wants

to graze, but if he wants to lead the pack, he won't be able to.

I must have scoped him a dozen times, and that's being conservative. No meatball. Strike three. I was beginning to question myself. It simply had to be one of those conditions, but we were coming up empty. In vet school, I prided myself on being one of the best when it came to the equine athlete. I never missed a diagnosis involving an airway problem. Now I was stumped. This called for dramatic measures.

We had a treadmill in the barn that we used during the wintertime to condition the horses. Most took to it fairly quickly and didn't fuss over the noise and motion under their feet. To Bad Honey was a good patient. He climbed on and quickly learned how to trot away at reasonable speeds. We thought if we could simulate a race, we could perhaps see what was going on during the mile.

I scoped him yet again. We had him going around eighteen miles an hour, a pretty fast speed from the treadmill, but not close enough to the high end of thirty-five that you would expect on the racetrack. The scope showed nothing. Or I should say, it didn't show nothing. The epiglottis was clearly visible, and it never turned into a meatball. I was already out of strikes, but I wasn't willing to stop swinging. This was becoming personal. This mystery ailment was a formidable foe. Game on.

The speed clearly wasn't enough on the treadmill. We had to try and simulate real racing speeds. This would take a bit of ingenuity and stupidity to pull off. I don't think anyone would have pushed any further. But we weren't just anyone. We had an old pickup truck that we used for towing horses when the weather was bad or we wanted to jog more than one horse at a time. A long, flat two-by-twelve board was placed over the two sides of the truck, sticking out about three feet on either side, like stubby wings on an airplane. The horses could be tied to this with ample slack in the line to prevent injury and they would trot alongside the vehicle. It may sound like we invented this technique, but we didn't. A lot of farms employed this system. The horses didn't seem to mind it and it was a heck of a lot easier than jogging them individually in ten-degree weather.

It wasn't without some problems, however. There were a few ornery stallions or sour mares that refused to cooperate. They had to be jogged the old-fashioned way. Our patient was good. He took to the truck easily. I sat in the back of the truck, my brother was by my side to help keep him steady, and Harryman was driving. It looked like a scene from a Hollywood set.

I put the scope in first because the thought of doing that at high speeds was logistically impossible and probably be more stupid than anything else about this freak show we were putting on. We got up to about twenty-five miles an hour. The scope once again showed nothing of significance. I pulled the tube out of his nose as we continued to roll tape. His breathing was labored. He seemed to be doing exactly what he was during the race. We were on to something here. Sitting so close to his head, we could see his nostrils were flapping badly with each inspiration. It was a source of noise. We weren't convinced it was THE source of the noise, but it was real.

We brought him back into the barn and examined his nostrils. He seemed to have some redundant tissue. The inner fold of his nostrils was hanging into the airway and fluttering when he breathed. It was unlikely, but possibly the answer we were looking for. In vet school, there is a saying, when you hear thundering hoofbeats, thinks horses, not zebras. We were beyond zebras, we were hearing armadillos.

It was worth a shot. We had to do something, as doing nothing would have been defeatist thinking. I took some suture material and some actual small plastic buttons and essentially stitched the excessive skin fold together so that the loose skin couldn't hang into his airway. We gave him the rest of the day off and tried him again the next day.

I should have listened to my professors. It wasn't armadillos at all. It was most definitely hoofbeats, and they were slowing down again after the half mile. He stopped at the three-quarter pole and exhibited the same roaring behavior he had before.

We had pretty much exhausted our search. We gave it some more thought and decided to race him with some equipment changes that might help. We would raise his head for the race and extend his tongue out of his throat ever so slightly to move his epiglottis forward a bit. This tended to reduce the chance of dorsal displacement of the soft palate. It was worth a shot. We didn't know what else to do. A second opinion was certainly next at a specialty clinic, but I was sure that they wouldn't find anything. Unless of course he by chance exhibited one of the aforementioned conditions that had somehow eluded my numerous scopings to date. Even through all of my negative findings, my money was still on epiglottic entrapment that I had yet to see. And if you can't actually see it, you can't fix it. With some equipment changes, we decided to race him again.

* * *

The second race was over and we had just one horse left to go. As the afternoon waned, I was finally able to go get To Bad Honey from the auxiliary paddock and put him in his correct stall. Thirteenth race, five-hole. The veterinarian on staff came by and drew blood from all of the horses in the thirteenth race as was customary about an hour before post time. This black box thing had been implemented over a month ago, so there were never any concerns anymore. At first a lot of people were apprehensive because they didn't know how accurate the machine was. Everything seemed to be going just fine, but no one had been caught with a positive bicarbonate level yet.

Just after having his blood drawn, we hooked up To Bad Honey to the bike and sent him out to the track with Doug to warm up. All of our horses jogged one hour out. It loosened up the muscles and got the blood pumping. Equipment checks were done during this time. It also gave us a gauge as to how the animal was feeling that day.

When he got back to the paddock, I wasn't available to pick him up off the track. I had been called into the paddock office. To Bad Honey's bicarbonate level was high. No big deal, it was some sort of mistake. I checked in with the technician, his level was twenty-seven. It was close enough to the danger zone for the track to be able to re-test to be sure he was legal.

I breathed a sigh of relief. At least he wasn't over the limit. At the same time, I was confused. It didn't make any sense. How could his levels be that high? All of our other horses weren't even close. This was To Bad Honey's first trip to the black box, as we had been trying to figure out this whole breathing situation for several weeks. It didn't matter. Just have them redraw the blood and move on.

I brought him over to the test stall where the veterinarian drew his blood again. It was a long fifteen minutes waiting for the results. Part of me was confident. Part of me was scared to death. Because I couldn't figure out why his first level was so high, I had no idea what to think his second one would be. I gave myself some comfort knowing that jogging him had to produce lactic acid, so whatever his bicarbonate level was would have to be neutralized to some degree.

Think again. He came back at thirty-two, four points over the legal limit.

They immediately scratched him. The three of us in the paddock were completely flustered. We were walking around each other not knowing what to do next. Questions were abounding. Did anyone give him more baking soda this morning? All of us answered in the negative. Where was he in the last two hours? Could anyone have given him anything while we weren't looking? A sinking feeling came over me. He was hidden away in that test barn for hours. Anyone could have given him a dose. Bicarbonate also came in an injectable form, so anybody with an agenda could have done it. It wouldn't be someone that had a vendetta against us; we didn't have enemies like that. We hypothesized that perhaps someone wanted to experiment with levels and used our horse to figure it out. The values of each animal were posted publicly, so giving a horse a drug and watching the values that followed would be helpful to ascertain future dosing schemes to sneak past the black box.

Paranoia had us frantic. We would later learn it was none of those reasons. We were facing a year suspension and a $1,000 fine and labeled as the first trainer that had been caught tubing their horses with baking soda. We were so confident that he was clean that we asked for a third test. Clearly, something was wrong with the machine. They reluctantly agreed to test him again. Mike Lynch was the guy in the trailer, and he felt bad for us. He did us a favor and allowed the third blood draw.

It came back even higher. Thirty-four. The world was crashing down on us. It was inexplicable. There was a familiar ringing in my ears, the kind I had heard when Hardwood Bret was "stolen" from us. I could feel the anger building. My inner conscience spoke to me.

"Deep breaths, Marc. Settle down. You're not dying or anything; it's just a thing about a horse. It's all going to be fine."

I wanted to wring my inner voice's little throat.

"It's not going to be fine, you idiot. We're done. Our stable is getting shut down. Now if you don't mind, keep quiet and let me have my moment. I've shut this anger thing down for ten years now. I think I know what I'm doing."

I really should have listened to that inner voice. A professional shouldn't behave the way I did that day. The F-bombs were flying and I was making a fool out of myself. Keeping it all inside would have been worse. I'm sure if I didn't pop off that I would have blown a gasket in my brain somewhere and dropped dead. It was worth it. But it didn't accomplish anything.

Mike Lynch was visibly upset and told my father not to worry. "We'll take care of this, Harry," he told him. He knew we hadn't done anything and was trying to comfort us. They would see what they could do about all of this. They asked if we wanted to draw one more blood.

"Draw another blood? Are you guys insane?"

His values were going up like a bottle rocket. I couldn't imagine what the next level would be. It was like being read your Miranda Rights. You have the right to remain silent; you have the right to not draw another blood.

"No more blood!" I yelled out.

That's how we got into this mess. We should have just left well enough alone after the first one and scratched him after the first draw when he was still legal. None of this would have happened. At the time, we had nothing to fear, so why wouldn't we ask for another sample? We couldn't have anticipated what was to happen. It was all too confusing.

We packed up our stuff and went home. The Rohrs were as shocked as we were. They couldn't understand how this could have transpired. Did we give him anything? The questions were starting. They had every right to think we had done it, but we knew that it wasn't the truth. Our horses were clean. There was an obvious problem with the system or someone had targeted him for experimentation while he was alone in the outside barn.

Nothing made sense. If they were going to target him, they would have to know who he was, what race he was in, and so on. Just hitting a random horse in the auxiliary barn didn't add up. No one had followed me out there. If it were a conspiracy, it was done by someone who was pretty intelligent. It would take quite a brainstorm to pull it off given the circumstances. Looking around the paddock area, nobody fit the description of a world class spy. It was still a theory, but we were shooting holes in it with an Uzi.

We waited for a decision. Four days went by. We all feared the worst. Mike Lynch's words echoed in my head. "We'll take care if this, Harry." We could only hope that he would.

The decision came down. One year suspension and a $1,000 fine. Harryman was officially the first trainer to get caught with high bicarbonate levels in the state of Maine, and they were going to make an example out of him. It was completely devastating. We would have to regroup and decide what we would do the rest of the way.

We had gone through this type of thing before when I didn't go to the urine stall with E.T. Vic several years back when we got a ten-day suspension. The fix was simple. We switched all of the horses over to Doug Mitchell as the trainer, removing Harry Mitchell from any paper trail associated with them. The ban from racing also banned him from the grounds. He couldn't come with us. He couldn't go into the grandstand area. The team was being dissolved. We had reached a crossroads. Keep racing or walk away.

It would have been a perfect time to quit. Our stable was pared down. We were losing the Rohrs because of the incident. We would have to wait a full year to get back to normal. We kept racing. We were going to try and fight this thing. We were sure we hadn't done anything wrong and needed an explanation as to what had happened.

Walking into the paddock, we could feel the eyes upon us. We had a scarlet letter branded on us for all to see. They all had the same look that said the same thing, "They finally caught the Mitchells." The irony was that we were perhaps the cleanest stable in the state. The injustice was maddening. Only a few trainers, the classy ones, would even talk to us. Elmer Ballard was one of them. He understood that things aren't always as they appear. We warned him that if *we* got "caught," more would follow. It wasn't possible to only have one glitch in the system. There was a problem with the machine.

No one listened. Almost all of them thought we were guilty. They reveled in the fact that we got caught. They had heard it all before. Just go to a prison and ask any of the inmates to tell you their story. There's not a single guilty man in the correctional system. It made it nearly impossible to be absolved. A year suspension and a $1,000 fine. It was ridiculous, seeing how Colen Mosher got thirty days for using a super narcotic that ended up killing horses. This was baking soda, for God's sake. And we didn't even tube our horse. It was as if we had been teleported into the bizarro world.

Our integrity was in question. The years we were successful with Honey were now being viewed through a tainted window. People wondered how long we had been cheating. No wonder we did so well in the eighties, they thought. It was all so obvious now. We must have been using this stuff for years. The bitter irony was that perhaps if we *had* been using baking soda all those years, Honey never would have had that muscle problem that sidelined her for nearly a year.

One by one, trainers started getting "caught." No one had listened, but it was finally happening. Positive after positive started to show up until there were nine of us bunched together. It was the most eclectic group of trainers imaginable. The big stables got nailed. The guy who shipped in with just one horse posted a high number. We became a little Leper colony that no one wanted to associate with. It had gotten the attention of everyone at the track.

Every time someone got a positive, they all said the same thing. "You were right, it happened to us." They felt the same frustration, the same shameful looks from the others who thought we had all gotten what we deserved. At this rate, by the end of the summer, there wouldn't be any trainers left to field a single race. Something had to be done.

The owner of Scarboro Downs got involved. Joe Ricci heard the testimony from my father first and then listened to all the rest of the trainers. It was fairly clear to him that an injustice had occurred. He hired several lawyers to represent us against the Maine State Racing Commission for wrongful prosecution. This was the owner of the track doing this, the same person that had established the testing and decided to clean up racing in the first place. After seeing what kind of nonsense had come of it, he wanted to right the wrong.

Meanwhile, our horses that had already been entered got scratched from their next start. Since Harry Mitchell was found guilty and they had been entered under his name, they penalized those horses as well. Consonance, Frugality, and Honey's Best all took the hit. Furthermore, any horse that was involved in this penalty got an additional thirty-day ban from racing.

None of them could race for a month. Too bad, Consonance. Too bad, Frugality. And yes, too bad, Honey.

Ed Rohr took his gelding and Flawless Almahurst out of our stable. I can't say that I blame him really, but I'm not sure if he believed what we were telling him. We had failed (at least I had) to fix his breathing problem, and now we had just gotten his horse a thirty-day suspension. He decided to bring him to another vet and see if they could figure it out.

Just about every fiber in me knew that they wouldn't find anything, just as I hadn't. But somewhere deep down, I was worried that maybe, just maybe, they would find an epiglottic entrapment if they got lottery lucky.

We had our day in court. By this time, we had a fairly strong team of defense. With so many different factions of trainers, any judge should have seen the inconsistencies in the charges. Eight of the nine trainers, including us, had never been tested positive for any substance whatsoever. Suddenly all eight decided to start to cheat? It didn't make any sense. None of the other horses in their stables were positive either? If someone were to cheat, wouldn't they do it more than once?

After two months in the court system, we got our verdict. Guilty. The judge saw the levels of bicarbonate on the piece of paper and the levels that were acceptable and heard nothing else. He didn't listen to the fact that the machine was supposed to be kept in an atmospherically protected environment. It was in a drafty portable trailer. The machine was supposed to be kept in a building with solid footing. Again, a portable trailer that moved when someone stepped on the stairs. The machine was supposed to be calibrated weekly. They never calibrated it once after it was installed. The judge looked at the numbers and lowered the gavel.

I'm sure he didn't understand how profoundly he was affecting these people. The maximum sentence horsemen had seen before this was thirty days for a first offense. This would cripple if not eliminate a small stable that had no other trainer to turn to. Luckily, we had another licensed trainer in Doug that we could switch the names over to. Others were not so fortunate. They would have to cut bait and run. They might never return to racing...for allegedly using baking soda. It was outrageous.

The sad truth remained that if someone got caught using anything else, whether it be a narcotic, pain killers, amphetamines, cocaine, or any other illicit drug other than baking soda, the penalty remained at thirty days loss of license. Did anyone else see the insanity in all this? Nine of us did.

Three weeks later we ran into Ed Rohr back home. He called Doug and me over and he was grinning as he walked up to us. "We found out was wrong with To Bad Honey!" he exclaimed. We were both silent, giving him a look that said, "Oh isn't that great," which really meant, "you have to be friggin' kidding me, and we thought things couldn't get worse."

Ed spoke again. "He had an epee-glo-pic entrapment," as he tried to pronounce it correctly and failed. "Have you ever heard of that?" he asked me.

There was a pause that lasted uncomfortably long as I was at a loss for words, trying to absorb what I had just heard and then respond without screaming.

I quickly composed myself. "No shit, good for you guys. I had a feeling that might have been it. Not sure if you remember me talking to you about exactly that, but I could never identify it to correct it."

"Oh yeah, well, Doc Anderson just scoped him the one time, saw it, and did surgery on him right then and there. He's racing next week, just as soon as the thirty days is up from your father's suspension."

He had just gutted us and then poured in a truckload of salt. Doug and I just smiled at him and wished him well. What else could we do? Just when we thought things were about as low as they could get, he tells us that. How nice.

To Bad Honey went on to be quite a nice little racehorse. He was now able to sustain the last quarter mile because he could finally breathe. I felt good for the horse as much as I felt bad for us.

As the weeks progressed, To Bad Honey was tested again for bicarbonates. He tested high again. Just as high as he had with us. Believe it or not, through all of the struggles with what we went through, they decided to raise the levels that horses were positive for. That's right, they changed the rules. It seems that To Bad Honey had an anomaly in his bicarbonate levels. He just ran high. The day he tested positive was the first time anyone had ever tested him, so he was higher than the standards they had set. They didn't realize that horses' blood gas averages are on a Bell Curve and To Bad Honey was way out at the far end. It didn't change our sentence. We were not grandfathered in. What was done was done.

We never raced in Maine again. They could take their rules on baking soda and their inability to use reason over righteousness and shove it. If they didn't want us racing there, we would grant them their wish. We decided we would rather quit racing altogether than to give them our business. Racetracks need horses just as much as horsemen need them. This was our way of voting "no" against the establishment.

It was a bit unfortunate in that the owner of the track actually was supportive, but the association was against us. No other industry in the world behaves that way. In almost every instance, the association backs its people and it's the company that fights them. Not Scarboro. It didn't matter. We put Maine in our rearview mirror and that's where it stayed. The book was forever closed on Scarboro, the black box, the mosquitoes, and Chuck Mangione.

It was the longest year of our racing life. I'm not sure how we kept it all together with the stress we were under. We lost an untold amount in purses in the weeks that we were down. We lost our owners that were paying us to train their horses. More importantly, we had lost a reputation that had taken twenty years to develop. And even more profoundly, we were losing our desire to race. It had killed something in all of us. We were affected like no other experience had before. We were hardened.

We shipped into the newly opened Plainridge Racecourse in Massachusetts and it became our new home away from home. The people seemed nicer. They actually understood what had happened to us and didn't look at us like criminals. We were back. Racing at Plainridge was fresh. The track was safer, the horses were of better quality, and the purses were richer. We were back to doing what we did best. We were a team, racing horses again.

The dark days of Scarboro were some of the worst times we had ever gone through. It's interesting to look back today and see how much of a microcosm it was. If there was something good that came out of all of that, it made us all stronger and somehow even closer. It was us against them and no one was going to tear us apart. So much so that we were willing to leave the business completely if it meant keeping the family tight. It showed us that there can be life beyond racing, more than just crossing the finish line first. It was a precursor of what was to come, as the end of our run was just around the corner. This was not the time to walk away. When we did walk away, it would be laughing, not crying.

FREE IMAGE

During the summer months on the farm, the barn was as alive as any living creature on the planet. Mid-mornings were the most animated. The main structure was originally a cow barn and was built at the turn of the century. Three of the remaining stalls of the old barn still have the cement trough where the manure was caught while the milking cows stood in their stanchions. The main frame of the building has a large hayloft over it that holds over ten thousand bales of hay. The peak tops out at about forty feet.

When we bought the place in the early seventies, it was painted in the classical New England red. After our purchase, it was repainted to its current soft slate blue with white trim. It's the only blue barn and house that I know of in a three-hundred-mile radius. My father has always been somewhat of a contrarian, and his choice of such a progressive color in what used to be a repressed and highly conservative country town certainly ruffled some feathers. As times have changed, and more liberal thinking has infiltrated the area, no one seems to mind the once eccentric look of the farm. As more and more farms have died all around us and housing developments have moved in, the steady heartbeat of Mitchell Farms has been pumping for over thirty-five years. Today, it has become a landmark of the town.

For the most part, racing Standardbreds in New England is a labor of love. Doing it for the money is extremely difficult to be successful at. We were able to race for a long time without going broke for several reasons. One was that my father was a school teacher and had the summers off. He would make enough money teaching to bail out the racing income if it went dry. Second, we rented stalls out to other horsemen.

We had a nice little Standarbred facility with a training track and plenty of turnout. At any given time of the year, there were four or five different trainers with a couple of horses that they raced out of the barn. They paid us a monthly fee for every horse they had at the farm. Finally, we were fortunate enough to raise Honey's Best, one of the richest fillies the state of Maine had ever seen. If not for her, our lives would have been very much different. She didn't just breathe new life into our stable; she was the essence of our survival in it.

When Mike Sherr came onto the scene, he had just quit his job coaching football at Central Catholic High School in northern Massachusetts. He had made the decision to race horses as his profession. Racing horses for a living is a bit of an oxymoron, especially in the Northeast. The purses were moderate at best, and the season wasn't year round. In order to make it, a second job was almost a necessity. Needless to say, we were all worried about his fate as a trainer.

He had never trained a horse in his life and now it was going to *be* his life.

Mike was an amiable guy with an infectious laugh that bordered on sounding like a witch in a fairy tale. His voice escalated to a shrieking staccato of "Ha-Ha-Ha-Ha" into a frenzy until his voiced cracked, forcing him to stop. We would joke that the fluorescent bulbs might shatter when something was particularly funny to him.

He was about six feet tall and weighed about two hundred pounds. Pictures of him from his days playing football showed him to be about eighty pounds heavier and his neck three inches thicker. Infer what you want, but he was huge, and then he wasn't. He had a full beard that was well trimmed and had oversized, hairy, meaty hands. Both Doug and I have large hands, but Mike's were even bigger. When I shook his hand when I met him, it was the first time in my life I was dwarfed in the exchange. They were freakish. If you were ever in the city and needed to hail a cab, you wanted Mike with you.

None of us knew what made him choose Standardbred racing as his career change, but he needed some stalls, and we obliged. He bought a couple of cheap horses to get started. He had been a conditioning coach for the football team as well. He had a plan to implement a thing called interval training that he used for human athletes and wanted to transpose it into the equine world. He had never sat behind a horse in his life, let alone trained one at high speeds. Now he wanted to do all this in a way no one else was doing. Good for him. We grabbed some popcorn, sat back in our seats, and got ready for the show.

Free Image was his first project. He was a short little gelding and he was stocky. Everything about him was thick. I laughed when I saw the horse for the first time. It figured that an ex-football coach would buy a horse that looked like a linebacker. He had a short, fat neck, thick legs, and muscles ripped over his body. He didn't look like a horse that would be good for anything remotely close to whatever interval training was. Plow a field maybe, but race at high speeds, now that was yet to be seen.

My father and brother worked with Mike every day. They taught him more in one month than most people learn in five years. He was a sponge. Soon he was on the track jogging little Free Image and starting his new training program. The first time he hooked him into the bike (jog cart), Free Image got a nickname. When he paced, he winged his front feet out to the side in what horsemen call paddling. His hooves would hit the ground flat, but he would then outwardly rotate them in a snapping motion as he advanced them forward and fling them to the side. It was not a very economical way of running. He was expending unnecessary energy with that extra flick to the side. His style of pacing earned him the new name, The Duck. And so, The Duck started his interval training.

Mike logged a ton of jog miles on him to start. Our horses went between four and five miles a day, while the Duck went six or seven. This went on for about a month until Mike had built a nice foundation of conditioning on which to work on. It was the same routine every day and everything was timed. Mike wore a wristwatch/stopwatch on his left arm and kept a close eye on it during his sessions. When his true training started, he had the little horse doing three-quarter mile wind sprints. The first of which was rather slow but as he did more, he increased the speed. Mike couldn't accurately gauge how fast he was traveling since he was a novice. That's where his watch came into play.

Mike didn't yet have that inner clock keeping time like experienced drivers have. His wristwatch was his co-pilot. During his cool-down sessions with The Duck, we would watch him reaching over with his right hand to reset the time and make mental notes as to what the horse just ran for three-quarters of a mile. As he passed by us, we could hear the beep-beep-beep of his digital sidekick working overtime.

The track at the farm wasn't always there. In the late sixties, the owner was into Standardbreds and decided to put in a racetrack. He had countless loads of sand and loam shipped in. He also redistributed soil from other parts of the farm for its creation. At the back of the barn, the track was about the same level as the rest of the landscape. On the far turn, however, it had been built up tremendously to fill in the swamp area that it had to occupy. The resulting build-up of sand created a very steep drop off on the turn farthest from the barn.

At the highest point at the top of the stretch, the outside part of the track stood about twenty feet above the wetlands below. The embankment from top to bottom was so steep that it was very difficult to climb up by foot. There really should have been a protective guardrail there to prevent anyone from going over, but in thirty years, no one had been so unlucky as to venture over the cliff.

It was in between one of his interval training trips that Mike was jogging his horse and poking away at his stopwatch. There are reasons why people shouldn't text while driving. Mike was about to learn first hand why it was a bad idea, and this was fifteen years before its time. He was at the top of the stretch heading toward the barn with his eyes fixated on that watch of his. As he reached over with his right arm to keep track of his interval splits or whatever he was trying to figure out, he inadvertently pulled on the right rein. He steered The Duck directly over the banking at the steepest point. They were gone in an instant. Horse, jog cart, and Mike...gone.

Mike was thrown from the seat and never touched ground until he hit the swamp below, burying himself up to his knees in the mud. The Duck had done two complete side rolls with the bike still attached as he tumbled down the slope. Miraculously, he landed on his feet, and he too was stuck in the mud. We ran down to help and found them both standing there in the muck and cat o' nine tails, helplessly waiting for someone to rescue them. Neither one of them was hurt. Most horses in that situation resort to the fight or flight wiring in their brains and panic. Not The Duck, he just stood there quietly, blinking, waiting for assistance. After his third three-quarter mile sprint, the last thing on his mind was running. Smart horse.

After a half hour or so, we managed to extract poor little Free Image from the mud. Somewhere at the bottom of the swamp, still buried, are one of Mike's boots and two of The Duck's shoes. When we got back to the barn, Mike checked on his wristwatch, reset the time, and went to work cleaning the mud off of himself and the horse. The very next day, they were back at it. Like the old saying says, when you fall off a horse, you get right back on. Right, but he fell off a cliff, not a horse. The familiar beeping from the watch indicated it was business as usual. The training continued.

Two months into his regimen, The Duck qualified to race. For a horse that had never won a race in his life, he looked fairly promising. Since Mike didn't have a driver's license for racing yet, he had Doug do the honors. His first start was non-winners of a race lifetime. There was some buzz in our barn from all the railbirds that had been clocking his workouts. No one was willing to give the rookie trainer much credit. All the usual suspects were talking about him...Bill Fiset, Dud Nason, Joe Schembri, and Don Jensen to name a few. They would sit out back of the barn and make off-color comments about what they were witnessing. Don't get me wrong, I was right in there with them.

Behind the barn, we had two cement blocks set on end with a twelve-foot slab of tree laid in between them. It could hold four or five men as a makeshift grandstand. It was an ideal spot to sit and chirp about other trainers while they were on the track. Mostly it was in fun, but the comments weren't exactly glowing. The seating arrangement became known as the Knocker's Bench. I could only imagine what they were saying about me when I was out jogging a horse. Not once did I hear a comment that was in praise of somebody while I sat there. It was all negative. Funny, but negative.

Mike disappointed everyone when Free Image won his first start handily. They so desperately wanted to see the newcomer fall on his face. He now had one

lifetime start as a trainer, and one win. Not bad. Surely it was a fluke. The following week, the little gelding was in non-winners of two races lifetime and won
again. The Knocker's Bench got awfully quiet. Maybe
there *was* something to this interval training thing.
People started asking questions. They were jealous
of his newfound success, but not stupid. If they could
get some inside track on what all this was about, they
were ready to listen.

Mike took the time to explain the system, but
when he was done, none of the trainers decided to
follow the plan. It was too complicated and seemed
like more work than they were willing to expend.
Some of the training exercises took forty-five minutes
or more to complete. They were not interested in adding to their workload.

Meanwhile, during this same run that he was having with his nouveau method, we were racing a horse
called Synek right out of the pasture. Synek was a nice
enough horse to be around, but on the racetrack he
was a nut. Whenever he was on the track, he would
pull so hard on the reins in an effort to want to go at
high speed at all times that he was often uncontrollable. Doug was the only one strong enough to actually
attempt to jog him. He pulled so hard that it would
cut the circulation off in your fingers from holding
the reins so tight. The one time I tried to jog him, I
lasted five laps before complete fatigue set in and I
became merely a piece of cargo on the Synek freight
train. We went six more laps at blinding speed until
he finally slowed down after he got tired. He wasn't
safe.

The option of towing him on the truck was tried
but he would pull on the chain enough to break it, or

his halter, over and over again. He was insane. We first adopted the idea of towing horses with a pickup truck back in the early seventies. My father taught school during the day, while Doug and I were in elementary school. My mother had to jog the horses herself. She wasn't afraid of work, that's for sure. But she was afraid of jogging them in the bike. She had a friend named Bev Cartmill that also had racehorses on the farm. The two of them looked out for each other and were quite a team in the early years. I'm not sure how Harryman talked the former city woman into becoming a farm girl, but he did. It didn't matter if it was ten below or the rain was driving down, Mama Pajama and Bev were out there working. They were remarkable. Those two women could have been teleported into the Civil War era and fit right in. They were tough as nails.

Synek was one of the few horses that couldn't be towed. We decided to race him cold. He got turned out in the morning and we called him in at night. Off the side of the barn was a door that led to a pasture that was about thirty acres in size. It was ideal for the riding horses that boarded there, retirees, broodmares, and of course Synek, provided they all got along. Because they were turned out using the side door, that group of horses affectionately became known as the "sidewinders."

Synek didn't jog or train a single mile. He watched from the paddock as Free Image went through his Rockyesque training program. He had to be laughing at him as he munched on the fresh clover.

The two of them happened to be racing on the same day on the weekend that The Duck was going for his third win in a row. The dichotomy between the two training styles was fascinating. One was training like a tri-athlete while the other sat on the couch watching television, eating cheese puffs.

We often left the sidewinders outside all day and into the night in the summer because it was so nice out. We had raced three horses the night before The Duck and Synek were in to go and got home around midnight. It was a long ride home as fog was rolling in thick off the ocean. We were ten miles from the coast but still felt the effects of the sea from time to time. My buddy Jim had joined us for the evening and was helping to unload the horses from the trailer. After giving the horses that raced fresh hay, we just needed to bring in the ones that were still outside.

Late at night, they were usually waiting in the little run-in shed that was used for cover when it rained. They were sick of the all-grass diet and eagerly awaited their night ration of grain. On this night, the fog cover had frozen them somewhere out in the back thirty. My father yelled for them to come in using the long-standing tradition of the farm.

"Come Oooooooooooooooooooon!" he boomed out. The sound deadened against the thick air.

Nothing. They were out there somewhere.

He called again. "Come oooooooooooooooooooooo ooooooooooooooon!"

This time he held the last syllable to carry it out further into the night. Still nothing.

As the years progressed, and more and more houses encroached upon our borders on the far edge of the property, Doug would enjoy yelling especially loud at one or two o'clock in the morning. He hated having those houses in view of what used to be a picturesque landscape.

"If they want to have a nice view of a country farm, they'll have to live with how we run things around here," he'd say bitterly with a laugh. And he would call them again at a level that was embarrassing. He held the last note so long that the echoes blended in with his booming voice, which created a chorus of "Come-ons." When he stopped, he smiled, and then gave them another one. Good stuff. We all had to laugh. We could only imagine what those people were thinking when they were so rudely awakened from their slumber.

Synek and the rest of the clan weren't coming. We would have to go get them by foot. Doug, Jim, and I headed out to wherever they might be lurking. We walked past the run-in shed on the left and kept walking. The paddock near the barn was only about twenty feet wide for about thirty paces and then it opened up into a vast field. It sloped down over a long meadow, and a small stream cut through the far end of it. On the other side of the brook was more pasture and then the boundary fence to the other farm that still existed before it was sold as a housing development.

We understood why they weren't coming. The fog was so thick that we couldn't see ten feet in front of us. We easily could have walked right into a horse before we saw them. As we got to the end of the fence line where the paddock opened up, we called out for them again. No sound of horses in the distance. Dead silence. We walked another fifty feet into the open field and Doug bellowed out another call to them. That time, they heard us alright.

They were clear on the other side of the stream when the twelve of them made a break for the barn. They hit the water three hundred yards from us and they were frantic. They had chosen the flight response from their two-choice repertoire in panic mode. After they cleared the stream, they were stampeding directly at us up the hill and were closing in fast.

One of us said, "Oh shit" and it spoke for all of us.

We had nowhere to go. Horses at high speed can cover a hundred and fifty yards in a matter of seconds. It was decision time. We could run to the side and try to make it to the fence line behind us. If we didn't get there in time, we would be caught in no man's land and likely flattened. Or we could huddle together behind a little four-foot bush that stood in front of us and hope they avoided it, knowing where it was from their many previous runs back to the barn.

There was no time for rational discussion. This wasn't an S.A.T. question that you had minutes to ponder over. *Twelve horses are running at you at thirty-five miles an hour and are four hundred feet away. A fence is located twenty feet to your right and fifty feet back that you can jump over to safety. How fast would you have to run to make it there before being killed?* The answer was E. "Not fast enough."

We stayed together and crouched down in a collective mass behind a single shrub, trying to make a smaller target. The sound of the oncoming hoofbeats wasn't half as scary as the rumble we could feel in the ground underfoot.

"How did we get ourselves into this situation?" I thought. "We certainly could have put a little more planning into this. What a way to die. In the middle of a paddock, in the fog, run over by horses."

In less than three seconds, twelve thousand pounds of horseflesh raced by, inches from trampling us. These so-called stupid animals avoided a bush that they knew was there but couldn't see. Our hearts were pounding out a drum solo. We all got out of our crouch and were speechless. That could have been as bad as it gets. We all did one of those "Are you alright?" checks and all of us answered in the affirmative. We knew how idiotic we were in what could have been a disaster. It was over, we were fine, and we didn't want to talk about it.

We made our way back to the barn where my father was as shaken up as we were. He hollered at us after they rushed by to find out if we were alive and we let him know that we made it. The horses were locked up and fed. After a few minutes, our nerves had settled and we all started to laugh. It was nervous laughter for sure, but it felt good to be alive. It was *that* close. It was a situation that we would never forget and one that we would never repeat.

The next day came quickly as the two horses that were worlds apart in training shipped up to Scarboro. I was there to groom Synek, and Mike would take care of his horse, The Duck. Synek was just as crazy on the racetrack as he was back home. To take some of the starch out of him, we were forced to warm him up four races out as was customary with all of our horses. Doug had all he could do to keep him from being a runaway.

When he went out to race, I had to follow him all the way out to the track to assist him at the gate. I usually hooked a ride on the arch of the sulky to Doug's left and sat facing backward with my legs hanging down. He would take me out to the head of

the stretch as horse and driver continued on to the
post parade in front of the grandstand. I had to then
trek across the infield of the track to where the starting gate was parked on the backside.

Synek was a true head case. He was so wound up
before a race that he became nearly impossible to
turn around and head him off in the right direction.
If he did turn around, he would often rear up and
dance and spin like he was on crack. Doug needed
me there to grab the reins and run with Synek toward
the gate.

I couldn't just face him in the right direction and
send him off. That would have been too easy. He
needed a running start in order to focus on the race.
I would grab both reins, manually turn him around
(all while he was doing his best to run me over), and
then start running alongside him while pulling him
toward the starting gate. If we didn't get up to my
sprinting speed, he would either stop abruptly or
spin around and face the other direction. Remember,
there were seven other horses around us that could
run us down if things went poorly. Fortunately that
never happened. I was clipped by a wheel or two, but
never got run over.

After a good sixty-yard dash, Synek would suddenly get engaged to race. The reins went from slack
in my hands to snap tight in an instant. Doug was
now in control and I could release him for the gate. I
peeled off and weaved around the oncoming horses
and headed over the hubrail. If I ran fast enough, I
could get to the head of the stretch before they came
around on the first lap. On cool nights, I walked and
got there after the race was over. On warm nights,
and most of them were just that at Scarboro, walk-

ing through the tall grass of the infield was a horror show. The mosquitoes would swarm up from the ground like little flying piranhas. If I didn't run, they may have taken me down. I'm not kidding. Their numbers were inconceivable. I would joke that one day they would drop me in the infield and I would yell to Doug as he came back from the race, "Go on without me, I'm not going to make it." Fortunately, I never actually succumbed. I would then jump back on the bike for an escort to the paddock.

Making my way across the middle of the track, I watched Synek go to the lead. He went to the top in every race he was ever in. There wasn't another option. There was no way anyone could control him enough to settle him back. It was the top or nothing. Doug got the front with him with ease. He won the race by five open lengths and was still pulling when he returned to the paddock. He was truly a phenomenon. With absolutely no training whatsoever, he had just destroyed a field of decent horses.

Next, it was The Duck's turn. He was in three races later. Doug needed the time for the feeling to come back to his hands. The Duck was now racing with some tougher company. It was going to be a real test. Because he was still fairly green and still learning, he could be a bit fractious behind the gate. Doug would need to nurse him along to keep him from breaking stride (gallop instead of pace) before the gate opened up to start the mile. Once he was racing, he calmed right down and paced cleanly.

Heading around the turn, the little horse got rough-gaited and tried to make a break, which would have taken him out of the race. Doug eased into him, talked to him through the reins with a soft touch, and kept him flat (on stride). Just like Synek, he won wire to wire.

Three wins in a row. There are a lot of horses out there that have never won three races in a row. Free Image had done it in his first three starts for new trainer Mike Sherr. In retrospect, it may have been the worst thing that could ever have happened to Mike. He must have been thinking to himself, "This is an easy game. Buy a horse, train him with my new technique, and win. No problem."

It wouldn't be that easy forever. Free Image was the right horse at the right time. And his run wasn't over. In fact, it was just beginning.

He paddled his way to his fourth straight win the following week. Things couldn't have been going any better. Doug was teaching him how to race and the little horse was responding and seemingly getting stronger. His race times were improving. When he came back to the paddock he was hardly even winded. While the rest of the horses would be blowing from the rigors of the workout, he was ready to go three more. He had incredible stamina. He was stepping up in class dramatically in his fifth start, and he would need it.

He was becoming quite the sensation and a crowd favorite. He was the little horse that could. He had drawn the two-hole on a bright Sunday afternoon. His program had all wins on it to date. Since he hadn't lost or ever really been tested, there was no way of knowing how fast he could actually go if pressed. The bettors were counting on him having more under the hood than what his past performances told them. He was in fairly tough but was made the prohibitive favorite at 2:5. I wasn't convinced he was *that* much the best, but I was too close to the situation to be unbiased. I would reserve judgment until after the race.

Heading for the start, Free Image got rough-gaited once again. This time, Doug was unable to keep him from making a break. He had to ease him off the gate, slow him down until he started pacing, and then ask him to gain his momentum again. It happened just as the starting gate was at the top of the stretch and had started to accelerate. He spotted the field twenty-five lengths taking him out of contention. The crowd went ballistic.

Even though Doug was trying his best to keep him together and win the race, the bettors were convinced that he had purposely made the horse break stride. They assumed that a fix was on and the real money was laid in on some other horse in the race. They couldn't have been more wrong. Doug never fixed races, but that's not what their money was telling them. The heckling began as the two made their way in front of the grandstand.

"Fix!" one angry bettor screamed out.

"Stiff!" another one chimed in.

"Mitchell, you're a goddamn crook."

There was far worse language than that actually thrown at him, but you get the idea. I'm sure Doug heard them, but it didn't matter. He knew it was nonsense. He got The Duck back paddling and on stride, tapped him once with the whip, and shifted gears. Although he knew winning was out of the question, he wanted to show the public he was actually trying with him. He was at least thirty lengths behind the field when he finally hit full speed. For the first time, he was all out. This horse could really motor. By the quarter pole, he was only fifteen lengths off the last horse. I had seen so many horses try to catch the field like that only to completely pack it in once they got there. They had expended too much energy to carry that speed the rest of the mile.

It happened to us with the strapping filly Sparkle Road at the Rochester Fair when the starter failed to recognize she wasn't at the gate when the race started. She caught them at the half and then couldn't keep it up. She finished eighth and was exhausted for her effort. For a marathon runner, it would be the equivalent of hitting the wall.

Coming to the half, the crowd was still incensed and more barbs and expletives were cascading down. At that speed, with the wind rushing by and the muffling effect of a helmet, Doug told me he couldn't hear them...but he could feel them.

At the half mile, The Duck was only two lengths off the horse in seventh but had used up what had to be all of his energy just getting there. He was one courageous little horse. Heading into the clubhouse turn, he just kept creeping up on the last horse and Doug tipped him to the outside and rolled up alongside the horse at the end of the line.

"Where is he going?" I wondered. "There's no way this horse has anything left."

He had just laid it all on the table trying to catch them. To top it off, they were throwing down a pretty quick mile up front. Up the backside they rambled and Doug feathered him with the whip and suddenly he was fifth, then fourth as they hit the three-quarter pole. Midway through the last turn he was third on the outside grinding down on the leaders. I found myself cheering the little horse on. I couldn't help it. He was putting in a Herculean effort.

They rounded the final turn. Not only had The Duck spotted the field in the equivalent of six seconds, but he had raced on the outside the whole last half. He was just a half length off the front horse when they tipped for home. He was attempting what seemed to be the impossible. No horse could possibly have enough left in the tank to run down the leader.

The same people that were calling my brother a crook were now cheering him on. There was a roar from the grandstand. The Duck kept coming. He had been a monster mile, but he didn't know it. He probably thought he still had a few more laps to go as he just kept chugging. The wire was coming fast as he was closing in ever so slowly on the horse out front. A length, a half length, a neck, a head, a nose...

Incredible. He did it. Five in a row. He had certainly answered one question. He *was* much the best. I had never seen a horse do what he had just done. It was nothing short of heroic. It was something that legends are made of. It was one of the most fantastic performances I had witnessed in racing. If I hadn't seen it myself, I wouldn't have believed it. The proof of the accomplishment has been preserved on DVD. If any of us are looking for a little inspiration, we just throw that race on and enjoy.

When he got to the winner's circle, he was blowing pretty good. It was the first time he was ever really up against it. He had answered the bell and then some. There was no telling the true potential of this horse. We were all excited to see what lay ahead. Interval training. Maybe there was something to that after all.

The next day, both Synek and Free Image got the day off. The following day, The Duck was back to work and Synek was out with the sidewinders. The run-in shed that the horses went under in bad weather next to the barn was getting old. The horses had chewed on the main beams so badly in some places that they had chomped more than halfway through the posts. It was becoming unsafe. It was time to tear it down. There was no need to wait until it fell by attrition and potentially killed who knows how many horses.

The old run-in shed was an annex to the main barn. Part of the shed was just an open structure covering a forty-by-twenty-foot area that faced the paddock. This was where the horses could get under cover. The other half had two old stalls with a makeshift garage attached to it.

The garage area was filled with cordwood year round. It was the farmhouse's main source of heat. We had two woodstoves and we kept them burning twenty-four hours a day in the winter. It wasn't uncommon to go through eight or nine cord in a single season. Aside from racing, haying, gardening, fence repair, tractor repair, slaughtering animals for food, and going to school, we cut our own wood. It's no wonder Doug and I never got into trouble with drugs or any other extracurricular activities. We were either too busy or too tired to bother.

The stalls in the old shed formerly housed the pigs and sheep when we had them. When we started racing more horses, there was less time for the other farm animals so we stopped raising them. We were making enough money by then to be able to go out and buy our own meat rather than produce it ourselves. Besides, after our storage freezer died in the fall of 1980 and we lost hundreds of pounds of farm-harvested meat, we decided it was best to not bother with that aspect of farming.

Since we didn't have any pigs or sheep anymore, the old stalls were defunct. Access to them was difficult due to the layout of the barn, so using them for racehorses wasn't a plausible option. The doorway was small, the lighting was poor, and the walls were drafty. Their time of usefulness had come and gone.

The rest of the barn was plenty big enough to accommodate all the horses we would ever need to house, even if we tore down the structure altogether. Doug was getting more serious about his music and always had a dream about being a sound engineer. It would enable him to not only record his own music but also make money doing recordings for other musicians. It was decided that we would tear down the old run-in shed and replace it with a state of the art recording studio on our own. It was a lofty goal. We got out the sledge hammers and crowbars and starting breaking down the old barn. We started the conversion of a nineteenth-century structure used for slaughter animals into a plush music studio.

Doug, Harryman, my buddy Jim, and I started the demolition. During all of this, we watched The Duck on the track. Mile after mile. It was unbelievable how much that horse worked. At least Mike was keeping him on the track and away from the steep banking. We hammered while The Duck paddled. Day after day this went on. We were close to completely gutting the whole place out and had removed all of the interior walls except for the six main support beams in the center of the building.

The clean-up was probably the most difficult task. The amount of old dirt, debris, and the loads of pig and sheep manure we hauled out of there was staggering. Broken boards, old moldy bales of hay, hundreds of pounds of bent rusty nails, a few beer bottles from the early nineteen hundreds, and a half-dozen dead rats all got taken out of there. The first phase of our mission was almost complete. The two dogs we had at the time, Snuff and Beaker, were constantly sniffing around and checking things out as we moved stuff around. They were fascinated with all of the old smells.

It was somewhere in mid-afternoon and we were almost to the point of hooking up the tractor to one of the supporting posts and pull it down. My mother brought us out some lemonade and we came out of the shell of the building to enjoy a break. The Duck wasn't so lucky. He was on the track, doing a three-quarter-mile sprint.

"All that workload has to catch up to him at some point," I said to the rest of the guys drinking lemonade.

"I agree," Doug replied. "He's going to burn him out sooner or later, but so far it's working."

It was peaceful standing just outside of our little project. Sweat dripped down off of us and we were covered in dirt. The clinking of ice in our glasses and the distant hoofbeats of Free Image was a welcome tranquil break from the hammering and destruction. Jim was the last to just come out from underneath the building and grab a fresh glass of lemonade. There was a sudden deep crack of wood that emanated from one of the main support beams. It had a hollow, echoing type of sound. It was the kind of sound a thickly frozen pond makes when the ice cracks under shifting weight. We all could sense it wasn't good. In less than the time we could even speak, the entire structure collapsed to the ground. Dust billowed out from the three exposed sides. The crashing sound was horrific.

We were all stunned. We had been under that thing just moments before. We all looked around to make sure everyone was accounted for. All the humans had made it out. The dogs. Where were the dogs?

"Beaker!??!" My mother screamed for the tri-colored collie. He wasn't there.

"Beaker???!" Doug yelled for him again.

He came running around from the side of the house. He had obviously been scared and ran off when it came down. Thank God.

"Where's Snuffy?" my mother asked in a panic.

No one knew where he was when it happened. Snuffy was a small mixed breed dog. He was mostly black with a few white spots on him. His most endearing feature was a dramatic overbite that made him look a bit mentally challenged. He was a sweet little dog but a genetic faux pas for sure. We looked around and couldn't find him. He had to have been under there.

"Here he is!" Doug yelled out. He had scurried under the front porch of the house and was cowering from the incident. Everyone was accounted for. Too close.

In matter of three weeks, Doug, Jim, and I had had two near death experiences. People talk about near death experiences lots of times. Most of those instances are nothing more than close calls that seemed dangerous enough, but weren't really life threatening. Theses two events were not that at all. They were real, and they had occurred merely fifty feet from each other. We still don't know why the roof collapsed since none of the weight-bearing beams had been removed. We felt that we hadn't done anything to structurally weaken the barn other than remove the boards that connected the beams. We hypothesized that they were holding them together enough, so that when removed, the building shifted laterally. This caused too much stress on what was left of the posts that the half-ton equine termites had chewed out of boredom.

Thinking back, the scariest part about the whole incident was how fast it came down. Even if we had heard the crack while we were still underneath it, there was no possible way anyone of us could have run for safety. When we almost got trampled by the horses just a few weeks earlier, we knew we were just foolish and never should have put ourselves in that position. This time, however, we all felt that it was perfectly safe before it collapsed. On the farm, my father always preached to us kids that almost all accidents are avoidable. I'm not sure this one would have been.

The conversation outside the rubble was one filled with relief and expletives. We talked about how fortunate we all were to be alive. It was one of those high testosterone moments that showcases each sentence with about forty percent F-bombs and sixty percent real dialogue. Unlike the fog debacle, we didn't laugh. We couldn't. Nothing about it was funny. The thought of one (or more) of us being flattened underneath tons of rafters was sobering to say the least.

After ten minutes or so of making ourselves feel better that we couldn't have foreseen this happening, we got back to work cleaning up. We worked slowly and safely. The track behind the barn was clearly visible from the front of the property now that the entire run-in shed was on the ground. It had been twenty minutes since the incident. The Duck was still out there on the track but was apparently just about done for the day as Mike had him walking back to the barn.

"Jesus," my brother said, "he's going to kill that poor horse."

"At least he doesn't have him underneath a run-in shed that is about to fall down," I answered him.

We all finally laughed. Mike was just finishing up with The Duck and was unhooking him from the jog cart when he looked up to see that the left side of the barn was gone. He yelled from across the paddock. "What are you guys trying to do, kill yourselves?" and he let out one of his cartoonish laughs as he disappeared into the back of the barn.

If he only knew. No, we weren't trying, but we came pretty darn close.

Free Image went on to win eight races in a row. Along the way, he kept stepping up in class and beating everyone they threw at him. He was tireless. The rigorous training that he had undergone had served him well. His sturdy frame and willingness to put the hours in was the perfect recipe for Mike's new program to work. Some horses were too frail to handle the workload. Still others would have become sour and refused to do it.

Free Image was a good soldier. Mike would say "jump," and The Duck would ask "how high?" As far as Mike was concerned, the sky was the limit. Eight times the stocky gelding did battle with some of

Maine's finest Standardbreds, and each time he came
out victorious. On his ninth start, after hundreds of
jog miles, dozens of training trips, three sets of shoes,
two new batteries for Mike's stopwatch, and a flip over
a twenty foot cliff, The Duck had had enough. He laid
down his sword and quit fighting for his colonel.

The grueling schedule finally caught up with him.
He finished last in his miraculous run for nine in a
row. He didn't even try. There was nothing physically
wrong with him. When Mike asked him to jump this
time, he responded with, "Why?". It was clear during
that last race that he had lost his spark.

Doug didn't press him. He realized the little
horse was tired and respected his previous valor. He
coasted him through the last half-mile and brought
him back to the paddock. The Duck hadn't even
broken a sweat, and he was barely blowing. His own
goal to be the best he could had already been accomplished and now there was nothing left to prove.
To Mike's credit, he listened to his horse. He stopped
with him for the season and gave him the next five
months off.

In the spring, he was back at it. The interval training was resumed as Mike tried to rekindle the flame
that had so quickly been extinguished last fall. The
stopwatch beeped just like it had the last year, and
Mike set up his schedule in the exact same manner
that brought him success before. Free Image would
have nothing of it. He was making a stand. No matter how much Mike asked him to train, he would only
jog. He never got interested in going fast enough to
even remotely look like he was racing.

Once again, Mike listened to his horse. He
stopped the interval training. In actuality, he never

really started it. He decided to train him in the conventional manner with just one-mile training trips per week. It failed miserably. Free Image had officially called it quits. He was willing to jog and paddle along, but he refused to hit top speed. His demeanor was still the same. He wasn't angry or sour. He just rejected the notion of running.

Despite his protest at the farm, Mike decided to continue to try and race the once brave little racehorse. In eight starts, he was one of the toughest horses I had watched run. It took Mike only three starts of embarrassing performances to stop with him. It was clear that he wasn't going to race for him anymore.

Dan McCarthy was a good friend of Mike's and asked if he could lease him for a while to see if a change in trainers would help his mind. Dan really liked The Duck and thought that maybe if he pampered him and just did some slow jog miles with him, that he could get him interested in racing again. Since Mike planned on selling him as a riding horse at some point, there was no harm in seeing how Dan could do with him for a few months.

Dan had a few horses in the barn as well. He was in his early thirties and loved harness racing. He had the prototypical eighties' mullet going on and glasses that had a slight reddish tint to them. He walked around with an empty Mountain Dew can in his hand at all times. He used it to spit out the juices that he produced from the constant giant wad of Skoal he packed in his mouth. He went through two or three canisters a day. Every pair of his jeans had a perfect outline of a little canister in the right front pocket. When he smiled, his front teeth were darkly stained from the tobacco.

His father was fairly well off and staked him to a few horses to let him have some fun with them. He easily could have bought a different horse that was racing better than Free Image, but it wasn't about the money. He really liked the horse and wanted to give him one more shot.

Dan tried for about two months with The Duck. No stopwatches. No training trips. No grueling sessions on the track. It didn't matter. In his mind, The Duck had retired when he won his eighth race. A switch went off in his head that told him it was over. The decision had been made, and at the young age of eight, his career was finished.

He was given to a woman named Diane that we knew who was looking for a small riding horse. The Duck had never been under saddle but his attitude was spectacular. Horse people talk about horses being "bombproof." It's an expression that describes an animal that is very difficult to spook, say even if a bomb went off. Police equines undergo extensive training to become as close to this as possible. Although the term is widely used, there is no such thing as a bombproof horse. They can be close, but there's always some stimulus that would cause even the most even-keeled animal to panic. The Duck was about as close to it as a horse can get. We first witnessed this when he went over the cliff and just stood there.

The best example of his calm nature, however, can be explained by an incident that he had in his stall one day at the farm. One of the screw-eyes that held his water bucket up had broken and left a sharp curved point protruding from it. Somehow he caught his nose on the hook, and it drove clear through his skin and he was hung up by the flesh of his left nostril. We're not sure how long he was there, but when we found him in his stall, he was just standing there calmly looking around, waiting for someone to unhook his nose from the metal. Most horses would have freaked out when it initially happened and promptly ripped themselves free. Not The Duck. He was one smart, cool horse. He had to be asking himself how he got into such a predicament, but he never panicked. Doug went into his stall, petted him on the forehead, and gently released him from his plight. Without missing a beat, he leaned over to his grain bucket and started eating.

The resulting wound was no more than a small piercing that healed uneventfully on its own with the aid of some antibiotics. We had been around horses a long time, and we all agreed that there wasn't a single other horse we could name that wouldn't have torn himself away from that hook. Maybe he wasn't bomb-proof, but it was likely his new owner wouldn't be exposing him to any explosives.

He spent the next twenty-two years with Diane. I remained his vet throughout the rest of his life. Through all his intensive workouts with Mike and his many years on the trails with his new owner, he never took a lame step. He was one of the most durable horses I have ever met. In fact, he *was* the most durable animal I have ever met. Twenty-four years without a leg injury. He was the Cal Ripken of the equine world.

After his last win, making his improbable run of eight victories in a row, The Duck shut it down. Diane often complained that she never could get him to gallop at high speeds. He just plodded along. His days of being a speedboat were over. He was now a paddleboat. Often times, she and The Duck would go out together with Paula and her horse Ouzo. Ouzo was a homegrown speedster that never wanted to race but relished the life of a riding horse. Ouzo never started a single race in his life, forget winning one. When Diane tried to race Paula across the Plains in town, it was comical. The Duck would lope across the grass as Ouzo left him at the starting line.

Free Image, for a summer, was a local legend. He knew how good he was. He had already proven to all that watched and himself what caliber of racehorse he was. He was done proving it. Not even a silly challenge from an obviously lesser opponent could get him to exert unnecessary energy. Those days were behind him.

When we're young and foolish, there are so many times that we try to show how tough we are, or how good we are. Countless fights in bars and senseless games are played by young men who are out to show they have what it takes to be a man. They fight and win, or they fight and lose, but they fight nonetheless. As we mature, it may be wise to take some advice from a horse called The Duck. Sometimes it's best just to walk away. Life is too short to spend it defending what most of us know in our hearts. Just because you can win a fight doesn't mean you have to start one. The heart of a true champion is pure and not tainted by self-admiration. Pride is something that should not be flaunted. It should be coveted with humility.

FRUGALITY

It was 1992, and I had just graduated Veterinary School from The Ohio State University. I'm not sure why they have to put the "THE" in front of the name of the school, but apparently it's a big deal to them. I always felt a bit self-conscious saying it that way, but that's the way they prefer it. I guess they had to distinguish themselves from the other Ohio State University? Whatever. I was just glad to be able to move on. The people I met and the experiences I had over those four years were incredible. But something was missing. The farm, the mountains, the ocean, my family, and the Rochester Fair all called me home.

Through all of our success in the late eighties and early nineties, we had attracted some fairly wealthy owners. Honey's Best had not only put money in the bank by winning, but she continued to do so by exposing us as a legitimate stable that attracted owners. Bill Narjarian was one of them. He owned a butcher shop, and apparently selling meat was a lucrative profession.

He was a very large man. So large, in fact, that he rarely ever got out of his car to speak to anyone. He got winded just walking twenty feet. He would pull up and people would have to approach him to talk to His Highness. And they would.

He drove a silver four-door Cadillac sedan and had the seat pushed as far back as he could to accommodate his girth. I never got a chance to look inside because I never saw his car without him in it, but I'm sure he had to have some sort of extensions on the foot pedals to allow him to reach them.

He had a lot of money. Not Fortune 500 kind of money, but he had enough to feel self-important. He was Armenian, although second generation, so he didn't have an accent. Most people had a very difficult time dealing with him, but my father and him hit it off early in the relationship. Harryman is a second-generation Greek immigrant himself, so they shared some common ground. He could talk to him like no one else could. Later on, as the relationship got strained, it was Doug that was the only one that conversed with him. As it turned out, the Mediterranean blood mixed together was a bit too hot to handle.

The relationship deteriorated because my father never bought into the idea that Bill wanted to be placed on a pedestal. He spoke to him like he spoke to everyone else, like an equal. Bill didn't like that. If he ever did get out of his car, which he didn't, I think he would have wanted rose petals thrown at his feet. He could have waited three lifetimes. My father was never going to treat him like royalty. First off, he wasn't. He was from an immigrant family. Second, he treated people poorly, and my father didn't respect him for it. As time passed, it started to come out.

Doug was different. He could get along with just about anybody. He has an uncanny ability to not sweat the small stuff and turn the other cheek. Although he has one hundred percent hot Greek blood coursing through his veins, he almost never lost his cool. He has one gear: cruise control.

He was able to put up with Bill's arrogance and look past it. He knew that Bill buttered at least some of our bread and didn't want to do anything at the time to stop the money from flowing in. I've only seen him angry (and I mean Greek angry) three times in my life. After seeing those rare episodes, I'm glad he has the demeanor that he does. It reminded me of the Bruce Banner line in the *Incredible Hulk* opening, "Mr. Magee, don't make me angry, you wouldn't like me when I'm angry."

We were racing two or three lower-end claimers for Bill, and he decided it was time to invest in some really nice stock. The problem was Maine was thin for the pickings for the type of animals we were looking for. We would have to look elsewhere. I had a connection with a classmate who also raced harness horses. He hooked us up with a trainer at Yonkers who had some nice young stock. We had about $30,000 to spend. Harryman and I took the drive to New York and decided to scope it out.

The trip was eerily reminiscent of the Hardwood Bret fiasco. We drove over four hours with an empty trailer to pick up these horses. It made me uneasy. The trainer we met was a bit of a shady character. He was a little too smooth. He didn't seem like a straight shooter, but not many people in the horse racing industry are when they are selling horses. We looked at four or five young horses and finally decided on a deal for three of them.

Consonance, Frugality, and Sky High Skipper. They were three- and four-year-olds, but all showed tremendous speed. On paper, they were better than anything we ever had, aside from Honey. Although we didn't want to get screwed in the deal, it ultimately wasn't our money, so we couldn't really lose. We bought Consonance and Frugality outright for somewhere in the neighborhood of $20,000 for the package. Consonance accounted for a bigger percentage of the sale.

Sky High Skipper was taken on a trial basis since she was very green and, quite honestly, a bit dangerous on the track. She had crazy speed, but that's because she *was* crazy. Her speed was uncontrollable. She would pull so hard that she would ram the gate or start galloping to a point where you became merely a passenger rather than a driver. When she got tired, if she got tired, you could get off the ride. Until then, it was anybody's guess what was going to happen. We were fairly confident we could figure her out with Doug driving and taking her off the track to the farm where her environment would be a little more relaxed.

We were wrong. She really was crazy.

She was fast, though. Faster than any animal I ever sat behind, although I actually never sat behind her. I left that to the professional. Okay, so I was scared to drive her. But you never saw this thing. She was out of her mind. We tried qualifying her two weeks after getting her, and she looked like a rabid gazelle going to the gate, jumping and bouncing around out there in a frenzy. Her name was fitting, because she would

jump "sky high" going to the gate. She broke her
head check more than once pulling her stunts. The
head check is a strap that goes from the top of her
bridle to the top center of the harness. This keeps the
horse manageable for the driver sitting behind her.
But when she paced, she was a machine.

In the qualifier that day, she spotted the field
twenty lengths at the start with her antics before the
race (the starting gate doesn't wait for you in a qualifier), and she ended up not only catching the field,
but circling them at the half. She then made a speed
break (overpacing herself and going off stride) and
that was that. We kept her around for about four
weeks, and it was becoming clear that although her
speed was fantastic, she was more dangerous than we
were willing to put up with. We shipped her back to
New York.

We settled down with Consonance and Frugality, and since they were in racing form, we decided
to train them once at Rochester, just to get a feel for
them, and let *them* get a feel for Rochester, before actually racing on those tight turns.

It was September 11, 1992 and a simply gorgeous
fall day in New England. I had just graduated vet
school, we had just bought two real nice young fillies
and my wife, Jen, had come to New England to live
with me. Life couldn't have been better. Knowing now
the historic significance of the date we were training
on, it comes as no shock that things were about to go
horribly wrong.

Doug was to drive Consonance, who was bull-
headed like Sky High Skipper but only a little more
controllable, and I was going to drive Frugality. She
was a little filly but her legs could motor. The third

horse in the mile was driven by a guy who made the trip with us to tighten up his little stud horse named Empire Jack. Ron Johnson was a big dude. He had to be six feet five inches tall. It was awkward to see him in the sulky because his knees were bent badly in the stirrups. These bikes weren't made for ridiculously tall people (my apologies to all the ridiculously tall people out there). When he sat behind Jack in the bike, his head was taller than the horse's. It looked like Ron should have been pulling the horse.

The plan was that I would cut the mile (go first to the top), Doug would sit second, and Ron would settle in third. It was a simple plan. This was merely a training trip and not a race, so we wanted to be sure everyone knew their roles. These two young fillies were untested for us, and we didn't want anything unplanned going on out there. We were feeling them out and trying to find out what to expect in race conditions. We figured at the half, Doug could pull out as I held onto Frugality to allow them to close in on me, and Ron could come three wide in a controlled pace. I wouldn't try to string them out. I would hold Frugality back to ensure a close finish and make all of the horses "win" at the wire. This was a learning trip as much as it was a tightener for the upcoming fair meet.

At the head of the stretch, Frugy was pacing solidly and felt nice as she picked up speed to start the mile. Doug had settled in the hard-pulling Consonance behind me and was doing his best to settle her down. She was hot. She was a tough mare to control early in the mile. We later had to rig an unorthodox overcheck, which consisted of a piece of two-by-three that extended eighteen inches over her head to act as a lever to keep her from ramming her head down. People would question its legality, but as it had never been used, there was no rule against it. She would be the brunt of many jokes, and many in the business would call her the "Indian" in reference to what looked like a big head feather coming off the top of her head. Whatever the case, it worked. It made her much more manageable to drive. She wasn't wearing it that day.

Consonance with her patented "Indian" head gear.

Just past the start line, I looked over my right shoulder as I heard hoofbeats coming at me. It was Ron with the little horse Jack, and he had him revved up going into the turn.

"Where the hell is he going?" I thought. "We had a strategy in place. He was going to settle third and come late."

Apparently he didn't care about the plan. He was going for the top.

"This isn't a race, you idiot, we didn't want this." I looked over at him incredulously and told him to settle back.

He didn't listen. He didn't even look over. He wanted the top.

"This is unbelievable," I thought to myself. "This guy can't be that stupid."

He got up even with Frugy just before the first turn, and the little filly got racy. She bore down hard on the bit and her legs were starting to churn. I knew I didn't want a speed battle on the front end; this was a training trip after all, and there was no need to get into a duel here. Frugy didn't like the idea of being reined in and was still driving hard going into the first turn. Jack was just starting to cut across to the top when disaster struck.

It happened so quickly it was difficult to ascertain exactly what took place. She was pacing so fast and pulling so hard that she started to outpace herself. Going into the first turn at Rochester, there is a drainage culvert that runs under the track. It carries a two-foot path from the rail to the outside fence giving the surface a slight dip due to softer footing. She hit that soft spot and just dropped like a stone. Her legs got confused and she literally tripped herself up. Her head hit the ground in an instant. For a brief moment, I was calm. I was still in the seat, still pulling back on the reins, but Frugy's head was on the track, bending back grotesquely underneath her.

As the half ton of horse flesh came to a stop, I was sent flying over the top of her. The tangent of the turn threw me over her right shoulder. I completely cleared her body in the air, and Carl Lewis would have been proud. But I failed to stick the landing. Perhaps he could have hit the ground running at thirty miles an hour, but I was not given the gift of that kind of speed. I tried, but only managed two running steps before tucking and rolling through the crash onto the almost rock-hard surface of a harness track. As I cart-wheeled through the roll, my left wrist took the brunt of the hit, snapping on contact. On my first tumble through, as I was upside down the first time, I saw Consonance bearing down on me. I knew I was going to get run over. Consonance was too strong to pull up that quickly. It's why in auto driving school you're taught to leave a two-second gap between you and the car in front of you. If the car in front stops abruptly, most drivers require two seconds to react in time to stop before hitting the car up ahead.

In harness racing, the gap is a mere one-fifth of a second. It is almost humanly impossible to react that quickly, especially if the horse in front of you goes down. Doug had been following a length back, which gave him exactly two-fifths of a second to react.

As I made my second roll and was upside down again, Consonance was gone. Doug had yanked hard on the left rein and driven the big mare over the hubrail to avoid running me down. In the process, he too was thrown from the bike and was in the air just behind me. He was still suspended when he asked me if I was alright. That's not an exaggeration; he was actually in the air when he asked me. I knew I wasn't dead, so I responded before our bodies came to rest with, "Yeah, I'm okay."

I also knew I wasn't okay, but he wanted to know if I was alive, not just hurt. My first reaction was to see how the horses were. Consonance was in the infield and seemed to be reasonably intact. Frugality had gotten up and was pacing again, now without her pilot, as the sulky was broken into pieces and the fractured skeleton of what used to be the bike bounced wildly behind her. Focusing my attention to my own injuries, I saw that my left wrist was obviously broken. It was shaking badly as I supported it with my right hand.

In denial, I hinged my wrist up and down to test it. The grinding noise it made only reassured me of what I already knew. I tried again. Still grinding.

"Okay, moron, it's still broken. Stop doing that." I said to myself. My head was pounding. We hadn't been wearing helmets, and I had banged it on one of my rolls. No blood. "Superficial," I thought, "it's just your wrist, you'll be fine."

Jen was in the same spot she was when she witnessed the miracle mile by Honey's Best. Hardly the encore she was hoping for. She had to have been horrified. Having no real large animal experience, she had to stay behind and tend to the horses' injuries as I was driven to the hospital. They finally tracked down Frugy before she did any serious damage to herself, and Jen was busy suturing up both horses' multiple lacerations. Superficial. They would be fine.

Surgery to correct my fracture took place three days later. I often laugh when my clients today get upset with me when I tell them that their animal will have to wait a day or two to have surgery for lesser issues. My break involved the joint, so my surgeon needed to place an external fixator on my arm to ensure it would heal properly. What's an external fixator, you ask? It's a medieval torture device, that's what it is. Pins are driven into your bone and stick out at a ninety degree angle to the skin. These pins are then connected on the outside with a straight bar. In my case, the bar extended two inches from the skin. A day didn't go by that I didn't rap that thing on something, sending shooting pain into the bone. Eleven weeks of this.

My new boss at the small animal hospital was not happy. His new grad that he had just hired to shoulder a major load in his busy hospital in Concord, N.H., was now on injured reserve. I went back to work two days later. Giving vaccines to animals was difficult, but I found a way. At least once a day a fractious dog or cat would move quickly and send another pain wave through me as I moved to get out of the way of teeth or claws. Surgery and other procedures that required two functional arms were out of the question, but I'd like to think I earned my paycheck. It was a long eleven weeks.

We actually raced both horses at the fair that week. They got off much easier in the accident than I did. Other than a few bruises, Doug was also fine. As I stood in the grandstand watching Frugy go into the first turn that Saturday night following my accident, I almost couldn't watch. We hadn't had a chance to get her back on the track and test her out again. Horses remember pain. Surely she would be nervous going into the turn that took her down. There was no way of knowing if she would balk when she returned to the scene, or maybe even take the same bad step and go down again.

Several days prior to bringing her back to Rochester, one of the railbirds that witnessed my crash made the comment that Frugality was a dangerous horse. He was a tiny little man in his early fifties who thought he knew everything about racehorses but had owned only one horse his whole life. His face looked like he could have been a Muppet. His chin sloped backward at the same angle that his nose sloped upward. He also had pointy little front teeth that were fitting for his small head. If he got miniaturized, he could have been a mole. He never had anything good to say, and his training abilities were seriously in question. As I heard an old-timer say one day, "He couldn't train a fart to stink."

He said he saw her "stick 'em in" that day. This term was used to describe a horse that suddenly decides during a race that they don't want to continue running. These horses are few and far between, and when you do come across one, they don't race for very long after one of these performances. It's one of the most dangerous maneuvers a horse can pull on the track. Most of the time, horses that "stick 'em in" have been in an accident and they will do this when they see something that reminds them of a bad experience they had in the past.

To witness a horse do this is scary. To have the horse you're driving do it is a nightmare. One second you're cruising along at top speed, the next second the horse stabs his front legs into the ground and suddenly puts on the brakes. Horses that do this look like they're hopping as they slam both front legs into the dirt repeatedly until they stop. There is no way of knowing when it will happen, and there is no way to prevent it once they decide to do it. If there are six or seven horses following behind you in a race when this happens, it is devastating. I was certain Frugality didn't "stick 'em in" that day. She didn't hop to a stop. She fell.

This guy wouldn't let it go. After I explained that she didn't do what he was saying, he kept pressing it. No one liked this guy, and I'm not sure why he was even in the barn, but he was pissing me off. My arm hurt, our horses were hurt, and now he was telling us she was dangerous. I couldn't take it. This guy didn't know shit even if he stepped in it, and now he was insisting he knew what happened. Did he forget that I had been driving the horse? His negativity was not something I needed right then. Not ever. I snapped.

"Jesus Christ. She didn't stick 'em in. I was *on* her. Enough!" I didn't like this little bastard before all this, and this wasn't helping my opinion of him. I never spoke a word to him ever again.

As the starting gate opened up and Frugy entered the first turn, his words echoed in my head, and although I knew she didn't "stick 'em in" that day, I was now worried that maybe she would tonight out of fear of what she went through just four days before.

She didn't. Doug eased her over the culvert, through the turn, and on up the backside. Second time around past the half, I held my breath one more time. She made it easily. We were unconcerned with where she finished that night, just keeping her on her feet was the goal. She finished fourth, raced a reasonable mile, and we were happy with the results.

The mares we bought took two years to become what we thought they would. We were warned about the trainer we bought them from by the race secretary after we had bought them. His statement was, "He's a hard man to buy a horse from."

His warning was too late. We already had made the purchase. Reading between the lines of what he was saying was simple. He was using some sort of performance enhancing drug that was making his horses look great on paper. Most people that got stock from him were sorely disappointed after the purchase as the drug was no longer used by the new trainers. Years later, I deduced that he was likely using Epogen, which is a red blood cell promoter. It is basically a blood doping scenario that creates more red blood cells and therefore greater oxygen carrying capacity.

After two starts, the two fillies crashed metabolically. Their bone marrow had been ramped up to produce red blood cells from an outside source. When that source dried up, there was a lag phase until the internal system started to produce its own Epogen (called Erythropoeitin) and triggered new red cell production. During this down time, horses race extremely poorly. Consonance and Frugality took a full year to recover.

It was a rough year. Mr. Narjarian started to question his choice of trainers, and the tension between him and Harryman was mounting. As the years progressed, the two mares came around and started racing to the form we thought they would. Sadly, we lost a fair amount of the prime of their racing careers waiting for their blood to normalize.

As our relationship with Bill broke down, we ended up buying both mares from him for a total of $4,000. The mares were now seven and eight years old. They had a nice run through the late nineties, and Frugality set a lifetime mark of 1:58.2 in a gutty performance at Plainridge Racecourse. They had done their job. They won races and made money. But they were getting old. Bill Narjarian was sick of racing, sick of us, and wanted out. It wasn't the best business decision we ever made to buy them, but like most divorces, we did what we had to in order to just walk away.

Doug was performing his music a lot more those days, and I was now practicing veterinary medicine. We had retired Honey's Best. The handwriting was on the wall. Our days of racing Standardbreds were coming to an end. We just didn't know it yet. In retrospect, we should have retired with her. But racing was in our blood. Walking away at that point didn't seem like an option. It would have been a good choice. We were like the boxer who doesn't know when to stop fighting. After a brilliant career, he thinks he can still get in the ring and win. His mind is willing but the body isn't. We were in the ring, getting beat up but still swinging. Someone should have stopped the fight, but none of us were willing to throw in the towel.

It was the end of 1998, and the days of having enough soldiers to go to battle to win Doug a driver's championship had long passed. He won it in 1987 and had some good runs at it over the following three or four years. Once we pared back the stable to a handful of animals, he logistically didn't have a chance. His catch drives (horses he drove for other trainers other than our own) steadily declined as his physical presence at the track declined, as we were only racing two days a week. Out of sight, out of mind.

Besides, owners and trainers didn't know if he would be available on any given night. There were some hold-outs that would race their horses the nights they knew he would be there, but as time wore on, those owners soon moved on too. Having continuity week to week with horse and driver was extremely important to most owners and trainers. We were left with two horses, throwbacks from a different era, and they were getting old. We were all getting older.

Consonance and Frugality turned out to be really nice horses. From two young fillies that were hard to handle and pumped full of exogenous drugs to make them super horses, they became well-mannered mares that were just plain nice to be around. As they aged, their speed waned and we were forced to race them in lower and lower classes to make them competitive.

In September 1998, the Rochester Fair had come around again. We used to get excited about the fair. It was what we waited for. The fall colors were bright, the air was crisp, and we always looked forward to giving Doug a chance at the driver's title. Now the colors were a reminder of the coming winter, and the air was not crisp, it was just damp. Doug had won the title in 1987, and now he would be lucky to even get a single victory. The year he won the championship, he got to the winner's circle nineteen times in nine days. By the end of the week, he had driven only six horses and hadn't made it to the winner's circle even once.

It was the last race of the meet, race fourteen on Saturday night. Frugality drew the four-hole and was our last chance of not getting shut out at Rochester for the first time in twenty-two years. Frugy had been racing fairly well and seemed to be hitting her stride late in the season. After she had finished a strong second on the first night of the fair, we thought she had a chance to break the losing streak. She was in with colts and geldings, much like Honey was relegated to in her illustrious career. It was the only class available to race her in, and we were desperate to get just one more start before the fair ended. We needed this for our emotional well-being. She was going off a long shot, but it didn't matter. Games you never play, you never win.

Rain was lightly starting to fall when the race got underway. Doug pushed her hard out of the gate and sat in the two-hole. We had a shot. She was getting a great trip. I had seen thousands of races, and at the half, I liked our chances. It was setting up just perfectly. At the head of the stretch, Doug eased her out and inched up to the front horse. It was going to be close. It didn't matter, I could see the wire, I saw her speed, and she was getting up. I was remarkably calm on the inside, knowing she was going to win, but on the outside I was urging her on. This meant so much to us. She almost *had* to win.

She did. She won by a head, but she won easy. It was an odd feeling. It was as if it was meant to be. I don't really believe in fate and destiny, but this was something that was meant to happen. In a way, it was a curse. It gave us hope. Hope that next year would start the way this one ended, and racing would be fun like it used to be.

Those days were far behind us. We were still a team. A strong team. Nothing had happened between us as a family, but the racing was starting to take its toll on all of us. We started having discussions about whether we should continue racing anymore. It was difficult to talk about. As spring rolled around, our two-horse stable started up again. Gone were the days that we would all be in the barn, jogging horses side by side, two by two, until the morning turned into afternoon, and then when afternoon turned into evening, and we would be off to the track.

Now Doug would jog the horses, I was off working, and we only raced once a week. It was becoming a chore, like mowing the lawn. The winning was still exhilarating. But with only two horses in the stable, the wins were few. Racing had gotten tougher, as trainers turned to medications more and more to keep up with the times. Our stable stayed clean, which made it more frustrating when we lost and more and more difficult to be competitive.

Through the summer of 1999, we had won only twelve races all year. In comparison to ten years before, Doug had won over sixty-five races that summer. It was disheartening. As the leaves changed and the brilliant colors of fall in New England painted the landscape, it was Rochester Fair time again. The mares were status quo. They were racing as well as they could, but had won enough money to put them in conditions that were a little over their heads. They would need good trips to have a chance, the type of trip that Frugy got in the finale last year.

As the week rolled on, Doug had a couple wins with some catch drives, but our horses still hadn't found the winner's circle. Both mares were in on Saturday night, and they were our last chance to once again avoid getting shut out at Rochester. Last year, Frugy had bailed us out, but things were looking a bit less optimistic. Consonance raced a giant mile and only finished second that night. A better trip would have done it, but she drew the six-hole and had to overcome the track bias, which at Rochester was sometimes impossible. As fate would have it, Frugy drew the last race of the meet again. An unlikely scenario, I know, but I'm not making this up.

This seemed to be it. The year no horses would win. The script had been written by the muses. There were no typos. Wins that used to come like flashes of lightning in a thunderstorm now seemed unthinkable in the drought at Rochester.

In years past, this was our best time of the racing season. We lived for these ten days in the fall. It was shades of Rochester all over again. The air was right, the smells were perfect, the lights of the midway flashed, the sounds of laughing children in the distance drifted faintly across the track, but we weren't winning. Now, fond memories and pictures of all of us in the winner's circle in the Hall of Fame under the grandstand were all we had to cling to.

It was like déjà vu. Not only had Frugy drawn the last race, but she once again hooked "the boys." She drew the five-hole. At Rochester, the track was so narrow that the gate only started six across, and the seven and eight horse followed behind the one and two horses when they started. It made for some crazy starts with so many horses jammed up going into the tightest turn in America. It was the scene of many accidents as well. Things weren't as bad as they could have been, I guess; she didn't have the six-hole.

It was Saturday night, and it had been a long, depressing week. Harryman and Gooch told me they could handle things in the paddock without me, so I went to the grandstand with Mama Pajama to watch the last race of the meet. The beer tent was open, and I had a few libations while waiting for the race. I was feeling pretty good. Little Frugy came out into the post parade and she was dwarfed by the rest of the field. Maybe it was the alcohol talking, but the rest of the field seemed uncommonly large. The number four horse looked like he had to be seventeen hands. The others weren't much smaller. Frugy came into the ring at fifteen hands tops.

Horses are measured in hands. Each hand is four inches, and they are measured to the withers (top of the shoulders). As an equine veterinarian, it is required that I can tell clients the height of their horses without necessarily using a tape. You weren't much of a vet if you couldn't size up a horse with the naked eye. Pull out a tape and you probably wouldn't get called back to that farm again. This came easy for me. Sixteen hands (five feet, four inches) is exactly my eye level. Frugy came up to my bottom lip. Fifteen hands.

As the crowd waned and the chill of late September crept in, the final chapter of the sad story of Rochester was being permanently inked onto the last pages of the book. The weight of our world was on Frugality's shoulders. I smiled as I watched our little horse parade in front of the grandstand. She didn't care that she was small. We were kindred spirits, she and I. Neither was gifted with height, but we pressed hard to overcome it. She would have to dig deep tonight. No one was coming in to help.

There is a line from a song by the group Nickleback that goes, "They say a hero will save us, I'm not going to stand here and wait." Words to live by. She would have to beat the boys on her own.

I was fairly lubricated from my stint in the beer tent when the race started and I had little hope she would pull off a repeat performance like last year. She got away sixth going into the turn, and it didn't look promising. It would take something special. At the half, Doug sat chilly, and the horse that was seventh moved alongside her and covered her up (raced right up beside her giving her no room to get out). The favorite had been parked (raced on the outside of other horses) the whole way and the half-mile time was wicked. They had to slow down at some point.

The horse fourth pulled out and was following the dead cover (a tired horse), which was the favorite that was going nowhere. My radar perked up. Things were looking better. We were still seventh up the backside but the field was bunching up and the pace was slowing. Doug tipped Frugy three wide going into the last turn, and the field of giants in front of her were on their hands and knees. There were six horses in front of her; two by two by two. As she swept the field going around the final turn, I was screaming for her to bring them home. The crowd noise around me was so loud that I wasn't making a fool out of myself this time.

We had won hundreds upon hundreds of races over the years. Some big races. For some reason, this one meant more. I desperately needed her to win. *We* needed her to win. Coming off the last turn, her little legs were doing double time to the large, fading strides of the leaders.

"Come on, Frugy! Bring 'em home, girl!"

The heartbreak at Lewiston, the anger with Hardwood Bret, the injustice with To Bad Honey...they haunted me as I watched her come down the lane.

It was hard to shake the feeling that this just wasn't meant to be

We had a connection. And a history. After taking that misstep over eight years ago, she never once took a bad step again. Tonight was no different. Smooth as glass, she was striding down the homestretch, uncaring that she was a foot shorter than the rest of the horses she was passing.

Halfway down the lane, she started to tire. The huge move she made on the last turn had stung her. Her heart alone would have to carry her home. The emotion of her winning this thing was getting the better of me. My voice was cracking and my vision was blurred as my eyes welled up. I found myself unable to yell. My shouts were now a clenched whisper as they approached the wire.

"Come on, girl, hang on, dig deep."

She had a determined stare and I could see that she was pressing, pressing for just a little more. She wasn't giving in. The big colt on the rail was hanging tough, but she wanted it. Quietly I spoke to her again.

"Come on, Frugy, don't give up."

At the wire, Doug asked her for one final surge as they just barely got up for the win. The little filly had stood in the ring with these monsters and taken them down. I was so proud of her.

Little "Frugy" gets up at the wire.

She had done it again, on the last day. It over-
whelmed me. My little Frugy. On the same track that
took us both down, she had shaken off the demons
and conquered her fear. I ran to the winner's circle,
took her check off, and gave her a giant hug around
her neck, something I had never done with any horse.

I couldn't believe how much this race meant. I realized then that I wanted this win for her as much as
I wanted it for us. We would have accepted a loss that
night. We didn't expect her to win, but winning this
one was inspirational. She had overcome a sex bias,
a size bias, and the post position. She showed us that
no matter how bad your chances are, or how much
things are stacked against you, you don't give up. You
never give up.

That night, she was our hero. And she saved us.
After the picture was taken, the delirium of a win
that really should have been insignificant faded. The
four of us were quiet in the paddock. We could sense
that an era of racing was coming to an end, but the

bond between us was as tight as it had ever been. The clean night air, the smell of Sam, Joe and Ed's sausages, the steam rising through the blankets of tired racehorses…shades of Rochester. This was how it was supposed to be.

Madam Ruth at the beginning of our career. Pictured from left to right: Elaine Mitchell, Jane Miliotis (aunt), Jay Pappas (cousin), George Miliotis (uncle), Doug Mitchell, Harry Mitchell (driver), Marc Mitchell.

EPILOGUE

My father bought his first race horse in 1968. His name was Kimberly Jacque. He was up in Buckfield, Maine, visiting his good friends Tom and Jean Boyd. The Boyds had just moved into their new home that had no running water and an outhouse for a toilet. Tom and Harry were both teachers in Massachusetts and thought it would be nice to spend their summers running a camp for underprivileged kids. Times were tough but they were young and ready to give it a go in the North Country.

My mother, Elaine, had started a lifelong friendship with Jean that was as close as any two sisters. The same can be said for that of Harry and Tom. They were like brothers. The piece of property in Buckfield was purchased for a mere $4,000 in a collaborative effort by these two couples. It came with an old brick farmhouse, a half-mile racetrack that they were unaware of when they bought it, and the land covered over three hundred acres of beautiful Maine landscape. It was at the foot of Streaked (pronounced stree-ked) Mountain and was nestled at the bottom of the foothills.

Tom and Jean moved into the brick house and started their new life there. Harry and Elaine stayed in Massachusetts, but they set up a mobile home across the street on the same property for the summer months. Interestingly, the dirt road in front of the brick house at the base of the mountain bisected the property. The old racetrack was way out in the back, a thousand yards behind where they had placed the mobile home. Neither Harry nor Tom had walked the property before they bought it so they didn't know it was there. One day some harness horse trainers stopped over and asked if they could use their facility for training. Shocked that it was even there, and figuring it wouldn't harm anyone if they did use it, they obliged the gentlemen's request.

Curiosity got the better of the two of them, and they made the trek all the way out to the track. One of the trainers asked Harry if he wanted to get on and try it. He was young and daring and hopped aboard. It was the first time in his life that he was even *close* to a horse, let alone driven one. He nervously went around the track once. The infield of the old track was completely grown over by pine trees and underbrush. Once you got on the backside, it was just you and the horse up in God's country. It was peaceful out there. No highway sounds, no telephone wires, no cell phones, and no one to help you if something went wrong. The thought of that crossed my father's mind as he hit the other side of the world on the backstretch. He said it was one of the most exhilarating feelings in his life.

He went around again. And again. Each time he picked up some speed and started to feel the wind in his face and the rush and power of a racehorse. He was hooked. A week later, Harry and Tom built a makeshift two-horse barn out of old scrap wood and soon after that Kimberly Jacque was its first inhabitant. In a wildly serendipitous string of events, the Mitchell family started their sensational thirty-year odyssey into the Standardbred racing industry.

In the early seventies, harness racing in New England was at its peak. Everyone knew someone in the business. There were no casinos, no off track betting parlors, no Keno outlets, no Internet gambling sites, and the lottery was in its infancy. Racing was the only game in town. Crowds of thousands would be packed into the grandstand, and the excitement when the horses thundered for home was electric. It was a thrill to be on the track as a driver. Some of the drivers reached local celebrity status. It was the golden years.

Harry Hiltz was the grandfather of Jean Boyd and owned a racehorse named Honey Sparkle Way. She was as game a mare as there was. She had decent speed for her era but her heart was legendary. The old-timers would boast that, for a whole summer, she raced with a cracked bone in her hock and never missed a start. It was an injury that was nagging and painful but not serious enough to cause permanent damage to her. When she was about ten years old, Grandpa Hiltz gave her away to my father, Harry Mitchell.

Honey Sparkle Way (Honey's Best's mom) back in the old days at Rochester Fair. Pictured left to right: Trophy presenter (unknown), Harry Mitchell in the sulky, Doug Mitchell, Marc Mitchell, Dick Rogers (holding the horse), and Luann Rogers.

She raced for us for about three years before retiring. Leah Boyd, the daughter of Tom and Jean Boyd, asked if she could take her back up to Buckfield and spend her days on the farm there. She spent the next ten years as a riding horse and companion for Leah.

As Leah got older and rode the old mare less, Harry asked if we could breed Honey Sparkle to a Maine stallion. We were trying to produce a foal that might be competitive in the Sire Stakes program that had lucrative purses. The Boyds were more than happy to oblige, knowing that after her breeding stint, she would once again retire to the farm. One of the resulting foals was Honey's Best.

Honey's Best changed our world. She became the richest filly in Maine history at the time and went on to win fifty-five lifetime starts. Her career spanned the eighties when harness racing was still popular but losing its fan base. Fewer people were in the stands, and the excitement was waning for the sport. Instead of thousands of cheering fans, there were only hundreds.

In the nineties, the downturn continued. Honey was retired in 1994. Something in all of us died the day we hung up her harness. Even when we were racing her, we knew that there was only going to be one horse like her in our lifetime. Each week that she raced, we all looked forward to it with great anticipation. While the other horses were exciting to watch, they weren't Honey. She was born on the farm, born from family ties, and was part of our team from the day she hit the ground. All the others came and went. She stayed.

As the nineties were coming to a close, the thrill of winning wasn't enough anymore. The crowds were embarrassingly small. There might have been fifty people on any given day watching live racing. Most of the bettors were at off track parlors or stopped going altogether. So many forms of gaming had cropped up that it had saturated the market. Harness racing was becoming a dinosaur. It was clear that our end was near, but we were struggling with the thought of giving up the very thing that defined us.

In 2001, we raced our last race. We had the two mares, Consonance and Frugality, who had been with us for nine years. They had become a huge part of our lives. They were too old to compete with the young stock that was coming at them. They were game, though, winning their share of races even at the end. The idea of getting rid of them was not an easy one to consider, but it didn't make a lot of sense to keep them.

Doug taught them how to be saddle horses. He broke them to ride in just a few short weeks and both of them took to it willingly. After another year on the farm, we finally found the right home for them. They had lived side by side for eleven years and had shipped together to race in almost every start over their careers with us. It didn't seem fair to separate them at that point. We gave them away to a school for handicapped children as riding horses where they could spend the rest of their lives. The only contingency we gave the new owners was that they were to stay together. If, for any reason, they needed to get rid of them, we would take them back.

As kids up in Buckfield, Maine, every summer we would take a ride up Streaked Mountain in the old Chevy station wagon. Tom and Jean and their three children, Leah, Hal, and Chris, would join my parents and Doug and me. We may not have been related to the Boyds, but we were family. We would pack a lunch and make a day of it. The mountain wasn't anything enormous but it was a good climb up the old dirt road nonetheless. With all nine of us packed in there, we would start our way up to the peak.

The going at the beginning was tough, but the steepest parts were up ahead. The car would struggle when we hit the big inclines and the engine would strain to press on. Several plateaus were along the way that eased the motor and then we would have to drive hard into another upgrade. At the summit, the old Chevy had all it could do just to get us there, but it always did.

After our successful journey, we would get out and enjoy the beautiful view and we kids would venture up the steps to the lookout tower. We were on top of the world, or at least ours. We would all sit down and laugh and talk about the summer and the horses, and what kind of ice cream we would get at the Lone Pine ice cream stand later. After finishing our lunch that the moms had perfectly packed for us, we reluctantly started back down toward home.

The ride down was even better than the ride up. My father or Tom, whoever was driving, knew the deal. They couldn't use the accelerator after we broke the first crest. The idea was to coast the whole way home. The first part of the trip was hair-raising. There weren't any patrol cars up in Buckfield and we rarely saw even one car during our descent going the other way. It was a quiet little town in northern Maine. We would reach speeds that I'm sure none of the parents would admit to today going down some of the steepest points. The kids would boo loudly when we sensed our driver was using the brakes.

If it started to rain, there was a song that we sang on the way down. Sometimes we sang it anyway, even if it wasn't raining. It was a simple little folk ditty that started off at a whisper, and with each successive time through, we would all sing a bit louder.

"It's raining, it's pouring, the old man is snoring. He went to bed and he bumped his head, and he didn't get up in the morning."

The car made its way down and the singing got louder. I don't know how we ever talked the adults into singing it each time because I don't think I could take the screaming today. It got deafening. The adults sang too. "IT'S RAINING, IT'S POURING, THE OLD MAN IS SNORING. HE WENT TO BED AND HE BUMPED HIS HEAD AND HE DIDN'T GET UP IN THE MORNING!" At the end of the trip, we were singing as loud as we possibly could. We actually coined the phrase "screaming at the top of your lungs." That's right. It was created back in 1970 in Buckfield, Maine, somewhere on the other side of Streaked Mountain.

As we neared the bottom, the car was just creeping along. A few little hills at the end gave us some momentum to carry us just a bit more. It was always fun to see if we could actually make it to the driveway without ever using the gas pedal. If our driver was brave enough and didn't brake too much at key points in the trip, we could roll right into the yard at walking speed. The ride was over. The singing was over. Our throats hurt from all the screaming. The engine got shut off and the quietness was a stark contrast to the noise that the car had just been filled with. We were all sad that it was done.

"Who wants ice cream?!" the moms would yell, breaking the silence.

All of us, of course. The journey had ended but a new one was just beginning. We were still all together, ready to start something else as a family.

The ride we took through thirty years of racing was just a trip up Streaked Mountain. Honey's Best was our Chevy. She put us on her back and she carried us to the top. There were struggles and trying times on the way up, but somehow we got there. Reaching the summit was only a bonus. The journey getting there and the memories we created were equally as important as the conquest. When it rained, and sometimes it poured, we found a song to change the mood. We embraced every moment as we made our way back down, always knowing that the end was in sight. When the ride was over, we had to move on. It was depressing at first, but the idea of what lay ahead was new and inviting. Our lives were just beginning again.

Some people never even get the chance to try to get to the peak. It takes desire, passion, luck, and persistence. Life isn't worth living if you don't have goals and aspirations. Sometimes you attain them and sometimes you don't, but you can't reach the top unless you're willing to make the climb. Find your mountain. The effort and sweat you expend getting to the summit is well worth the ride back down. Trust me. Better still...trust yourself.

GLOSSARY OF GENERAL TERMS

BOXED IN: A horse that is racing on the rails (or fence) and is surrounded by other horses in front, outside, and behind it. A horse that is boxed in is held up and unable to gain a clear passage.

BREAK: To start galloping and lose natural trotting or pacing rhythm. It occurs more with trotters than pacers.

BROODMARE: A female horse, generally retired from racing, used for breeding purposes.

CARD: Another term for program of racing. For example, a person may refer to there being eight races on the card, which simply means eight races will be staged on that particular day.

CATCH-DRIVER: A driver who doesn't train his or her own horses and is engaged by other trainers and owners to drive their horses.

CLAIMING RACE: A race where any of the entrants may be claimed (purchased) for a specified amount.

CLASS: The category of racing in which a horse competes, such as a claimer, conditioned event, stake race, etc.

COLORS: The special colorful jacket worn by drivers when in a race. Unlike Thoroughbred racing, drivers register their own colors and wear them every time they race.

COLT: A male horse three years of age or less.

CONDITIONED RACE: A race where eligibility is based on age, sex, money won, or races won. For example, "three-year-old fillies, non-winners of $10,000, or four races."

COVER: A horse that races with another horse in front of him is said to race with cover, as the leading horse cuts the wind resistance.

DAM: The female parent, or mother, of a horse.

DEAD HEAT: A situation in which the judges, using a photograph, cannot separate two or more horses when judging the outcome of a race.

DISTANCED: A horse that is out of touch with the rest of the field at the end of the race. This is often referred to as finished distanced.

DRIVER: The person holding a license or permit to drive harness horses. There are different types of licenses, which correspond to differing levels of experience.

EARLY/LATE CLOSER: A race requiring payments that start much closer to the actual race date than a stake. "Early" and "Late" involve specified periods of time.

FILLY: A female horse three years of age or less.

FIRST-OVER: The first horse to make a move on the leader in a race, moving up on the outside.

FOAL: A newly born horse. Also describes the act of a mare giving birth.

FREE-LEGGED: A pacer that races without wearing hopples.

GELDING: A castrated male horse of any age.

HARNESS: The gear that is used to attach the sulky to a horse, to carry the hobbles, and to enable the driver to steer the horse.

HEAD POLE: A sliding device that is strapped to the side of the horse's neck running from the side of the head halter to the top of the harness. If needed, it aids in keeping the horse's head straight.

HOME STRETCH: The straight length of the track, nearest the spectators, where the finish line is situated. It is called this because it is the final part of the track a horse travels down during a race on its run "home" (or to the finish line).

HOPPLES: The straps that connect the front and rear legs on the same side of a horse. Most pacers wear hopples to help balance their stride and maintain a pacing gait. The length of hopples is adjustable, and a trainer registers the length that best suits his or her horse. There are also trotting hopples that work through a pulley system to help trotters maintain their gait.

HORSE: A male four years of age or older.

INVITATIONAL: A race for the top horses in the area. Also known as Open or Free-For-All.

INQUIRY: Stewards may conduct an inquiry as a result of any incident that may have occurred during a race, to determine whether or not certain drivers and/or horses were responsible for the incident and whether they should receive due punishment.

JAN. 1: All Standardbreds share this date as their birthday.

JOG CART: A cart that is attached to the harness and carries the trainer, and which the horse pulls. Used when horses are training or warming up for a race. It is larger, longer, and heavier than a SULKY.

LAME: The term used to describe a horse that is limping or has difficulty walking properly.

LEASING: As opposed to buying a harness horse, people have the option of leasing one. Just like some people lease a car instead of paying the money up-front, leasing a horse gives people use of a horse without large capital outlay. An agreement or contract must be drawn up between the two parties, and the lease must be registered with the relevant controlling body.

MAIDEN: A horse that has not yet won a race.

MARE: A female four years of age or more.

OVERCHECK: A strap that runs from the top of the bridle to the top of the harness which aids in holding the horse's head up.

PACER: Describes the Standardbred whose racing gait is the pace. This gait features legs on the same side moving forward and backward at the same time.

PARI-MUTUEL RACE: A race in which wagering is allowed, held at a track licensed by a state's racing commission. Pari-mutuel races are held at licensed pari-mutuel racetracks or fairs.

PARKED: A horse racing on the outside, with at least one horse between it and the inside rail.

PERFECTA: A bet in which the bettor must choose the first and second place finishers in exact order.

PHOTO FINISH: When two horses cross the finish too closely to identify a winner, officials call for a photograph of the race, taken exactly at the finish line, to help them determine who was ahead.

POCKET: A horse in a pocket is unable to obtain a clear run because it has other horses situated in front, behind, and to the side of it.

POST POSITION: Generally, the closer a horse starts to the inside rail or barrier of the track (especially on smaller tracks), the better its chance of winning. At the start, horses must either "leave" (start quickly) to get a good position, or else find a place on the rail to avoid racing on the outside of other horses. When racing on the outside the horse is said to be "parked out," and loses ground on every turn. A horse on the inside has a better chance to get to the rail or quickly get a good position.

QUALIFIER: A race in which a horse must go a mile below an established time standard to prove itself capable of competing in pari-mutuel races.

SCRATCH: A horse that is withdrawn (or scratched) from a race before the start.

SIRE: The male parent, or father, of a horse.

SIRE STAKE: Stake races designed to promote Standardbred breeding and racing within a state. Different states have different rules regulating eligibility to that state's sire stakes program. Rules include: a horse must be the offspring of a stallion standing in the state or a mare living in that state, owned by a resident of that state, or the horse was born in that state.

STAKE RACE: A race where owners make a series of payments, starting well in advance, to keep a horse eligible. If an owner misses a payment to a stakes race, the horse becomes ineligible.

STARTER: The person responsible for starting a harness race. The starter controls the start of the race from the back of the mobile vehicle.

SULKY: Also known as the racebike, the sulky is attached to the harness, pulled by the horse, and carries the driver. It is lighter and more streamlined than a jog cart.

THREE-WIDE: When a horse is two horses out from the rail.

TIME TRIAL: An attempt to have a horse beat its own best time in a non-competitive event. A time trial is not a race. Galloping horses hitched to sulkies, called prompters, are used to push a horse to its best effort.

TOTE BOARD: An electronic board, usually in the infield of a track, which posts the odds, amount of money bet, results of a race, and the wagering payoffs.

TRIFECTA: A bet in which the bettor must choose the first, second and third place finishers in exact order.

TROTTER: Describes the Standardbred whose racing gait is the trot. This gait features legs on opposite corners moving at the same time.

WEANLING: A baby horse, up to its first birthday.

YEARLING: Any horse between its first and second birthday.

4998347R0

Made in the USA
Lexington, KY
24 March 2010